THE URBAN
HOMESTEADING
COOKBOOK

Forage, Farm, Ferment and Feast for a Better World

MICHELLE CATHERINE NELSON
with photography by ALISON PAGE

Douglas & McIntyre

Douglas and McIntyre (2013) Ltd.
P.O. Box 219, Madeira Park, BC, V0N 2H0
www.douglas-mcintyre.com

Photography by Alison Page except where otherwise noted;
  photo styling by Alison Page and Michelle Catherine Nelson
Edited by Carol Pope and Nicola Goshulak
Indexing by Nicola Goshulak
Cover and text design by Diane Robertson
Typesetting by Roger Handling
Printed and bound in Canada
Printed on chlorine-free paper made with
  10% post-consumer waste

Douglas & McIntyre acknowledges the support of the Canada
Council for the Arts, which last year invested $157 million to
bring the arts to Canadians throughout the country.

We also gratefully acknowledge financial support from the
Government of Canada through the Canada Book Fund and
from the Province of British Columbia through the BC Arts
Council and the Book Publishing Tax Credit.

Cataloguing data available from Library and Archives Canada
ISBN 978-1-77162-081-9 (paper)
ISBN 978-1-77162-082-6 (ebook)

For my grandma,
Catherine Nelson

CONTENTS

PREFACE | 9

INTRODUCTION | 10

A NOTE ON INGREDIENTS | 15

FORAGING | 17

KEEPING | 81

GROWING | 147

PRESERVING | 183

ACKNOWLEDGEMENTS | 252

INDEX | 253

ABOUT THE AUTHOR & PHOTOGRAPHER | 256

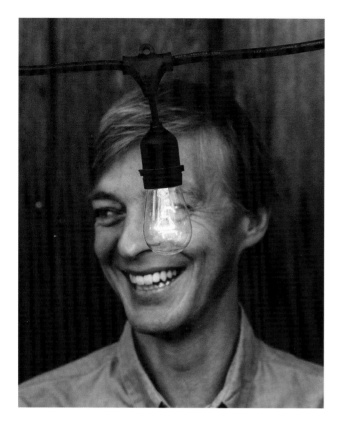

PREFACE

Can you actually improve the world by what you eat? A passionate ecologist living in a high-rise apartment smack-dab in the centre of the city, Dr. Michelle Catherine Nelson was conflicted about how to feed herself in a *sustainable* way. Following years of research in agriculture, ecology and conservation across North America and in the cloud forests of Ecuador, grasslands of Kenya and even the sub-arctic tundra of the Yukon, she has become convinced nothing is more critical to our planet's survival than for each of us to eat with our environment in mind.

Nelson wanted to grow and gather fresh and delicious ethically-produced local food rather than buy into pesticide-laden crops from supermarkets or the eggs and meat spit out by torturous factory farms. She wanted to take control of her own nourishment... leaving the environment better off because of how she ate rather than worse than ever.

But is it possible to homestead while living in a small space several floors up? Can the urbanite *truly* forage, ferment and farm for an ongoing delicious feast of authentic, healthy *and ethical* food? And can your food choices actually benefit the environment instead of damaging it further?

With her partner, Chris Mull, a marine biologist equally devoted to a DIY lifestyle that supports adventuresome earth-wise eating, Nelson embarked on an odyssey to answer this question... and the outcome is empowering for all of us!

Yes, you *can* forage in the city. Did you know that many of our urban weeds are the descendants of food plants brought to North America by immigrants generations ago? A short city walk can be an exciting scavenging expedition resulting in a delightful tea or salad of fresh (and free) greens and edible flowers. Or, if you happen to be seaside, scoop up some sea lettuce for a Sesame Seaweed Salad that will rival anything you will find at the downtown sushi shop.

You *can* keep microlivestock. Within your walls, it's easy to raise such microlivestock as rabbits in a way that integrates well into urban life and ensures a comfortable existence for the creatures you keep. Meanwhile, a small balcony humanely hosts tiny quail, perhaps the most prolific and reliable egg layers in all the poultry clan. Add to this a tank of edible aquatic animals, and consider growing your own crickets to feed your fowl and fish—or maybe even to dry and grind into a protein-rich flour for Dark and Stormy Chocolate Cupcakes.

You *can* grow food in any urban setting. Tree collards on the patio, crimini mushrooms cultured in a cupboard, microgreens on the counter, a mini pond to grow aquatic plants for Smoked Chili Water Lotus and Taro Root Chips . . . yes, it's possible to grow a mountain of food even without access to land. Add to this a honeybee hive for a win-win of supporting pollinators and feasting on your own herb-infused honey.

You *can* preserve and ferment delicious food and drink in the smallest of spaces. Simmer a fall harvest into Seasonal Fruit Leather or store protein in the form of Teriyaki Pineapple Rabbit Jerky or Canned Deer. With a few introductory fermenting skills, you can enjoy daily bread in the form of Rustic Rosemary Sourdough, or healthful homemade Pink Kohlrabi Cabbage Sauerkraut and Seaweed Kimchi. And don't forget dairy ferments—from Easy Greek-style Yogurt to 30-Minute Mozzarella to decadent Plum, Honey, Bourbon and Kefir Pops. Toast your efforts with a Kombucha-Pickled Beet and Ginger Bellini or Bee's Knees Cocktail with Homemade Bitters.

And, yes, the answer is, undoubtedly, that you *can* improve the world by what you eat. In addition to your other worthy food endeavours, by learning to identify a few edible invasive species you can literally eat this ecological problem in the form of Roasted Japanese Knotweed Pannacotta or Creamy Braised Purple Loosestrife and Mushroom Risotto or Wild Greens Pasta with Periwinkle Sea Snails.

With 85 inspiring and delicious recipes and tons of tips and advice for foraging, fermenting, farming and unforgettable feasting, urbanites everywhere can take inspiration from this innovative guide to eating better and with life-embracing bravado within any setting.

—Carol Pope, Associate Editor

INTRODUCTION

Before I started homesteading, I was a frustrated farm-lover living in the heart of the city. Despite growing up in typical suburbs complete with shopping malls and soccer practice, I was lucky enough to spend summers in my grandma's magical garden and hobby farm on the wild Sunshine Coast of British Columbia. I remember waking up early to collect eggs in Grandma's way-too-big rubber boots, giggling at the pigs snuffling my brother's pajamas, picking crisp green apples from the gnarled tree with the rope swing, and collecting endless wild berries that Grandma patiently taught me to make into pies, crisps and preserves.

By renowned artist Steve Moore, my sleeve represents my strong concerns about the commodification of nature that is so severely threatening earth's ecosystems: A river with spawning salmon marred by bar codes passes a hungry bear and imperilled forest before transforming into an assembly line destined to feed a fume-spewing industrial complex.

My memories from her place loom large in my life, pictures of ecological diversity and cultivated abundance. I still often think about Grandma's garden and greenhouse: brimming with every kind of vegetable, berry, herb and edible flower she could think of growing, and nurturing a thriving natural ecosystem too. I remember the bough-bending bounty of the fruit trees . . . the soft croaking of frogs hiding in the rainwater barrels . . . the thrumming of the beehives on the roof of the old wooden shed . . . the turtle that lived in the little pond by the yellow rosebush and finally got eaten by the black bear . . . the tree frog that would steal in through the kitchen window at night to snooze behind the water tap. And the most delectable and wholesome homegrown culinary delights: warm and fluffy buttermilk biscuits smeared with sweet strawberry jam; savoury roasted free-range chicken served with jewel-hued dill-pickled beets; slices of bread still steaming from the oven and slathered with liver pâté; simmering pots of garden green-pea soup with salty smoked ham; sizzling fried sausages and bacon made from happily raised pigs; and simple lunches of sun-warmed tomatoes, luscious greens and brilliant nasturtium flowers.

But Grandma got older and eventually didn't live on her farm anymore. And I grew up. Fleeing the suburbs, I moved into the heart of Vancouver and then Toronto for university, and found that I relished the urban life too. There was always so much to do in the art and music scenes, and as a dedicated foodie I revelled in the gustatory delights on offer around every corner. Yet living a high-rise life felt so removed from the homestead life I also loved. There were two conflicted sides of me: one in a black pencil dress and stiletto heels walking the red carpet on Queen Street, the other daydreaming about keeping fluffy heritage chickens, growing food, stocking preserves . . . about not being dependent on the grocery store.

City Michelle and Country Michelle, as a friend once summed it up, and I had a hard time reconciling these two for a long time. During those days, I researched about what I wanted to do One Day, read DIY books about what I wanted to do One Day, and finished degrees in agriculture and conservation while sneaking in homesteading and permaculture courses to help prepare for my One Day. This agonizing back and forth went on for years while I lived in the city and waited and waited for the right time and rural space, and finally I thought: you know what? No more One Day.

So, in my small apartment in a downtown neighbourhood in East Vancouver, along with my incredible and talented partner, Chris, I set out to learn, mostly by trial and error (so many errors!) how to homestead in the heart of the city. Starting in the little living room with a pair of contented rabbits destined for our dinner plates, we soon found out how easy it was to humanely keep egg-laying quail on the patio, brew first-rate craft beers and ciders in a broom closet, catch invasive bullfrogs in the local park for delicious tempura, and pick through the lawn for greens for salads, sides and pasta dishes. I planted edible landscaping around the building for all our apartment neighbours to enjoy, installed a pocket pond on the balcony to grow aquatic edibles like lotus, taro root and rice, and learned that even a small ground-floor patio provides room enough to grow seafood using a compact aquaponics system, or plant a mini food forest by stacking plants to support each other and native ecosystems at the same time.

Preserving is also a whole world of opportunity for the DIY urban foodie. In only 400 square feet of shared living space, Chris and I ferment kombucha and kefir, bake beautiful sourdough bread, craft our own cheese, infuse oils, honey and spirits with foraged flowers and container-grown herbs, smoke meat and fish, prepare jerky and pâté, and go crazy pickling, canning, freezing and drying everything we can get our hands on when it's in season locally.

Homesteading doesn't have to be defined by where we live, but rather by the choices we make. It's about slowing down and taking the time to do it yourself. About empowering ourselves to do what we think is right, for ourselves, for the environment and for the animals that provide our food—which often doesn't fit with the status quo of industrialized agriculture. By making a few choices with regard to how we eat, we can be more self-sufficient, humane and sustainable all at the same time. And, perhaps best of all, with just a little effort, along with the satisfaction of doing it yourself, urban homesteading rewards you with sophisticated and impressive meals to enjoy.

As a conservation biologist, I believe that supporting and growing sustainable food may be the most important contribution to our ecosystems that any person can make. Imagine the difference if we all looked to alternative proteins to minimize our eco-footprints, grew or locally sourced our produce and made our own preserves instead of relying on big business to make all the decisions for us, used "weeds" in our neighbourhoods as part of our daily food, worked to control invasive species by eating them, and—perhaps most important of all—sustainably raised our own meat and eggs, allowing livestock to live in ways that honour their natures, instead of supporting industries that mistreat animals from birth to death. And, yes, this is all possible—even in the city.

So, whether you are a frustrated farm-lover, homestead dreamer or conscientious urban foodie, I hope this book helps you to make the same connections we did—that you can create your own incredible food while conserving the environment, eating ethically and living well no matter where you live, and that your own One Day can start Today.

—Michelle Catherine Nelson

A NOTE ON INGREDIENTS

SOURCING FOOD YOU CAN'T PRODUCE YOURSELF

While there are a great many ways to grow, find or make food for yourself while living in the midst of a city, as we will see in this book, urban environments are also surprisingly rich places to connect with others doing good work in the area of ethical, sustainable food. Where you don't have the time or inclination to DIY, find conscientious growers and artisans at the farmers' market, local food fairs and even in your own neighbourhood. Speak to the producer of your food directly if you can to ensure fruits, herbs and vegetables are grown without chemicals in environmentally responsible ways, and animals are humanely raised and respected. Free-range (not free-run) eggs and meat are a good start, and we speak more about this in the pages that follow. Another option for acquiring ethical, environmentally sound food is to start trading with your neighbours. Maybe someone down the street has a prolific kale patch or extra eggs from their flock of backyard laying hens, which you can trade for your homemade beer or herb-infused olive oil. This way, you don't have to do everything yourself and you get to know your neighbours better, all the while empowering yourself and your local community to be more sustainable.

GENERAL WARNINGS ABOUT SAFE EATING

Before eating any plants (including those provided by other growers or foragers), always keep a few concerns in mind. Never harvest or purchase plants that have been treated with pesticides or herbicides—they are toxic for both you and the environment in which they grow. If you have any health concerns or are pregnant, speak to your doctor about your food choices before adding foraged food to your menu. And regardless of your health status, always keep a good balance in your diet and avoid relying too heavily on one food source—some nutritional compounds that are healthful and necessary in typical portions can cause imbalances in metabolism if too much is consumed. When foraging your own food it is crucial to your safety to make sure you have properly identified what you eat: use field guides and get help from experts until you are very confident in distinguishing your foraged food.

AS YOU COOK . . .

All recipes assume washing of produce before using. Remove any hard or fibrous parts as well as any debris on foraged ingredients. When cutting away plant stems and removing bones or seafood shells from meat, put them to good use as a base for soup, even storing these ingredients in the freezer until you're ready to make stock. Stems and other fibrous parts also make great fodder for rabbits and chickens, if you have them, or for your worm bin, and we talk more about the many ways to make full use of your food in the pages that follow. Keeping all the nutrients from your food waste within your own food-production system is healthier for both you and the environment.

FORAGING

FORAGING FOR EDIBLES

When I was little, my Uncle Eric lived on a tugboat on the rugged and wild Sunshine Coast of British Columbia; he had a log-salvage licence, so was a real-life beachcomber. One of the most interesting people I know, Eric can build a boat or a house, and has taught me all about surviving in the woods. When we were just toddling around the boat, he and my dad spent time teaching me and my brother where to find all kinds of sea beasties and how to use a handline baited with mussels to fish for shiner perch from the dock. Eric became involved in marine conservation, and it was through him that I started salmon-ecosystem research, which I studied for several years for my doctorate. And he also inspired me to learn about foraging; in fact, the first time I tried eating stinging nettles was on Uncle Eric's boat. They were steamed in an enamel pot on the woodstove and served simply with butter and lemon juice—surprisingly delicious, and there were no stings!

Since then, I've learned to identify all kinds of edibles to forage for, even within the city, and delight in sharing with friends just how many of the weeds in lawns and gardens are good for dinner. Edible wild creatures and plants abound just about everywhere, and foraging is accessible to everyone, whether it's in an empty lot, backyard, forest, or on the seashore. And, while it does involve a little effort to learn to correctly identify what's safe to eat, once you get to know a few reliable favourites, you can take advantage of nature's bounty—for free! Even better, if you become familiar with a few edible invasive species, you can do your part in conservation by literally eating the problem.

These delicious and nutritious stinging nettles are just one example of free food for the taking and grow rampantly as "weeds" in urban areas—on roadsides and in sprawling gardens and empty lots.

STINGING NETTLE PESTO

Traditionally made from pine nuts blended with basil, pesto works well with other leaves too. My favourite is stinging nettle—pesto is a perfect way to preserve these super healthy greens when they are abundant for picking in spring (make sure to wear gloves and long sleeves). As pine nuts are not locally available to me, I use walnuts instead.

4 cups (1 L) stinging nettle leaves
¼ cup (60 mL) walnuts, lightly
   toasted
¼ cup (60 mL) grated Parmesan
   or Asiago cheese

2 garlic cloves
4 Tbsp (60 mL) olive oil, divided

1. Blanch nettles to remove sting by steaming for 2 minutes.

2. Use mortar and pestle (or food processor) to grind walnuts, cheese and garlic with 2 tablespoons (30 mL) of the olive oil. Add nettle leaves in batches to mortar, pounding with pestle and gradually adding remaining olive oil.

MAKES 1 CUP (250 ML)

GET A FIELD GUIDE AND ASK FOR HELP

Before beginning your foraging, be sure to get at least one very good local plant, mushroom, animal or seashore field guide (depending on what you are foraging for) to help with identification. And, if you can, ask a seasoned forager to accompany you when starting out. People can be guarded about their favourite spots (especially for mushrooms), but weeds and invasive species are abundant and easy to share. Also, consider joining a local foraging group or nature club that has meet-ups or find a chef-forager who hosts identification and cooking workshops—search online for the resources available in your area. And check websites on edible invasive species to learn how to spot these too.

To keep things simple, consider starting with a laminated pocket guide with photos and descriptions of a few easy-to-identify species. Then, over time, as you become more serious and knowledgeable about foraging, upgrade with comprehensive guides. While you won't need to learn to identify everything that's listed, when you do discover something new, it's nice to have a good reference on hand.

Once you think you have identified an edible for foraging—whether it's a salad green, mushroom, berry, root or some seaweed—double-check that the preferred habitat and range, as well as every single aspect of its description, matches your field guide. If you are unsure, show it to experienced foraging friends, or take a photo to post online in foraging forums.

The bottom line is . . . when foraging, do not eat anything until you are certain it is safe to ingest. It's integral to put a support system in place that enables you to be 100 percent sure of the identity of anything you eat.

TAKE ONLY A LITTLE . . . EATING WILD EDIBLES

When collecting wild food, it's very important to be aware that those plants, mushrooms and animals are part of an ecosystem that provides food and shelter for other species. Don't collect so much that you remove the entire population. Picking up to one-quarter of the foliage in the patch you've found and no more than half the fruit should be safe for the ecosystem, but take no more than that. Leave spores behind when you pick mushrooms to encourage future populations (see pages 152–153). Be aware of sensitive areas, such as wetlands, and stay on pathways to prevent damage from your footsteps.

OR A LOT! . . . EATING INVASIVES

You have probably heard of the locavore food movement (eating local) but you may not have heard of the invasivore food movement—eating invasive species!

The genius behind this is to relish the joy of cooking highly invasive edibles such as Japanese knotweed or purple loosestrife, or (as you'll see in later sections of this book) even American bullfrogs, garden snails and Chinese mitten crabs, to help ensure the survival of our native plants and animals.

You don't have to be careful about taking just a little to leave populations intact when collecting non-native invasives because they aren't part of the local evolved ecosystem. In fact, in the case of invasive species, you can aid in conservation by collecting as much as you can to minimize their damage to the native environment. Community and government conservation projects to remove invasive species from both urban and rural areas often involve a lot of time and money, so you are doing your part by removing (and eating) those that are edible.

So What's a Native Edible and What's an Invasive?

Calling something native simply means the plant or animal naturally grows in the landscape where you live, as opposed to being an introduced, or exotic, species.

Introductions of exotic species occurred in North America when Europeans first settled and started growing food familiar to them in their homeland (which may be why many "weeds" in North America are edible), and these new introductions continue today, especially through garden-centre imports. Not all exotics become invasive—many introduced species, like dandelions, may seem prolific but are simply negligible (and edible) additions to our urban landscapes, while others don't find much of a foothold at all.

Some introductions, however, become invasive when they displace native species, at times taking over large areas of a landscape. As all the indigenous plants and animals within a habitat have evolved as part of an ecosystem—dependent on each other for survival—this can be ecologically devastating, with the invasives out-competing native species for food and shelter. Some invasives, such as purple loosestrife in wetlands, can cause a complete collapse of a native environment.

How to Identify Invasives

It is often easy to determine if a species is non-native to North America simply by its name—as in the case of Japanese knotweed or European grove snail. Otherwise, check your identification guide for words like "introduced" or "naturalized," which indicate the plant or animal is not native—and I've noted this in the plant and animal lists that follow. Check online, too, for updates and advice regarding invasives in your area.

ROASTED JAPANESE KNOTWEED PANNACOTTA

Japanese knotweed is a very invasive plant in many neighbourhoods throughout North America. It is notoriously hard to kill, but luckily the rhubarb-like plant stems are edible and delicious. Encourage everyone you know to harvest as much knotweed as they can in the springtime to reduce the vigour of knotweed stands and eventually kill the plants. This dessert is a smooth and sophisticated way to enjoy the tart and sweet taste of knotweed, and to show off your conservation efforts.

3 cups (710 mL) knotweed stems
¼ cup (60 mL) apple juice
2 Tbsp (30 mL) + ¼ cup (60 mL) sugar, divided
¼ cup (60 mL) 2 percent milk
1½ cup (350 mL) whipping cream, divided
1 vanilla pod, scored and seeded (or 1 Tbsp/15 mL vanilla extract)
Zest of half a lemon
1 Tbsp (15 mL) gelatin
2 Tbsp (30 mL) grated fresh ginger
⅛ tsp (0.5 mL) cinnamon
½ cup (120 mL) champagne or apple juice
4 small moulds, such as espresso cups

1. Preheat oven to 400F (205C). Remove leaves from stems of knotweed and snap off tough lower stems (like asparagus). Peel outer skin to remove stringy parts on knotweed stem, then chop. Place in roasting pan, sprinkle apple juice and 2 tablespoons (30 mL) of the sugar on top and place into oven until it starts to brown, about 10 minutes.

2. Simmer milk, ¾ cup (180 mL) of the whipping cream, vanilla seeds and pod and lemon zest in saucepan on medium-low heat for 10 minutes. Take simmering mixture off heat, remove vanilla pod and add gelatin, mixing to dissolve.

3. Remove roasted knotweed from oven and coarsely blend in a food processor, then add to creamy gelatin mixture. Allow to cool slightly.

4. Meanwhile, whip the remaining ¾ cup (180 mL) cream and ¼ cup (60 mL) sugar together. Once gelatin mixture has cooled, stir in whipped cream. Divide into 4 moulds, and chill for at least one hour.

5. To make the sauce, simmer ginger, cinnamon and champagne on medium heat until reduced by three-quarters. Remove pannacotta from moulds by dipping each mould into boiled water and turning upside down. Drizzle with sauce.

SERVES 4

CHOOSE SITES FREE FROM CONTAMINATION

When foraging for food, always look for uncontaminated areas. Avoid seashores near busy ports, wetlands downstream of industrial complexes, polluted lakes or rivers, and lands that have housed gas stations or industrial sites—all of which can accumulate toxic heavy metals and other impurities. That said, some long-neglected urban areas do start reverting back to "wild" landscapes and can be excellent places to forage for native plants, such as empty residential lots or unused railway corridors (but only several feet back from the tracks to reduce risk of such toxins as creosote).

QUICK GUIDE TO FORAGING FOR EDIBLES

Once you have the resources needed for correct identification of a species you are after and have found a good place to look, it's time to start foraging! Here's a quick guide to get you going:

Edible	Equipment Needed	Method of Collection
Plants	Plant field guide, scissors, basket, bag or bucket, optional gloves and digging tool	Pick by hand or with scissors, dig roots or tubers
Mushrooms	Mushroom field guide, cloth bag or wooden basket, pocket knife	Cut caps from stem with knife
Invasive snails	Paper bag or glass jar with air holes drilled through lid	After heavy rain, remove from plants by hand
Invasive bullfrogs	Rubber boots or waders, flashlight, large dip net, ikejime spike, food-safe bucket with air holes drilled through lid	At night, find reflective eyes with flashlight and use dip net to capture while shining light
Invasive crayfish	Rubber boots or waders, large dip net, food-safe bucket	Find under rocks, scoop into net
Seaweed and sea asparagus	Seashore field guide, knife, food-safe plastic bag or bucket	Cut from rocks at mid to low tide
Invasive sea snails	Seashore field guide, knife or prying tool, food-safe plastic bag or bucket	Pry off rocks at mid to low tide
Mussels and oysters	Fishing licence, seashore field guide, food-safe plastic bag or bucket	Pull from rocks at mid to low tide
Clams	Fishing licence, seashore field guide, shovel, food-safe plastic bucket	Dig from sand at mid to low tide
Invasive crabs	Seashore field guide, food-safe plastic bucket	Find under rocks and collect by hand
Dungeness crabs	Fishing licence, snorkel mask, dive weights, fins, mesh collection bag. Optional wetsuit and gloves	Free dive down to 15 feet (4.5 m) below sea level

WILD AND INVASIVE EDIBLE PLANTS

I realize that if you haven't tried foraging yet, collecting and eating wild food may seem daunting or even dangerous, particularly given my precautions. We've all heard the urban legends about people poisoned by wild mushrooms or plants. But while you absolutely need to be careful, there are many wild edibles in both urban and outlying settings that are fairly foolproof—simple to identify and easy to find.

TAKE IT ONE PLANT AT A TIME

Almost everyone knows what a blackberry bush looks like and can safely identify this fruit for eating. While a few species can be hard to pinpoint, many plants are distinct enough that you will not be confused once you come to know them, and you can happily harvest when you have the chance.

LET NATURE GUIDE YOUR SEARCH

When foraging, instead of having a set idea of exactly what you expect to come home with, it works better to simply let nature show you what is available and go from there. Think of the landscape as you would your local farmers' market—you wouldn't be looking for ripe peaches in the middle of winter!

Generally, plants follow a sequence: sprouting in spring; leafing out, flowering and fruiting through the summer; setting seed and storing sugars in roots in fall. Different parts of a plant are available at particular times of the year.

Once you learn where a certain plant grows, you can visit when it is producing the bounty you want. For example, asparagus plants are common roadside "weeds" and very visible in the summer with their bright red berries, so take note and return to this spot early next spring to snap off some of the soft-green sprouts.

PLANTS TO AVOID

It's always better to be safe than sorry when foraging for plants, so when you are starting out, particularly avoid those with a three-leaved growth pattern, milky sap, bitter or soapy taste, spines or thorns, unless you are certain they are safe to eat. Many toxic plants have one or more of these attributes—although, as in our example of blackberry fruit borne on thorny bushes, having these characteristics does not necessarily mean a plant is dangerous; you simply want to be sure of its identity before eating it. Never pick any plants growing in water if they have carrot-like foliage and flowers similar to dill or fennel, as they may be water hemlock (*Cicuta* spp.), which is highly toxic and can be deadly.

When collecting wild, invasive or garden plants, ensure no one has been spraying pesticides or herbicides wherever you are collecting, especially

Preceding pages: Chris and I love to forage in spring, when tender new growth—like these maple flowers collected in our local park—provides endless opportunities for salads, sides, soups, dips, desserts, preserves and drink flavourings.

if you are not in your own yard or on land where you know the caretakers.

Pesticides are commonly sprayed in agricultural areas, for example, and herbicides often depended on to control weeds and such invasive plants as Japanese knotweed and purple loosestrife in municipal areas. Pesticides and herbicides can be highly toxic (as well as long-lasting and devastating to local ecosystems), especially those not approved for food crops and used on lawns and roadsides . . . as well as in parks; if foraging there, check with your parks board first.

Some cities have gotten smart to the drastic negative effects of pesticides and banned them, while others still allow and use them extensively, so check with your local city hall or municipality website to review local bylaws before collecting on roadsides, by railroad lines or in empty lots. And remember that even if pesticides have been banned by forward-thinking governments, not everyone has educated themselves, so ask neighbours about their possible use of weed sprays before collecting near their yards.

WHERE TO START—URBAN FORAGING

So you're ready to start foraging—but where?

Lawns

A good place to begin is to look for "weeds" in your own or a friend's backyard, or in the grassy area surrounding your apartment building. Weeds in urban areas are simply plants (either native or introduced) that have figured out how to survive the higher disturbance and adverse conditions that urban environments offer. Look for common weeds you already may know, such as easy-to-recognize dandelion and clover. Do leave some of these plants behind, though, because the bees and native pollinators love their flowers—and more pollinators mean higher production and biodiversity in nature and the garden.

When you are first learning to identify plants, a lawn free of pesticides and herbicides is a great place to start. There are a limited number of plants that can compete with grass, so you aren't likely to encounter a lot of different species.

Once you've sourced some nutritious dandelion and clover, look up a few additional easy-to-find edibles—such as sorrel, dock, plantain and purslane—in your plant guide or online, and then find them. Pay attention to the shape and orientation of the leaves (round and smooth, or thin and toothed; all along the stalk or only at the base?) and note the colour and contour of the flowers. Keep in mind that each plant likes to grow in certain conditions . . . so even though the mysterious plant you've found has a flower that looks just like a swamp rose, if it's growing in a dried-up, brown-looking summer lawn, it most likely is not.

Verges, Empty Lots and Parks

After you've gotten comfortable identifying a few plants, start looking farther afield in the neighbourhood for more of these weeds (a.k.a. untapped resources). Often local parks will have untended areas where edibles abound. Again, beware of pesticide and herbicide use, and also of bylaws that may prohibit collection (although usually no one will complain if you're picking dandelion greens or other well-known weeds). Call your local parks board or city hall to find out.

Good Neighbours

Another great way to forage is to ask neighbours with edible flowers, herbs or fruit not being harvested if they would mind sharing. A surprisingly large number of people are growing food unwittingly, and are delighted with a jar of plum sauce made from fruit that would usually just drop and rot on their grass.

There may even be groups in your community that organize harvests of unused fruits, berries and nuts on private land. Also, most neighbours would be delighted to have you pick the edible weeds out of their garden or lawn, saving them from doing this chore themselves.

FORAGED SPRING GREENS SALAD

In the springtime, when plants begin to sprout and unfurl their fresh soft leaves and delicate flowers, the urban forager can find plenty of variety for a beautiful and unique salad. As plants mature, their flavour becomes more pungent, so nibble your fresh-picked edibles to decide if you want to add a base of overwintered greens such as kale, or if the foraged leaves are mild enough on their own. Either way, you are going for about 5 cups (1.2 L) of fresh chopped greens—and I always aim to include several different types of plants for a multiplicity of tastes, as shown in the examples listed in this recipe. Do use this recipe as inspiration only and substitute greens freely based on what you have available. If you have it, use homemade IPA Beer Vinegar (page 230) in the dressing!

DRESSING
1 tsp (5 mL) Beer Vinegar (page 230) or any light vinegar
¼ tsp (1 mL) Dijon mustard
3 Tbsp (45 mL) safflower or canola oil
Salt and pepper to taste

MY FAVOURITE SALAD COMBO
2 cups (475 mL) chopped chickweed, clover, lamb's quarters, amaranth, miner's lettuce and/or goldenrod leaves
1 cup (250 mL) sheep sorrel, wood sorrel, purslane, field mustard, garlic mustard, watercress, chicory, dandelion, mint and/or fennel, chopped
2 cups (475 mL) kale and/or tree collard leaves, chopped
1–2 handfuls of any of the following edible flowers: chicory, clover, dandelion, fireweed, goldenrod, kudzu, mint, blackberry, maple, field mustard, pineapple weed, field mustard and/or watercress

1. Combine vinegar, mustard and oil in a jar. Screw on the lid and shake until well emulsified. Season with salt and pepper.

2. Toss salad dressing with leafy greens, and then top with flowers.

3. Serve immediately.

SERVES 6

LEARNING TO IDENTIFY WILD PLANTS

Chris and I are lucky to live by a park that has some natural forest and seashore. In the spring, we collect stinging nettles and Douglas fir tree tips. We eat the stinging nettles steamed and as pesto, the tree tips as tea and syrup.

Foraging in wild spaces can be more challenging than in urban areas because the diversity, or variety, of species can be much higher, making it more challenging to identify edibles. However, if you have access to a natural forest, wetland, meadow or seashore, learning to collect and prepare wild food is a very rewarding way to interact with the landscape. I remember how daunting it seemed when I first started identifying plants in the forest for my work as a biologist, but then the real satisfaction that followed when I was able to figure out, based on leaves and/or flowers, which family a plant was in without referencing my field guide.

The going does get easier, and after you've identified a few good edibles available nearby, you can start experimenting with different recipes and impressing your guests. If you can find a wild edible similar to a commonly used ingredient, it's an easy substitute in your favourite recipes. For example, steamed wild stinging nettles are similar in taste and consistency to spinach, so perfect in lasagna, quiche, soup or other cooked recipes that include spinach.

Remember that what you forage for depends on the time of year. In spring, hunt for new leaves or shoots of cress, sorrel, dandelion, stinging nettle and more, as well as fiddleheads and the tips of spruce, fir and pine trees. In summer, keep looking for those tender leaves and, as the season progresses, hunt for fruits and rosehips. In fall, keep your eye out for amaranth and mustard seeds, mushrooms, wapato tubers and kudzu root.

OXALIC ACID—ENJOY IN MODERATION

Many plants, particularly those belonging to the amaranth family (including amaranth, spinach, chard, beets, quinoa and lamb's quarters), the knotweed family (particularly sheep sorrel, curly dock, Japanese knotweed and rhubarb), the purslane family (including purslane and miner's lettuce) and the wood sorrel family contain a compound called oxalic acid, particularly concentrated in the leaves. Like the citric acid found in citrus fruits, oxalic acid imparts a lemony tart tang, and these plants make flavourful additions to recipes, either as fresh greens in salads or cooked in sauces (especially sheep and wood sorrel, dock and purslane). The stems of plants like rhubarb and Japanese knotweed add a tart kick to sweet desserts.

Warning: Moderation is advised: in very large quantities (several cups per day), oxalic acid can bind with the body's calcium, occasionally causing symptoms for those with arthritis or rheumatism, and creates calcium oxalate crystals that can form kidney stones in people who are susceptible to them.

Common Name	Description and Habitat	Edible Parts and Harvest Times	Cooking and Eating
Amaranth or pigweed (e.g. *Amaranthus retroflexus*)	Invasive. Tender herb to 9 feet (3 m) tall with lance-shaped or oval leaves with visible veins and reddish flowers growing in dense, long, furry upright or drooping clusters. Gardens, roadsides, empty lots	Leaves and stems in spring and early summer; flowers in summer; seeds in late summer and early fall	Use raw or cook leaves, stems and flowers like lemony spinach. Seeds like quinoa
Asparagus (*Asparagus officinalis*)	Large patches 3 to 5 feet (0.9 to 1.5 m) tall with feathery, green foliage and small red berries. Roadsides, railway lines	Source plants in summer and fall; return in spring for the edible shoots. Do not eat berries	Like store-bought spears (shoots)
Autumnberry, autumn olive or Japanese silverberry (*Elaeagnus umbellata*)	Invasive. Dense thickets of tall shrubs up to 16 feet (5 m) with thorns, leathery, silver-flaked, oval leaves and bright orange-red, oval, currant-sized berries. Disturbed and eroded areas	Berries in late summer	Desserts and preserves
Bamboo (e.g. *Phyllostachys dulcis* and *P. edulis*)	Invasive. Very tall grass usually up to 20 feet (6 m) in urban areas, with hollow, cane-like stems and long, thin, lance-shaped leaves off smaller branches. Shoots are conical and deep-rooted. Landscaping and parks	Shoots in spring. Dig shoots with a sharp spade when 1 inch (2.5 cm) high	Peel off woody exterior and steam or boil for 20 minutes, then roast, stirfry or add to soup
Blueberry and huckleberry (*Vaccinium* spp.)	Native. Shrubs up to 9 feet (3 m) tall with alternate, toothed, oval or egg-shaped leaves, pink or white bell-shaped flowers and plump round berries. Forest edges and parks	Berries in late summer	Salads, desserts, preserves
Burdock (*Arctium lappa* and *A. minus*)	Tall herb to 5 feet (150 cm) with alternate, large egg- to heart-shaped hairy leaves, and flowers that are tufts of pink to purple on marble-sized burrs covered in tiny hooks. Roadsides and empty lots	Stems in summer, roots in late fall	Peel, shred or julienne, then soak for 10 minutes. Use in vegetable dishes, to pickle or as a bittering agent
Cattail or bulrush (*Typha* spp.)	Native. Aquatic plant to 9 feet (3 m) tall with flat, long, thin, basal, grass-like leaves, and single, tall stems bearing familiar fuzzy cattail flower cluster. Wetlands, parks	Shoots in spring, flowers in early summer, pollen in late summer, roots in winter	Cook shoots like leeks, flowers like corn on the cob and roots like potatoes
Chamomile (e.g. *Matricaria recutita* and *Chamaemelum nobile*)	Tender herb to 2 feet (60 cm) tall with narrow, deeply divided leaves and small daisy-like flowers. Gardens, empty lots and parks	Flowers in summer	Dry flowers and brew for tea
Chickweed (*Stellaria media, S. pallida* and *S. neglecta*)	Small, tender herb forming creeping mats with paired egg-shaped leaves and tiny white star-shaped flowers. Disturbed soil in gardens, empty lots, parks	Leaves throughout the growing season	Use raw like lettuce or cook like spinach. Avoid if pregnant
Chicory (*Cichorium intybus*)	Shrub up to 5 feet (1.5 m) tall with alternating deeply toothed leaves and blue dandelion-like flowers. Roadsides, empty lots	Leaves in spring, flowers in summer	Use leaves like endive or radicchio, use flowers in salads or pickled
Clover (*Trifolium* spp.)	Tender herb up to 2 feet (60 cm) with 3 oval leaflets in a shamrock shape, and white or pink sphere-shaped flowers. Lawns, gardens, empty lots, parks	Young leaves in spring, flowers in summer, seeds in late summer and fall	Flowers raw or roasted, or dried for tea. Leaves like spinach. Seeds ground into flour

Common Name	Description and Habitat	Edible Parts and Harvest Times	Cooking and Eating
Curly dock (*Rumex crispus*)	Large tender herb up to 3 feet high (1 m) often tinged with red, with circular rosette of large elliptical leaves with curling edges and inconspicuous flowers. Lawns, gardens, empty lots, parks	Young leaves in spring	Cook like lemony spinach
Dandelion (*Taraxacum officinale*)	Small tender herb up to 2 feet (60 cm) with circular rosette of spoon-shaped, lobed leaves, milky sap and yellow daisy-like flowers. Lawns, gardens, empty lots, parks	Young leaves in spring and summer, roots in winter	Use raw like radicchio or cook like spinach. Use roots as bittering agent
Daylily (*Hemerocallis fulva*)	Tender herb up to 4 feet (120 cm) with long, thin, basal leaves and large lily-like yellow or orange flowers growing 10 to 20 on a single stalk. Gardens, roadsides and parks	Young leaves and stems in spring, flowers in summer and tubers in fall and winter	Leaves and stems like mild onions. Flowers like squash flowers. Tubers like potatoes
Elderberry, red and blue (*Sambucus racemosa* or *S. cerulean*)	Native. Large shrub up to 30 feet (9 m) tall, with leaves divided into 5 to 7 opposite, lance-shaped, toothed leaflets, white to cream pyramid-shaped clusters of flowers, and small, round, red or blue berries. Landscaping and parks	Flowers in spring and berries in summer	Flowers and berries can be used to flavour preserves, beer, wine and cider. Do not eat raw
Fennel (*Foeniculum vulgare*)	Invasive. Tall herb up to 7 feet (2.5 m) with several hollow stems, feathery foliage of thread-like leaves and large disc-shaped clusters of tiny yellow flowers. Gardens, roadsides and parks	Leaves in spring and summer. Seeds in late summer and fall	Leaves like anise-flavoured spinach. Seeds dried and ground as anise-flavoured spice
Fiddlehead ferns, ostrich and lady ferns (*Matteuccia struthiopteris* and *Athyrium filix-femina*)	Native. Funnel-shaped rosettes up to 6 feet (2 m) tall with unbranched tender fronds either tri-angle or diamond shaped. Shoots (fiddleheads) smooth and scale-less with brown, papery flakes and trough on upper side of stalk. Landscaping, gardens, forest edges	Shoots in spring	Cook like asparagus. Do not eat raw
Field mustard and garlic mustard (*Brassica rapa, B. campestris, B. vulgaris* and *Alliaria petiolata*)	Native (field mustard). Invasive (garlic mustard). Tender herb up to 3 feet (1 m) tall with alternate, arrow- or lyre-shaped leaves and clusters of small, cross-shaped 4-petalled white or yellow flowers. Roadsides and parks	Young leaves and flowers in spring, or early summer. Seeds in late summer and fall	Leaves and flowers like watercress and/or garlic greens. Seeds can be dried and ground into mustard powder
Fireweed (*Epilobium angustifolium*)	Native. Tall herb up to 10 feet (3 m) with un-branched reddish stems, alternate, lance-shaped leaves with distinct veins and cone-shaped, showy clusters of red to purple 4-petaled flowers. Ditch sides, wetland edges, roadsides, empty lots, parks	Young leaves in spring, flowers in summer	Leaves raw or cooked like spinach, or dried as tea. Flowers dried for tea or used for desserts and preserves
Goldenrod (*Solidago canadensis* or *S. odora*)	Native. Fairly tall herb up to 5 feet (150 cm) with hairy stems, alternate, long, lance-shaped leaves and tiny yellow flowers in pyramidal clusters. Roadsides, wetland edges, empty lots, parks	Young leaves and stems in spring, flowers in summer	Cook leaves like spinach or dry for tea. Flowers can be dried or used in desserts or preserves. Stems peeled and pickled

Common Name	Description and Habitat	Edible Parts and Harvest Times	Cooking and Eating
Himalayan blackberry (*Rubus armeniacus* or *R. discolor*)	Invasive. Thickets of thorny canes climbing over each other and structures with leaves divided into 3 or 5 oval, toothed leaflets, white to pink 5-petalled flowers with many stamens in centre, and dark-purple to black compound berries. Roadsides, empty lots, parks	Flowers in spring, berries in late summer	Desserts, preserves and for flavouring cider and wine
Japanese knotweed (*Fallopia japonica*)	Invasive. Big patches of tall herbs up to 10 feet (3 m) of hollow, bamboo-like stems with large egg-shaped leaves and erect, linear clusters of small cream or white flowers. Roadsides, empty lots, parks	Shoots are best in spring, or peel stems in summer	Cook like rhubarb
Kudzu (*Pueraria montana*)	Invasive. Climbing vine with hairy stems up to 100 feet (30 m), dense, hairy leaves divided into 3 leaflets with 2 to 3 lobes, and red to purple flowers in large, showy, linear clusters with grape-like aroma. Disturbed soil, agricultural areas	Shoots and leaves in spring. Leaves and flowers in summer. Roots in fall and winter	Cook shoots like asparagus. Use leaves like kale. Flowers can be dried for tea, or used in desserts or preserves. Roots like potatoes
Lamb's quarters, goose-foot (*Chenopodium* spp.)	Tender herb usually 2 to 3 feet (60 to 90 cm) tall but up to 8 feet (250 cm) with alternate silvery-green diamond- or goosefoot-shaped leaves, and inconspicuous clusters of flowers at end of stems. Gardens, roadsides, parks	Young leaves in spring, flowering shoots in early summer, seeds in fall	Use leaves raw or cooked like lemony spinach. Cook flowering shoots like broccoli. Seeds like quinoa
Maple (*Acer* spp. including sugar, red, black, silver, Norway or bigleaf)	Native. Tree with opposite, veined and 5 to 7 lobed leaves with characteristic "maple leaf" shape, and hanging clusters of small green, yellow, orange or red flowers. Landscaping, roadsides and parks	Tap trunk for sap in early spring, pick flowers in late spring and early summer	Boil down sap to concentrate for syrup. Use flowers fresh in salads or pickled
Miner's lettuce (*Claytonia perfoliata*)	Native. Small, delicate herb up to 1 foot (30 cm) with spoon-shaped, basal leaves with 1 disc-like leaf near the top of the stem, and white to pink 5-petalled flowers in clusters of 3 to 7	Leaves and flowers in spring and summer	Use raw leaves and flowers like lettuce, or cook like spinach
Mint and lemon balm (e.g. *Mentha arvensis* and *Melissa officinalis*)	Native. Tender herb up to 3 feet (90 cm) tall with distinctly square stems, opposite lance- to oval-shaped, toothed leaves, and white, purple or pink whorled or cylindrical clusters of flowers	Leaves and flowers in spring and summer	Raw leaves and flowers can be used as a flavouring for salads, desserts and preserves, or dried for tea
Mugwort (*Artemisia vulgaris*)	Invasive. Tall herb up to 5 feet (1.5 m) with silvery deeply lobed leaves covered with white or grey hairs on the underside. Distinct absinthe-like aroma. Gardens, landscaping, roadsides, empty lots	Shoots in early spring, young leaves in spring and summer, flowers in summer	Use shoots and young leaves as flavouring for savoury dishes and beer. Dry leaves and flowers for tea
Oregon grape (*Mahonia aquifolium*)	Native. Small evergreen shrub up to 2 feet (60 cm) with shiny, holly-like leaves divided into spiny-toothed, opposite leaflets, bright-yellow upright clusters of flowers, and blue berries dusted with whitish powder. Landscaping, forest edges	Flowers in late spring/early summer, and berries in late summer	Use flowers and berries in desserts, preserves and to flavour cider and wine

Common Name	Description and Habitat	Edible Parts and Harvest Times	Cooking and Eating
Oxeye daisy (*Leucanthemum vulgare*)	Invasive. Tall herb up to 3 feet (1 m) with mostly unbranched stems with spoon-shaped, toothed leaves and large daisy-like flowers. Roadsides, empty lots, parks	Unopened flower buds in spring, and flowers in summer	Pickle unopened flower buds like capers. Use flowers in salads or desserts
Pineapple weed (*Matricaria discoidea* or *M. matricarioides*)	Native. Small herb up to 8 inches (20 cm) tall with feathery green foliage and yellow half-cone or sphere-shaped flowers	Flowers in summer	Pick flowers to dry for tea like chamomile, or use raw in salads
Plantain, Alaska and English (*Plantago* spp.)	Small herb up to 2 feet (60 cm) with basal-, lance-, elliptic- or egg-shaped leaves with prominent lengthwise veins and a cylindrical cluster of inconspicuous flowers or an egg-shaped cluster of flowers surrounded by a cloud of white stamens. Lawns, driveways, roadsides, parks	Young leaves in spring	Cook leaves like spinach
Prickly pear cactus (*Opuntia* spp.)	Mat-forming shrubby succulent cactus with large, paddle-shaped pads covered in large spines, yellow flowers and red or pink fruits. Dry soils in parks or beach sides	Young pads in spring, fruit in summer. Use gloves and tongs to harvest to avoid spines	Spray strongly with hose water to remove small bristles, then burn off larger spines. Peel pads and cook like eggplant, and use fruits like strawberries or raspberries
Purple loosestrife (*Lythrum salicaria*)	Invasive. Tall herb up to 6 feet (2 m) with short, lance-shaped leaves and showy spikey clusters of red to purple 5-petalled flowers with yellow centres. Wetland edges, parks	Young leaves in spring, flowers in summer	Cook leaves like spinach. Flowers for desserts and preserves or dried for tea
Purslane (*Portulaca oleracea*)	Creeping, mat-forming succulent with reddish stems, clear sap, alternate, fleshy, paddle-shaped leaves and small yellow 5-petalled flowers. Gardens, lawns, parks	Leaves, stems and flowers in spring and summer	Use leaves, stems and flowers raw or cooked like lemony spinach
Rose (*Rosa* spp.)	Native. Thorny shrubs or vines with leaves divided into leaflets that are opposite, oval and toothed, 5 to several-petalled white, yellow, pink or red flowers with many stamens in the summer, and large, conspicuous hips	Flowers in summer and hips in fall	Use whole flowers to flavour preserves, syrup, and wine. Dry hips for tea
Salal (*Gaultheria shallon*)	Native. Creeping to erect shrubs up to 13 feet (4 m) tall with opposite, round, waxy and toothed leaves, small white or pink bell-shaped flowers, and dark-purple, somewhat fuzzy berries	Fruit in summer	Use in preserves and desserts
Sheep sorrel, garden sorrel or sour grass (*Rumex acetosella* and *R. acetosa*)	Small herb up to 1.5 feet (50 cm) tall with prostrate arrowhead-shaped leaves and reddish erect flowering stems, and small red or yellow cylindrical clusters of flowers. Roadsides, lawns, parks, gardens, beaches	Leaves in spring to fall	Use leaves raw or cooked like lemony spinach

Common Name	Description and Habitat	Edible Parts and Harvest Times	Cooking and Eating
Shiso (*Perilla frutescens*)	Invasive. Tender herb growing up to 3 feet (1 m) tall with square stems and opposite, diamond-shaped, toothed leaves that are green on top and purple underneath	Leaves any time	Use as spicy flavouring for savoury dishes
Staghorn sumac (*Rhus typhina*)	Native. Large shrub or tall tree to 16 feet (5 m) with velvety red hairs on trunk and branches, leaves divided into alternate, lance-shaped, toothed leaflets, conical clusters of red flowers, and clusters of red berries. Landscaping, parks, roadsides	Berries in late summer	Soak berries in water, strain and use water to flavour preserves and drinks. Dry leftover berries and grind to use as spice
Stinging nettle (*Urtica chamaedryoides*)	Native. Large patches of tall herbs up to 9 feet (3 m) with stinging hairs on stem and leaves, opposite, lance- to heart-shaped, toothed and pointed leaves, and drooping clusters of tiny greenish flowers. Ditches, roadsides, forest and wetland edges	Young leaves in spring. Use gloves to harvest and handle to avoid getting stung	Cook to remove sting, like spinach
Tree tips: spruce (*Picea* spp.), fir (*Abies* spp. and *Pseudotsuga menziesii*) and pine (*Pinus* spp.)	Native. Coniferous trees often used in landscaping, parks and forests	Tips (bright-green new growth) in spring, just as the brown papery coating is coming off	Pickle, use for infusions, or dry for tea
Wapato, arrowhead or duck potato (*Sagittaria latifolia*)	Native. Aquatic plant in shallow water, growing up to 3 feet (1 m) tall with arrowhead-shaped basal leaves and white, 3-petalled flowers on long stalks	Flowers in summer, roots in fall or winter	Use flowers in salads or desserts. Roots like potatoes
Water hyacinth (*Eichhornia crassipes*)	Invasive. Free-floating mats of aquatic plants with air-filled floats on bulbous stems, smooth, glossy, round to oval leaves, showy erect clusters of large blue to purple flowers with yellow spots on 1 petal, and feathery black roots. Slow moving and standing water in ditches and wetlands	Leaves, stems and flowers in spring, summer and fall	Cook leaves and stems like cabbage. Use flowers in desserts and preserves. Start with a small amount to test for allergic reactions
Watercress (*Nasturtium officinale*)	Aquatic or semi-aquatic mat-forming herb with hollow stems, lyre-shaped leaves and small white or green cross-shaped, 4-petalled flowers. In or near flowing water in streams, ditches and wetlands	Leaves, stems and flowers in spring and summer	Raw or cooked leaves like store-bought watercress
Wolfberry, Christmas-berry or Goji (*Lycium* spp. including *L. barbarum* and *L. carolinianum*)	Native. Tall shrub up to 6 feet (2 m) with spines, small, narrow leaves, purple to blue 4-petalled flowers and currant-sized, oval, red to orange berries	Berries in fall to winter	Use in desserts and preserves, or dry for snacks and tea
Wood sorrel (e.g. *Oxalis acetosella*, *O. montana* and *O. oregana*)	Native. Small, delicate herb up to 0.5 feet (15 cm) with 3 heart-shaped leaflets on single stalks in shamrock shape, and white or pale pink or yellow flowers	Leaves and flowers in spring or summer	Use raw or cooked like lemony spinach

FORAGER'S TEA

Perhaps because Chris's mom is British, we make a lot of tea in our house. Despite some extreme coffee expeditions in my earlier years (see page 163), I no longer do caffeine (doctor's orders) and lean now toward herbal tea. We bought a lot of packaged chamomile and mint until realizing we could simply harvest herbs growing rampant around the neighbourhood. A lot of foraged edible plants dry well and can be stored for months for use as tea all through the winter. These plants also grow well in patio containers (except perhaps for the stinging nettle!).

COLLECT IN SPRING
Stinging nettles (wear gloves to
   pick fresh leaves; the sting will
   go away once dry)
Tree tips: Douglas fir, spruce or
   pine

COLLECT IN SUMMER
Chamomile
Mint
Lemon balm
Clover flowers
Pineapple weed

COLLECT IN FALL
Rosehips
Hops

1. Preparing these plants for tea is as simple as collecting and drying them thoroughly for storage. Tie the stems of small bundles tightly with twine and hang the plants upside-down for several weeks in an airy and dry out-of-the-way spot. Small bits of green, like tree tips and chamomile, must be dried on a rack. You can make your own drying rack by tying cheesecloth onto a wooden or wire frame (metal clothes hangers bent into rectangles work in a pinch).

2. Once dried, store your teas in a dark and cool place in airtight containers, such as glass jars.

3. To enjoy the tea, simply steep in boiling water—about 1 tablespoon (15 mL) crushed dry tea per cup (250 mL) of water, or to taste.

Opposite, clockwise from top left: stinging
nettle, red clover, lemon balm, hops.

ROSEWATER SYRUP

Chris used to live in a house belonging to a university professor who loved plants. The yard was stuffed to the brim with fruit trees, flowering vines and beautiful scented flowers and herbs, including an impressive clump of rose bushes along the sidewalk. Being a gardener and loving to be in the middle of these lovely beasts, I liked to remove their spent flowers to prolong the blooming. But, as a result, I ended up with a ton—literally garbage bags full—of spent roses, and had to think of something useful to do with them; they were just too beautiful to compost. Hearing that hummingbirds like rosewater, I made some for them, and then thought, "I bet I would like this stuff, too!" So I stewed a simple syrup from the rosewater, and now have a sweet and floral latte or tea flavouring. It lasts for a long time in the fridge, too.

4 cups (1 L) water
2 cups (475 mL) rose petals
3 cups (710 mL) sugar

1. Bring water to a boil in a large pot on the stove. Turn down heat to medium, add rose petals and simmer for 30 minutes. Turn off the heat and strain out the rose petals. At this point, you have rosewater, which you can freeze to make hummingbird food or homemade body care items.

2. To make syrup, put the rosewater back on the stovetop. Add sugar and stir to dissolve. Bring the syrup to a boil, then take off heat and let cool.

3. Store in glass jars in the fridge for 4 weeks or more.

MAKES 3 CUPS (710 ML)

VANCOUVER RAIN LATTE

Now, instead of a London Fog (which is an Earl Grey latte with vanilla syrup), I enjoy a Vancouver Rain—a green-tea latte with rosewater syrup. A nice taste of summer on a rainy fall or winter day.

1 tsp (5 mL) green tea (or 1 teabag)
½ cup (120 mL) water
½ cup (120 mL) whole milk
1 tsp (5 mL) Rosewater Syrup (above), or to taste

1. Boil water and pour over tea leaves to half fill your mug (you want this to be concentrated). Steep for about 2 minutes.

2. While tea is steeping, add rosewater syrup to the milk, then steam it using an espresso machine.

3. Pour the sweetened steamed milk into the tea mug, using a spoon to reserve the foam for the top.

MAKES 1 BIG MUG

TREE TIP SYRUP

You would think evergreen tree tips would taste piney, but they're actually quite citrusy—which is a nice find for foragers who live where citrus trees don't grow. In the early spring, look for soft bright-green new growth bursting from the tips of spruce, fir and pine branches. This recipe uses sugar to extract the moisture and aromatics from the tips for a delicious syrup that lasts for ages. Pour onto waffles, into coffee, or make Baked Brie with Roasted Garlic and Tree Tip Toffee (below).

4 cups (1 L) fresh tree tips
3 cups (710 mL) brown sugar

1. Remove the papery coating from the tree tips.

2. Layer about ½ cup (120 mL) of sugar on the bottom of a clean 4-cup (1-L) glass mason jar, then add one layer of tree tips, then cover in sugar, then another layer of tree tips and so on.

3. Put a lid on the jar and place on a shelf until the sugar dissolves, about a week in total. After the sugar has started to turn liquid (about 1 to 2 days), shake the jar once a day to mix.

4. Once all the sugar has dissolved, strain syrup to remove the tree tips.

5. Store the syrup in the fridge for 4 weeks or more.

MAKES 4 CUPS (1 L)

BAKED BRIE, ROASTED GARLIC & TREE TIP TOFFEE

This is an easy dish to make for friends—and an impressive way to feature your homemade Tree Tip Syrup (above). Be sure to use high-quality brie for best results.

1 whole head of garlic
4-inch (10-cm) round of brie
¼ cup (60 mL) Tree Tip Syrup (above)
¼ cup (60 mL) water

1. Preheat oven to 350F (180C).

2. Cut off top of garlic, drizzle with olive oil and wrap in foil. Place in oven and roast until soft and browned, about 30 minutes.

3. Remove top rind of brie and place cut side up in small baking dish. Place in oven and bake until soft, about 10 minutes.

4. Meanwhile, make tree tip toffee by mixing syrup and water in a small saucepan over medium heat. Simmer until the mixture begins to caramelize and turn golden, about 10 minutes. Do not overcook, as the mixture will become too thick.

5. While toffee is simmering, remove garlic from oven and squeeze cloves from outer husks by pressing with the flat edge of a butcher knife. Remove brie from oven and top with garlic, then as soon as toffee is ready, pour over brie and garlic. Serve immediately.

SERVES 4 AS AN APPETIZER

BROWN BUTTER FIDDLEHEADS WITH CARAMELIZED CATTAIL SHOOTS

Fiddleheads and cattail shoots start coming out around the same time in spring, and are fairly easy to find in urban areas. Both are used in landscaping and can be commonly found in parks. This dish would make a lovely accompaniment to chicken or fish, all washed down with a Pinot Gris.

1 cup (250 mL) fiddleheads, whole
1 cup (250 mL) cattail shoots, chopped
1 Tbsp (15 mL) olive oil
4 Tbsp (60 mL) butter, divided
½ tsp (2.5 mL) sugar
Pinch of salt
1 lemon

1. Thoroughly rinse fiddleheads and cattail shoots in water. Prepare cattail shoots the same way as leeks: trim red or green parts and discard any damaged outer parts, so you are left with only white. Remove any damaged, dried or brown parts from the fiddleheads. Chop cattail shoots like you would leeks or scallions.

2. Over medium heat in a wide, shallow sauté pan, add the olive oil, 1 tablespoon (15 mL) of the butter and the sliced cattail shoots. Caramelize the cattail shoots the same way you would onions: cook for about 15 to 20 minutes, adding sugar and salt once they start to soften and scraping the pan often. Add a bit of water if they dry out or start to crisp.

3. About 5 minutes before the cattails are done, steam fiddleheads for 1 minute, and immediately immerse in cold water to stop cooking (steaming is especially important for tougher ferns; if the fiddleheads appear to be quite tender, though, you can skip this step).

4. At the same time, make brown butter by adding the remaining 3 tablespoons (45 mL) of butter to a saucepan over medium-high heat. Stir constantly as the butter starts to simmer and turn heat to medium-low once the butter browns (about 2 minutes). Add fiddleheads to brown butter and simmer on medium-low for 3 to 4 minutes, until they soften.

5. Remove fiddleheads from butter and plate over caramelized cattail shoots, garnishing with lemon wedges, and squeezing lemon juice over both.

SERVES 2 AS A SIDE

CREAMY ROASTED PEPPERS, CORN & SORREL

Springtime and early summer are optimum for searching for greens—when leaves are young and delicate, and haven't had time to develop a lot of the compounds that can make them too pungent later on. Along with curly dock, wood sorrel, amaranth, lamb's quarters and purslane, sheep sorrel is one of the common weeds that contains oxalic acid (see Oxalic Acid—Enjoy in Moderation on page 30), which gives it a pleasant lemony taste. This bite combines well with smoky roasted peppers and sweet corn, all of which are rounded out by yogurt.

4 red bell peppers
1 Tbsp (15 mL) butter
1 Tbsp (15 mL) olive oil
2 medium onions, diced
2 cloves garlic, minced
3 cups (710 mL) chopped sorrel leaves (or substitute dock or purslane)

4 ears of corn, kernels removed
1/3 cup (80 mL) Rabbit Stock, recipe on page 93 (or substitute quail or chicken stock)
1 cup (250 mL) Easy Greek-style Yogurt, recipe on page 240
Coarse salt to taste
Freshly ground pepper to taste

1. Preheat oven to 500F (260C).

2. On a baking sheet, place whole peppers in oven. Cook peppers on each side for about 15 minutes, or until charred, then turn. Remove from oven, cover in foil and set aside to cool for 30 minutes. Once cooled, remove skin, stems and seeds. Roughly dice and set aside.

3. In a large saucepan over medium heat, heat butter and oil, add onions and garlic and sauté until translucent. Stir in the sorrel and sauté until wilted, about 1 minute. Add the corn, peppers and rabbit stock. Mix well and simmer until the liquid has evaporated, about 10 minutes. Stir in yogurt and heat through. Season with salt and pepper and serve immediately.

SERVES 6 AS A SIDE DISH

Opposite: Sheep sorrel or sour grass grows as a "weed" in many urban gardens and parks, as well as on roadsides and beaches. It can easily be harvested in spring and summer for use as a pleasant lemony green in many dishes.

COOKING SHORTLIST

Tea
- Chamomile
- Chicory root (coffee-like)
- Clover flowers
- Goldenrod leaves and flowers
- Kudzu leaves and flowers
- Mint leaves and flowers
- Mugwort leaves and flowers
- Pineapple weed
- Rosehips
- Wolfberries (goji berries)

Salad Greens—Peppery
- Field mustard and cresses
- Garlic mustard
- Watercress

Salad Greens—Lemony
- Amaranth
- Lamb's quarters
- Purslane
- Sheep sorrel
- Wood sorrel

Salad Greens—Slightly Bitter
- Chicory flowers and leaves, young
- Dandelion

Salad Greens—Subtle
- Chickweed
- Clover
- Daylily
- Goldenrod
- Kudzu
- Miner's lettuce

Salad Greens—Flavoured
- Fennel
- Fireweed
- Mint

Cooked Greens—Like Asparagus
- Asparagus shoots
- Fireweed shoots
- Kudzu shoots
- Water hyacinth stems, young

Cooked Greens—Like Spinach
- Amaranth
- Chickweed
- Clover
- Curly dock
- Dandelion
- Daylily shoots and leaves
- Field mustards and cresses
- Goldenrod
- Kudzu
- Lamb's quarters
- Plantain
- Purple loosestrife
- Purslane
- Sheep sorrel
- Stinging nettle
- Watercress
- Wood sorrel

Cooked Plants
- Bamboo shoots
- Burdock immature flowers (like artichokes)
- Cattail shoots (like leeks)
- Cattail immature flowers (like corn on the cob)
- Fiddlehead ferns
- Garlic mustard (like garlic and mustard)
- Japanese knotweed (like rhubarb)
- Lamb's quarters flower shoots (like broccoli)
- Prickly pear cactus pads (like eggplant)
- Water hyacinth leaves, young (like bok choy)

Edible Flowers
- Blueberry
- Chamomile
- Chickweed
- Chicory
- Clover
- Dandelion
- Daylily
- Fennel
- Field mustards and cresses
- Fireweed
- Garlic mustard
- Goldenrod
- Himalayan blackberry
- Huckleberry
- Kudzu
- Maple
- Mint
- Oregon grape
- Oxeye daisy
- Pineapple weed
- Prickly pear cactus
- Purple loosestrife
- Rose
- Salal
- Wapato

- Water hyacinth
- Watercress

Seeds for Toasting and as Flavouring
- Amaranth
- Garlic mustard
- Lamb's quarters (soak and rinse first)
- Mustard

Making Flour
- Amaranth seeds
- Cattail flower pollen
- Kudzu roots
- Lamb's quarters seeds (soak and rinse first)

Berries and Fruit
- Autumnberry
- Blueberry
- Elderberry (never eat raw)
- Himalayan blackberry
- Huckleberry
- Oregon grape
- Prickly pear cactus fruits
- Rosehips
- Salal
- Wolfberry (goji berry)

Roots—Like Potatoes
- Cattail
- Daylily
- Wapato

Roots—Like Root Vegetables
- Burdock
- Kudzu

Bittering Agents
- Burdock root
- Chicory root
- Dandelion root

Pickles
- Burdock root and stems
- Chicory flowers
- Goldenrod stems
- Kudzu flowers
- Oxeye daisy flower buds
- Tree tips
- Water hyacinth stems, young

Flavourings
- Elder flowers (slightly floral)
- Fennel (like black licorice)
- Field mustards and cresses, seeds (like mustard)
- Garlic mustard seeds (like garlic and mustard)
- Maple sap (sweet syrup)
- Mugwort leaves and shoots (bitter and slightly sage-like)
- Rose flower
- Shiso (like savoury herbs such as cilantro or basil)
- Staghorn sumac berries (spicy and sweet)
- Tree tips (citrusy)

Further references

A Field Guide to Edible Fruits & Berries of the Pacific Northwest by Richard Hebda

A Field Guide to Foraging for Wild Greens and Flowers by Michelle Catherine Nelson

Foraged Flavor by Tama Matsuoka Wong and Eddy Leroux

Hunt, Gather, Cook: Finding the Forgotten Feast by Hank Shaw

Lone Pine Field Guides (choose depending on your area: one of my favourite books of all time is *Plants of the Pacific Northwest Coast: Washington, Oregon, British Columbia and Alaska* by Jim Pojar and Andy MacKinnon)

Stalking the Wild Asparagus by Euell Gibbons

Eat the Weeds website (www.eattheweeds.com) by Green Deane, forager extraordinaire

WILD AND INVASIVE EDIBLES AT THE SEASHORE

Chris and I don't have a boat for fishing for such local marine goodies as salmon and spot prawns, although we wish we did. But there is a rocky beach nearby, and luckily there are lots of delicacies to forage for at the seashore.

Explore the intertidal zone (the area exposed between high and low tides) at low tide to collect seaweed, sea asparagus, clams, mussels, oysters, periwinkle sea snails and Chinese mitten and European green crabs. If you have the gear and gumption, you can even free dive for Dungeness crab.

First, though, check the regulations and openings in your local area, and get a fishing licence if necessary. Fishing supply stores can usually help with this, or visit the website of your local fish and wildlife branch. Ask around for advice on the safest places and best times to forage for whichever species you are looking for, checking with local fishing stores and guides, naturalist groups and even online forums. And ensure there are no red-tide alerts—see the sidebar on Shellfish Poisoning and Red Tide (page 49).

Lastly, check the tide tables and time your trip to the beach for low tide, when the most area is exposed for foraging.

AVOID FORAGING IN POLLUTED WATERS AND BUSY PORTS

When foraging for seafood, choose your spot carefully. Avoid busy ports, active boat areas or any locations tainted by sewer or industrial runoff when digging or foraging for seashore edibles.

A FORAGER'S LIST OF SEAFOOD

Clams, various hardshell species, including hard clam or quahog (*Mercenaria mercenaria*), native and Japanese littleneck (*Protothaca staminea* and *Tapes philippinarum*), butter clam (*Saxidomus giganteus*) and basket clam (*Clinocardium nuttallii*)

Seashore natives or introduced. Easy to do and fun for the whole family, digging clams is a traditional pastime for many coastal residents of North America.

Habitat

Clams eat by filtering plankton from sea water and live in protected bays and inlets, where sand and mud have accumulated to form long, level beaches. Dig for them on these flat beaches and in tidal marshes. Productive clam beds will be known to other foragers, so ask about where to find them when you are starting out.

Equipment

To dig for clams, you only need something to dig with, like a garden shovel, and a bucket.

Collection

First, look for the telltale holes in the mud that let water in for the clam to feed on and breathe. Next, dig down about 6 to 8 inches (15 to 20 cm), loosening the mud or sand so you can sift through it with your hands. Put the clams you find in the bucket if they are large enough—this may depend on the fishing regulations in your local area, but anything over 1 inch (2.5 cm) wide has enough meat to eat. Don't keep any clams that smell bad or with shells that are broken or don't close when you tap them. Rinse the clams in sea water, and bring home some sea water with them so that you can purge them of mud or sand.

Warnings: See Avoid Foraging in Polluted Waters and Busy Ports sidebar, page 48, and Shellfish Poisoning and Red Tide sidebar, below.

Processing

To purge clams of mud and sand, simply cover the bucket and leave them in the sea water for several hours or overnight. Keep the bucket out of direct sunlight since high temperatures will stress or kill the clams. Ideally, leave the bucket indoors in a cool spot. Rinse the clams after purging them of mud and sand to get them ready for cooking. Any clams that don't close when you tap on the shell or handle them are likely dead and should be discarded. When cooking clams, you will either boil or steam them whole (live), or shuck them first. To boil or steam, start a pot of salted water, or a steamer, on the stovetop and when the water is boiling, place the clams in the pot. Cook as directed in recipe.

To shuck, or remove the meat from the shell, insert a paring knife between the top and bottom shells, near the hinge. Sweep the knife around the shell toward the opposite end of the hinge, rotating the shell as you slice. Lift off the top shell and cut any attachments to the bottom shell. Cook as directed in recipe.

For large clams, such as good-sized butter clams, you may want to remove the siphon (or neck), which tends to get tough as the clam gets larger, as well as the brown mass containing the digestive organs.

Shucked clams can be frozen after cooking, covered with the water used to cook them.

SHELLFISH POISONING AND RED TIDE

Always be careful when collecting marine bivalve molluscs like mussels, oysters and clams because of possible shellfish toxicity or red tide, and never eat any shellfish, including crustaceans, that's been dead for longer than an hour before cooking.

Shellfish poisoning can have many serious symptoms including digestive, amnesiac, neurological and paralytic symptoms, which can sometimes be fatal. These syndromes are caused by a marine condition called red tide, which occurs when ocean water is warm enough to support large blooms of certain toxic plankton (small marine organisms). These are taken up and concentrated by filter-feeding bivalves (mussels, oysters and clams). Collecting bivalves in warm months (May through August) is never recommended. Check with local authority offices or websites, such as the fish and wildlife branch of your local government, for shellfish harvest openings.

Also, never eat marine molluscs or crustaceans of any kind that are dead for longer than an hour before cooking. Ideally they are cooked immediately upon harvesting. The bacteria that grow on dead marine organisms produce toxins, which cause the food poisoning symptoms associated with eating bad seafood. This type of food poisoning is not related to red tide and usually clears up on its own.

Chinese mitten crab (*Eriocheir sinensis*)

Identification

Look for brown to purplish crabs 2 to 4 inches (5 to 10 cm) wide and with dense patches of dark hair on white-tipped claws.

Seashore and freshwater invasive. Chinese mitten crabs are competitive with native species for food resources and their burrowing can cause damage to streamside and estuary habitats. They aren't huge, but they are plentiful, invasive and make for a great meal.

Habitat
They rear in fresh water but mate and spawn in salt-water estuaries, burrowing into the mud and sand.

Equipment
Mitten crabs are easy to catch with a bucket; plus, you'll probably want to wear rubber boots.

Collection
The best time to catch them is during mating season in late fall and winter, when the females will have roe (or eggs), especially prized in China as a delicacy. They can be caught by turning over rocks on beaches in or near estuaries and digging through the muddy sand to find their burrows.

Processing
Because the crabs are somewhat small and it can be tedious to remove the flesh, a good way to eat them is in a soup. First, kill the crabs by piercing their abdomen with a sharp spike or knife, then cutting them in half lengthwise. Use a rolling pin or meat tenderizer to break up the shells and meat a little, and then add it to the soup. Once the meat has been cooked, it will fall away more easily from the shell. Use a large-gauge strainer to remove the shells.

Warning: See Avoid Foraging in Polluted Waters and Busy Ports sidebar, page 48.

Dungeness crab (*Metacarcinus magister*)
Seashore and ocean native. At the seashore, I usually putter around the tide pools looking for seaweed, mussels, oysters, sea snails and shore crabs, while Chris (who has a fishing licence) free dives for Dungeness crabs.

Habitat

Dungeness crabs are found along the Pacific coast of North America, as far south as Point Conception, California. They like sandy or muddy bottoms, where they can be found at a minimum of 10 feet (3 m) deep.

Equipment

To forage for crabs, most people use crab pots (or traps), which you have to set with a boat. A motorboat works best, but you can also use a kayak or even a paddleboard if you have one; just be careful not to tip yourself over when hauling up the line and trap.

For those of us without boats, there is another option—free diving. All this involves is holding your breath, diving underwater and swimming to the bottom to catch the crabs by hand. This might sound difficult, but it's really not that hard. If you're a good swimmer, and especially if you're a diver, you should have no problem—Chris does it all the time. If you've never gone free diving in the ocean, consult with an expert to ensure you're following all the recommended safety precautions.

Once you feel comfortable with how free diving works, it's time to go out looking for crabs. To dive for crabs, you'll need a fishing licence, snorkel mask and fins, plus a wetsuit if the water is really cold. You may also want to wear diving gloves since the water will be colder at depth and you will lose dexterity with icy hands. A mesh collection bag (about 20 dollars at a diving supply store) helps—clip it to your belt to store the crabs in. Or ask a friend to hold the crabs for you between dives; it's always a good idea to have a spotter with you when you're diving in the ocean.

Collection

Go in the mid-morning or early afternoon for best light. It's wise to start from a buoy or piling, as this will help you orient yourself underwater (and crabs like pilings). Descend slowly to the ocean floor about 10 to 16 feet (3 to 5 m) down, checking for crabs.

Once you've located some, press down on the top of the shell with your hand so they can't pinch. Check if the crab is large enough to harvest—prior to diving, review your local regulations since this varies by area; often the requirement is that the crab should be at least 6 inches (15 cm) across the largest part of the shell. Next, grab the crab at its back end between the back two legs and flip it over to check whether it is male or female. You can only harvest males, so you're looking for crabs with a triangle-shaped abdomen (females have a round shape). If it's male (and large enough to harvest), grasp him firmly by the back end between the two smallest legs to avoid the pinchers. Place the crab in your collecting bag, or keep a firm hold on him while you ascend slowly.

Warning: See Avoid Foraging in Polluted Waters and Busy Ports sidebar, page 48.

Processing

I usually dispatch my crabs right at the ocean and return the unused portion for other sea creatures to feast on. Start by holding the crab right side up on either side of the shell, placing the heels of your hands against the shell and grasping it with your fingers above where the legs attach. You should be able to hold the crab like this without its pinchers being able to reach your fingers. Next, using a hatchet, a big rock with a sharp edge or the edge of a dock, swiftly and forcefully hit the crab's abdomen in a line down the centre from its nose to the back end. Apply enough pressure so that the abdomen cracks (this will also likely sever the nerves). Grab all the legs on one side and firmly pull them away from the shell, then repeat on the other side. The whole process should take about 30 seconds. Place your crab meat in a cooler and bring it back home to cook right away—when raw it does not keep.

Opposite: Dungeness crabs are gourmet seashore foraging finds, and can be caught without a boat—you need only a fishing licence, a few pieces of free-diving gear and a bit of gumption.

STEAMED DUNGENESS CRAB WITH GARLIC BUTTER

There is nothing like fresh-steamed crab—meaty, moist, slightly salty from the sea while also somewhat sweet. If you are able to forage for crabs, it's a very worthwhile endeavour. Chris loves to swim (and has a fishing licence), so he goes out free diving for crabs, but you can also look for trap-caught crab at your local seafood market. For the most humane way to kill crabs, see page 55. Although fresh crabmeat really needs no accompaniment, it's heavenly with garlic butter.

CRAB
1 Tbsp (15 mL) coarse salt
1 Tbsp (15 mL) freshly ground pepper
1 cup (250 mL) dry white wine
1 cup (250 mL) water

Legs and claws from 2 fresh Dungeness crabs

DRAWN GARLIC BUTTER
½ cup (120 mL) salted butter
2 garlic cloves

1. In a large pot, combine the salt, pepper, wine and water. Bring the liquid to a simmer, then add crab legs and claws, and cover the pot to steam them.

2. Meanwhile, in a small pan over low heat, melt butter. Skim off the solids that rise to the top (and keep for other uses). Add minced garlic and heat for a couple of minutes. Pour into ramekins.

3. Cook the crab just until the shells turn bright red and the flesh is solid white (about 5 to 6 minutes for the legs) and remove immediately. Rinse briefly under cool water to stop the cooking process.

SERVES 4

Preceding pages: Dungeness crab is a memorable centrepiece for a meal with friends—simply pass around some shell-cracking tools, garlic butter and napkins for all to enjoy the rewarding challenge of collecting the luscious sweet meat while chatting about the fun of foraging. Also pictured (clockwise from top left): Rustic Rosemary Sourdough Bread (page 214), Creamy Roasted Peppers, Corn and Sorrel (page 45), and Tree Collard, Mint and Microgreen Salad with Peanut Dressing (page 151).

European green crab (*Carcinus maenas*)

Invasive. Native to Europe, green crabs are invasive on both coasts of North America, and increasingly becoming a concern in conservation because they feed on native molluscs and crustaceans, including juvenile Dungeness crabs. Help to remove this invasive species by eating it. Because they are quite small, they are best eaten as soft-shell crabs. Venice is world-famous for moleche, or battered and fried soft-shell green crabs. Italian fishermen are expert at collecting soft-shell crabs, but it can be difficult for beginners. But if you can get the timing right, you will eat very well and help the ecosystem at the same time.

Identification
Green crabs are about 2 to 3 inches (5 to 7.5 cm) wide and have a mottled brown shell with dark green and yellow flecks on the top, and with green, orange or red underneath. The front of the shell has 5 spiky points on each side of the crab's eyes.

Habitat
Green crabs like fairly protected mud or sand beaches, salt marshes and especially estuaries. They tend to hide in submerged vegetation like eelgrass or salt marsh grasses.

Equipment
A bucket, dip net and just the right timing.

Collection
Although the equipment you need is simple, catching soft-shelled green crabs is tricky. You want to find crabs that are molting, or shedding their old hard shells (which they do so they can grow larger). As they do this in the fall and spring, and are only soft for about six hours between the time they shed their old shell and become protected once again by a new, larger shell that fills out and hardens, you have to find crabs that have just molted and are still soft . . .

kind of unlikely. Or you can use the Italian fisherman's trick: find crabs that are about to molt and keep them in a bucket of sea water for a few hours or days until they shed their old shells and become soft. These crabs all molt at the same time in the late summer or early fall, using marine conditions such as temperature to cue their collective shell-shedding. Crab fishers in North America are just beginning to get a sense of what these cues are for the newly invasive green crabs, so do some research to find out when the green crab fishery is open in your area and see if you can collect some yourself to keep in sea water until they molt, adding fresh sea water once or twice a day. Remember to immediately remove them from the water once they are in their new soft shells, since it is the calcium in the sea water that will harden the shells.

Warning: See Avoid Foraging in Polluted Waters and Busy Ports sidebar, page 48.

Processing
To prepare soft-shell crabs to eat, keep them alive until just before cooking.

In my opinion, the conventional method for killing soft-shell crabs is not the most humane. It involves cutting off their eyes, antennae, mouthparts, gills and apron (the flap on the abdomen) and then cooking them in boiling water or oil. At no point is the crab rendered senseless in this process. On the other hand, crabs have decentralized nervous systems and can't be killed quickly by a spike to the brain like fish. The only humane method of slaughter recommended by the Royal Society for the Prevention of Cruelty to Animals (RSPCA) is an electrical shock[1] but that is not a feasible solution for most people. So what to do?

The best way for people to kill soft-shell crab at home (and this also works on any crab) is to use a sharp spike or knife to pierce through the abdomen

1 "Humane Electrical Stun/killing of Crustacea," Royal Society for the Prevention of Cruelty to Animals, accessed November 2014, http://www.rspca.org.uk.

under the apron (the flap on the abdomen), guided by a hole or small indentation you will find there. Stab the crab through with a quick, sharp movement until you feel it hit the shell on the other side, then firmly and quickly slice the spike or knife towards the back end. This should pierce the major nerves, or ganglia, of the crab and kill it immediately. You can then cut the eyes, antenna and mouthparts off in one go with kitchen shears, lift the sides of the shell to tear off the gills (the off-white feathery things), and pull off the apron.

Mussels (blue, *Mytilus edulis,* and California, *M. californianus*)

Seashore natives. California and blue mussels are very similar and are both choice seaside foraging.

Habitat
Common along the coasts of North America (M. *californianus* is found only on the west coast), these mussels like to live on large slabs of rock in the intertidal zone, attaching themselves with green string-like filaments.

Equipment
All you need is a food-safe bucket and sharp pocket knife.

Collection
Find suitably sized mussels and cut the filaments that attach them to the rock. Collect only as many mussels as you need off the rock, being careful not to dislodge their neighbours. Fill your bucket with some sea water to keep the mussels alive until cooking. Don't keep any mussels that smell bad, have broken shells or don't close when you tap them.

Warnings: See Avoid Foraging in Polluted Waters and Busy Ports sidebar, page 48, and Shellfish Poisoning and Red Tide sidebar, page 49.

Processing
Like clams, mussels can collect sand, although not as much since they don't live in the muddy substrate itself. Just leave the mussels in the bucket of sea water for an hour or two to purge the sand out. Then steam or boil as directed in the recipe you are using.

Easy to collect at the seashore, blue and California mussels are meaty with just the right mix of salty and sweet.

MUSSELS TWO WAYS

Most of us have enjoyed mussels steamed with some kind of wine sauce and served with crusty bread in a good restaurant. Delicious! And totally possible to replicate (or even improve upon) at home. Here are two ways to enjoy those mussels freshly foraged from the seashore. Crusty bread is essential, better yet, freshly baked Rustic Rosemary Sourdough Bread, page 214).

BEER AND GARLIC MUSSELS

1 lb (455 gr) mussels
1 medium onion, finely chopped
2 cloves of garlic, minced
2 Tbsp (30 mL) butter
1 Tbsp (15 mL) olive oil
1 bottle of stout (a dark ale works well too; you want something sweet and malty)

1. Rinse each mussel under cold water and remove any sand, seaweed or other debris. Discard any mussels that stay open during handling and rinsing. Live mussels should close up to protect themselves when they get poked and prodded, so if they don't close they are likely dead and not safe to eat.

2. In a large saucepan over medium heat, sauté the onions and garlic in butter and olive oil until translucent. Add the beer and mussels to the pan and cover. Simmer until the mussels start to open (about 5 minutes) and wait another minute or two for the remaining mussels to open. If the mussels don't open, it's safest to discard, just in case they were dead before you collected them.

3. Serve with crusty rustic sourdough bread and butter.

SERVES 4 AS AN APPETIZER

SRIRACHA LIME BUTTER MUSSELS

1 lb (455 gr) mussels
1 medium onion, finely chopped
2 Tbsp (30 mL) butter
1 Tbsp (15 mL) olive oil
1 cup (250 mL) dry white wine
½ tsp (2.5 mL) sriracha sauce
½ Tbsp (7.5 mL) freshly squeezed lime juice
¼ tsp (1 mL) coarse salt
1 tsp (5 mL) minced cilantro

1. Rinse each mussel under cold water and remove any sand, seaweed or other debris. Discard any mussels that stay open during handling and rinsing. Live mussels should close up to protect themselves when they get poked and prodded, so if they don't close they are likely dead and not safe to eat.

2. In a large saucepan over medium heat, sauté onions in butter and olive oil until translucent. Add the wine and deglaze the pan. Add sriracha sauce, lime juice, salt and cilantro, stir well and cook for 1 minute. Add the mussels to the pan and cover. Simmer until the mussels start to open (about 5 minutes) and wait another minute or two for the remaining mussels to open. If the mussels don't open, it's safest to discard, just in case they were dead before you collected them.

3. Serve with crusty rustic sourdough bread and butter.

SERVES 4 AS AN APPETIZER

Oysters (*Crassostrea* spp. and *Ostrea* spp.)

Seashore natives or introduced. For commercial use they are farmed, but the same varieties you get at restaurants and markets can be found in the wild.

Habitat
Oysters are native to both the west and east coasts of North America. Oysters tend to prefer warm, protected rocky beaches and reefs, rather than sand beaches (like clams) or rock shelves (like mussels).

Equipment
Oysters attach themselves onto the rock they live on, using a glue-like substance. If they are only adhered at the hinge, you can remove them with a screwdriver. If they are connected along the whole shell, they are quite difficult to pry off and require a chisel to remove. You will also need a container and a sturdy knife or oyster shucker.

Collection
Pry or chisel oysters from the rocks at low tide. Discard any that do not close when the shell is tapped.

Warnings: See Avoid Foraging in Polluted Waters and Busy Ports sidebar, page 48, and Shellfish Poisoning and Red Tide sidebar, page 49.

Processing
Shuck oysters right away and leave the shells on the beach. Larval oysters attach to them, for more oysters in the future. Or you can leave half the shells on the beach, rinsing the rest to serve your oysters on.

To shuck the oyster, hold it level in your hand with the large side down. Insert the knife or oyster shucker between the top and bottom shells about 1 inch (2.5 cm) from the hinge. Twist to pry open the shell, being sure to keep the shell level so the liquid inside doesn't pour out. Carefully cut the flesh from the bottom shell, and tip the flesh and liquid into the jar.

At home, strain the liquid to remove any sand, and then you can freeze the oysters in the liquid, or cook them with the liquid immediately.

Periwinkle Sea Snails (*Littorina littorea*)

Seashore invasive. Periwinkles, or winkles, are sea snails native to Europe and are now invasive in North America, so the more we eat the better. While this small creature may appear harmless, it gobbles the eggs of native snails and destroys ecosystems in intertidal zones where it has virtually no predators. Periwinkles are very popular seaside snacks in Great Britain and around the world.

Identification
These marine snails have shells like land snails, which are dark brown or grey, sometimes with spiralling bands, a sharp point on the top and a white base. They are about ½ to 1½ inches (1 to 4 cm) wide.

Habitat
Periwinkles are very prevalent on North America's eastern shoreline and have now also been introduced on the west coast. They live in the intertidal zone of rocky beaches and can sometimes be found in tide pools and muddy estuaries.

Equipment
All you need is a bucket or bag.

Collection
Simply pick the snails off the rocks where you find them. Warnings: See Avoid Foraging in Polluted Waters and Busy Ports sidebar, page 48.

Processing
Rinse off thoroughly under cold running water. Heat water in a pot. When it is boiling, place the snails into the water. After three to four minutes, strain. Remove the flesh using a skewer or pin.

Opposite: While free diving for crabs requires a bit of skill, and a wetsuit when the water is cold, seaweeds like rockweed are easy to collect and a good source of protein and minerals.

WILD GREENS PASTA WITH PERIWINKLE SEA SNAILS

This is a nice, filling dish to whip up after a blustery day of foraging at the seashore. The pungency and slight bitterness of freshly gathered greens pairs well with the salty starchiness of pasta, further offset by the delicate sweetness of the periwinkles. Try collecting a variety of edible greens for a combination of flavours. If you only have one or two plant types available, that works too, and you can always add a bit of homegrown or farmers' market greens to boost the volume. If you have sorrel, dock or purslane handy, toss some in, but keep them to only about a quarter of the total volume of greens due to their pungent lemony taste. If you don't have access to invasive periwinkles, substitute sustainably collected or farmed mussels or clams.

1 lb (455 gr) live periwinkle sea snails (winkles)

4 Tbsp (60 mL) olive oil, divided

1 medium onion, chopped

8 garlic cloves, minced

9–12 cups (2.1–2.8 L) finely chopped amaranth, chickweed, dandelion, goldenrod, kudzu, lamb's quarters, plantain (ribs removed), purple loosestrife, and/or stinging nettle leaves

3 cups (710 mL) finely chopped extra-flavourful greens: sheep sorrel, wood sorrel, curly dock (ribs removed), purslane, field mustard, and/or garlic mustard (optional)

8 oz (225 gr) linguine

2 tsp (10 mL) fresh lemon juice (if not adding lemony greens)

2 Tbsp (30 mL) butter

½ cup (120 mL) grated Asiago cheese

A few pinches of coarse salt

1. Prepare the periwinkles by rinsing them under cold water and removing any sand, seaweed or other bits attached to them. Set aside in refrigerator to sedate them before cooking.

2. Heat 2 tablespoons (30 mL) of the olive oil in a large cast iron pan over medium heat. Add onion and cook until translucent; then add garlic and cook for another minute. Add all greens and another tablespoon (15 mL) of olive oil and toss. Cover pan and reduce heat to low. Continue cooking until leaves are tender but not too soft (keep a particularly close eye on the plantain and dock), about 5 to 6 minutes.

3. Meanwhile, bring salted water to a boil in a medium pot. Add linguine and cook until almost al dente. Drain pasta, reserving ¾ cup (180 mL) of cooking liquid. Return the pot with reserved liquid to the stove and bring to boil over medium heat.

4. Add drained pasta to greens mixture in the cast iron pan. Add lemon juice (if not using the lemony greens), the remaining 1 tablespoon (15 mL) olive oil and the butter. Toss quickly, cover with lid and turn off heat.

5. When the reserved pasta water is boiling, place winkles in pot, add a couple more pinches of salt, and cover with lid. Steam 3 minutes.

6. Plate pasta and greens, sprinkle with Asiago cheese, place winkles on top, and serve. Don't forget to provide your guests with utensils to remove the winkles from their shells. If you have them it's nice to provide an escargot fork and tongs, but a skewer works as well.

SERVES 4

Sea asparagus or glasswort (*Salicornia* spp.)

Seashore native. Sea asparagus is a delicious seashore plant with a crunchy texture and slightly salty taste, excellent steamed with butter and lemon juice.

Identification

Look near the high tide line for a mat-forming plant with long green stems topped by a cylindrical swelling and reminiscent of thin asparagus.

Habitat

Sea asparagus grows on protected tidal flats, salt marshes and beaches.

Equipment

All you need is a food-safe bucket or water-resistant bag.

Collection

Simply pick the plants, discarding woody stems. Warning: See Avoid Foraging in Polluted Waters and Busy Ports sidebar, page 48.

Processing

Take them home to rinse under cold running water.

Seaweed (*Ulva* spp./*Enteromorpha* spp., *Fucus* spp.)

Seashore native. Seaweed, or marine algae, is a great food to forage for if you're near the ocean because it's easily recognizable and super nutritious, being high in protein and iron especially (vegetarians take note!). Bring along an intertidal field guide on your first few beach foraging trips to help with identification. Common forms of green algae can be eaten raw, while many types of brown algae are tougher and more gelatinous and best pickled or fermented. You can dry seaweed to later rehydrate to add to soups, but if you live by the ocean it's very easy to collect for fresh use.

Identification

Green algae: Sea lettuce or sea hair (*Ulva* or *Enteromorpha* spp). Look for very common bright green mats of seaweed attached to rocks throughout the intertidal zone. The shape of the fronds ranges from long strings (sea hair) to flattened "leaves" (sea lettuce).

Brown algae: Bladderwrack or rockweed (*Fucus vesiculosus* or *Fucus spiralis*). Very common and easily identified by the flat brown fronds ending in spherical air bladders that pop when crushed.

Habitat

Edible green and brown marine algae (seaweeds) grow everywhere on both coasts of North America. They attach themselves to rocks in large mats in the intertidal zone.

Equipment

All you need is a food-safe bucket or water-resistant bag.

Collection

Simply pick the algae, discarding tough stems or attached molluscs.

Warning: See Avoid Foraging in Polluted Waters and Busy Ports sidebar, page 48.

Processing

Rinse the algae in cold running water to remove any debris. Discard pieces with barnacles attached and tough roots.

SESAME SEAWEED SALAD

The first time I made this salad, I was amazed that it took only three minutes to collect the seaweed and another three to whip it up—and it tasted as good as the salad at my favourite sushi restaurant! Look for green marine algae called sea lettuce or sea hair (Enteromorpha *or* Ulva *spp).*

2 Tbsp (30 mL) sesame seeds
1 cup (250 mL) sea lettuce or sea hair
2 Tbsp (30 mL) rice wine vinegar
3 Tbsp (45 mL) soy sauce
1 Tbsp (15 mL) sesame oil
1 tsp (5 mL) sugar

½ Tbsp (7.5 mL) shredded ginger
½ Tbsp (7.5 mL) crushed garlic
¼ cup (60 mL) finely sliced scallions
¼ cup (60 mL) shredded carrot

1. Toast sesame seeds in a cast iron frying pan over medium heat until the seeds start turning brown.

2. Soak the freshly collected seaweed in tap water for a minute, then rinse and squeeze out excess water (use a salad spinner for best results). Put vinegar, soy sauce, sesame oil, sugar, ginger and garlic in a small mason jar, screw on the lid, and shake to mix. Toss seaweed, scallions and carrot with the dressing, then top with toasted sesame seeds and serve.

SERVES 4 AS AN APPETIZER OR SIDE

Opposite: Sesame Seaweed Salad, Seaweed Kimchi (page 236) and extra sesame salad dressing for dipping sauce.

FRESHWATER AND INLAND INVASIVE ANIMALS

More and more invasive animals are displacing native species and disrupting ecosystems in North American wetlands, rivers, streams, lakes and even on land. Some of these invaders are edible, and if we seek them out as food, either by foraging for them ourselves or asking for them at restaurants and markets, we can remove them from the environment and help protect our native species.

There are three invaders that I would particularly recommend for eating, as they are common and accessible in urban environments and fairly easy to catch—snails, bullfrogs and crayfish. The others listed here require specialized equipment for capture either through fishing or hunting. And while I am providing information on them in case you want to seek them out, if you aren't able to forage for these creatures yourself, consider working to increase demand for their meat by asking for it at your local restaurants and markets (see Sustainable Foraging at the Fish or Meat Market, page 75).

If you do decide to forage for these critters yourself, check the regulations in your local area, and get a fishing or hunting licence if necessary. Although many areas don't have limitations on invasive species collection, this differs regionally, so visit the website of your local fish and wildlife branch to find out more information and make sure the methods you plan to use are allowed as well.

A FORAGER'S LIST OF EASY-TO-FIND EDIBLE INVASIVE CREATURES

American bullfrog (*Lithobates catesbeianus*)

Wetland invasive. While these bullfrogs are native to the eastern US, they have spread throughout North America and can do a lot of damage to wetland ecosystems. Being the largest of North American amphibians, they successfully outcompete and prey on native frogs, salamanders and even baby waterfowl. They are highly abundant in many areas and common in urban environments, easy to catch, and make a great meal. While most North Americans don't often eat frog legs, they are gourmet fare in Europe. In fact, this species was originally introduced in many areas as a food source, causing it to become invasive around the globe.

Identification

They are the largest frog in North America, reaching from 3 to 9 inches (7.5 to 22.5 cm) from nose to end and up to 2 pounds (900 gr) in weight. Light to dark olive, they usually have dark spots and blotches on their back and a creamy white or yellow belly. You can recognize bullfrogs by the loud "meep!" they make when startled.

Opposite, clockwise from top left: invasive signal crayfish (*photo Jonathan Moore*); the minimal equipment required to forage for crayfish and bullfrogs; the horrendously invasive but surprisingly tasty American bullfrog; and a typical bullfrog habitat.

Habitat

Bullfrogs live in freshwater wetlands, lakes and ponds. They do well in disturbed urban areas such as parks.

Equipment

Gear up with hip or chest waders, a strong flashlight, a big net (or sling spear), an ikejime spike (see Processing for more information), a knife and a good-sized bucket with a lid.

Collection

The easiest way to catch bullfrogs is to hunt at night with a flashlight. Find a nice muddy spot on the shore of a lake or pond—bullfrogs are often found hiding in vegetation or resting on rocks next to the water. Wade in slowly, shining the flashlight over the surface of a pond or lake. The frogs may be sitting by the edge of the water or on a rock, or floating near the shore. Their eyes will reflect the light and make them easy to spot. Keep the flashlight shining on them as you slowly move closer. Inch the dip net up and under them (or get it as close as you can if they are on a rock) and quickly scoop them up. They are very good jumpers, so you will need to immediately grab them from the net, put them in the bucket and pop on the lid. If you have a sling spear (for spear fishing), it is easy to spear them from a few feet away. Dispatch the bullfrogs on site if you can to avoid the stress of transport.

Processing

Although many bullfrog hunters stun frogs using a club to the head, the way you would with fish, bullfrogs are tough little critters and this may not render them unconscious. The most efficient and humane way to dispatch bullfrogs is to use a traditional method called ikejime, also known as pithing or, in the case of fish, spiking. This involves using a sharp spike, such as a thin, sharpened screwdriver, to pierce the brain. Hold the frog right side up with its head facing away from you, its back end toward you and the legs dangling towards the ground (don't rest its legs on anything or it will jump with surprising force). Find the soft spot at the base of the back of the skull, and then quickly and firmly insert the spike in towards the front of the head and between the eyes to pierce the brain. Next, use a sharp knife to sever the head from the body. This will disconnect the brain and spinal cord and ensure the frog feels the least possible pain in the process. Finally, cut through the body above the hips to detach the back legs, and through the shoulder for the front legs. Remove the feet and skin.

SESAME PANKO-CRUSTED FROG LEGS

I work with several biologists who specialize in amphibian conservation, and it is through them that I got the idea to include a recipe for the legs of that invasive predator Lithobates catesbeiana *or American bullfrog, which wreaks havoc on North America's wetlands. Enjoy these non-traditional Japanese-style frog legs for lunch or as an appetizer. If you can't find bullfrogs, invasive signal crayfish or homegrown aquaponics crayfish work well instead (see page 71 for more on foraging for invasive crayfish).*

2 Tbsp (30 mL) sesame seeds, toasted

2 Tbsp (30 mL) smoked salt

1 Tbsp (15 mL) lime zest

½ tsp (2.5 mL) sugar

1 cup (250 mL) flour

2 Tbsp (30 mL) cornstarch

1 tsp (5 mL) baking soda

1 egg

1 cup (250 mL) cold light beer (or sparkling water)

3 cups (710 mL) panko crumbs

½ cup (120 mL) canola oil (or vegetable oil)

16 skinned frog legs (from 4 frogs), or substitute 8 peeled crayfish

1. Mix sesame seeds, smoked salt, lime zest and sugar in a small bowl. Set aside.

2. Combine flour, cornstarch and baking soda in a bowl. Whisk egg and beer together. Fold egg mixture into flour mixture until just combined. Do not over-mix; some lumps are fine. Pour into a wide, shallow bowl (or pie plate). Pour panko bread crumbs into another wide, shallow bowl.

3. Heat canola oil in a skillet over high heat. Dip frog legs in egg and flour mixture, then panko bread crumbs, then place in skillet. Cook until golden brown on both sides, about 2 minutes per side.

4. Place legs on a paper towel-lined plate. Sprinkle sesame seed mixture on top and serve immediately.

SERVES 2 FOR LUNCH OR 4 AS AN APPETIZER

European grove and garden snail
(*Cepaea nemoralis* and *Cornu aspersum/Helix aspersa*)

Inland invasive. Like bullfrogs, snails are very accessible in the city and a delicacy. Many of us gardeners, especially food gardeners, have at some point battled snails—they can be quite the garden scourge, eating our succulent young seedlings and tender greens. Many common garden snails are exotic species imported from Europe, and they compete with our native snails for food and habitat. These snails are some of the same edible species raised in heliculture (snail farming). In fact, some of that expensive escargot imported from Europe into North America is the very same species we spend so much time getting rid of here in our gardens. Imagine that.

Habitat
Your garden, empty lots, verges and parks in the neighbourhood. These snails especially like tender, young greens like lettuce, spinach, peas and clover, as well as young fruits and slightly decayed vegetables.

Identification
The European grove snail (*Cepaea nemoralis*) can be recognized by its spiralling yellow and black or brown shell, while the European garden snail (*Cornu aspersum*, also known as *Helix aspersa*) has a brown shell with lighter flecks and colour bands. Use a field guide to make sure you aren't confusing the European snails with native species, some of which are threatened.

Equipment
You will need a large glass jar or food-safe bucket with ventilation for the snails to breathe.

Collection
The trick with preparing snails as escargot is that they require feeding and resting periods before they are ready to eat, to purge them of any potential toxic plant matter they may have ingested. This involves housing the snails for a couple of weeks.

First, in the early morning after a rain, start by collecting the snails feasting on young leaves.

Processing
After collection, keep the snails in a small container, such as a lidded food-grade bucket or large glass jar, making sure to add air holes. Feed and water the snails in their enclosure for a week to 10 days to purge their systems of anything they may have been eating that is unpalatable or potentially toxic. You can feed the snails water-soaked grains such as cornmeal or oat bran to fatten them up. If they are collected at the end of summer or fall, they don't need to be fattened, and do well on greens, apple cores, spent beer-making grains and stale bread. You can also supplement their diet with culinary herbs to imbue some of the flavour into the meat. Or do as the ancient Romans did and feed them on grape leaves. Ensure they always have access to food and a shallow dish of water, and keep the snail container in a cool place out of the sun.

After a week to 10 days, the fasting period begins. Remove the snails from their container and rinse well with cold water under the tap. Wash the bucket with soap and water, rinse and dry. Put the snails back in and cover (ensuring they still have ventilation), and fast them for 48 hours. You can also hang them in a mesh bag (or old stockings) like they do in commercial snail farming.

After the fasting period, the snails should have purged their digestive systems of any grit and each will have closed up in its shell with a membrane protecting it. Rinse them again and then place them in a covered, ventilated container and put them in the fridge for an hour or more. This will slow their metabolism down to minimize any pain during cooking. After refrigerating, add them to a pot of boiling water on the stovetop. Boil for 5 minutes, allow to cool, and then use a seafood fork, tweezers or a long pin to remove the meat from the shells. Place the meat in cold salted water for 15 minutes. At this point, the meat is ready to cook, or you can refrigerate for a day or two, or freeze for later use.

Opposite, clockwise from top left: Invasive American bullfrog, invasive European grove snail shells, Sesame Panko-crusted Frog Legs (recipe page 67).

CRISPY PAN-FRIED ESCARGOT & ARUGULA SALAD

This is a delicious way to enjoy the common European grove and garden snails many gardeners battle regularly—yes, these frustrating and invasive species happen to be edible! Funnily enough, we don't have a snail problem in our food garden, so I've enlisted my helpful mom to scourge her garden and neighbourhood to collect snails for me. She doesn't mind, but hasn't gone so far as to taste the result . . . yet. I'm confident it won't be for long, though: this sumptuous buttery meat pairs well with the herby dressing and peppery bite of the fresh greens.

3 or 4 dozen garden snails
½ cup (120 mL) Rabbit Stock, recipe on page 93
   (or substitute water)
½ cup (120 mL) dry white wine
½ cup (120 mL) cognac
1 bay leaf
1 small onion, halved
2 garlic cloves, minced
1 tsp (5 mL) fresh or dried thyme
1 Tbsp (15 mL) butter
Juice from half a lemon
½ cup (120 mL) finely chopped arugula leaves
½ cup (120 mL) finely chopped watercress leaves
⅓ cup (80 mL) finely chopped Belgian endive
2 Tbsp (30 mL) Stinging Nettle Pesto, recipe on
   page 19 (or substitute basil pesto)
Handful of pea shoots

1. Start with snails you have first fed and rested for a week to 10 days, precooked and removed from shells (instructions on page 68).

2. In a small pot over medium heat, add rabbit stock, wine, cognac, bay leaf, onion, garlic and thyme, and bring to a boil. Reduce heat, add snail meat and simmer until the snail meat is no longer rubbery (about 30 to 40 minutes).

3. Once snails are tenderized, remove from stock. Heat a skillet over medium heat and melt butter. Add snails, drizzle with lemon juice, stir and cook until browned and crispy. Remove from pan and allow to cool slightly.

4. Toss the arugula, watercress and endive with pesto. Plate and top with pea shoots and escargot.

SERVES 2 AS AN APPETIZER

Signal crayfish (*Pacifastacus leniusculus*)

Freshwater native and invasive in some areas. The signal crayfish is native to western North America, and has been transferred to Europe and Japan, where it is an invasive species, outcompeting native crayfish and transferring fatal diseases. It is also invasive in most of North America where it is not native—in California and everywhere east of the Rocky Mountains. If you live west of the Rockies in Canada, Washington or Oregon, signal crayfish are native, so limit your harvest with sustainability in mind.

Habitat
Crayfish like to hide on the rocky bottoms of streams, rivers and lakes.

Identification
About 5 to 7 inches (13 to 18 cm) long, crayfish are similar in appearance to a lobster. As there are several species of native crayfish that are threatened, be sure to distinguish the signal crayfish by the conspicuous white oval spot on each claw where the pincers meet.

Equipment
To catch signal crayfish you will need a dip net and some rubber boots or hip waders for wading into freshwater streams.

Collection
Look for them in the rocks on the bottom of the stream and slowly place the dip net behind them while standing in front of them. Crayfish swim backwards so when spooked they will swim right into your net.

Processing
If the crayfish are in muddy water, purge them of mud by keeping them in a bucket of clean water for a few hours. Dispatch by piercing their heads with a knife. Boil or steam to eat like lobster. The recipe for Sesame Panko-crusted Frog Legs can easily be adapted for a delicious crayfish dish (see page 67).

OTHER MORE ELUSIVE INVASIVES
There are several other invasive animals and fish that may not be as accessible to people in urban or outlying areas, due either to the need for specialized equipment and hunting or fishing skills, or because they are limited to specific areas. If you are motivated to pursue this ecological sourcing of food—and I hope you are—check with a local conservation group or government environmental agency to find out what edible invasive creatures are accessible in your area. Local governments often encourage invasive species removal by allowing hunting or fishing of invasives at any time of year with no limit on size or numbers. Just ensure you do your research to learn how to catch and dispatch them in the most humane way. If you're not able to fish or hunt these invaders yourself, look for them at restaurants and buy them if you can (see Sustainable Foraging at the Fish or Meat Market, page 75).

- Asian carp, various, including grass (*Ctenopharyngodon idella*), silver (*Hypophthalmichthys molitrix*), bighead (*H. nobilis*) and black (*Mylopharyngodon piceus*)
- Blue and flathead catfish (*Ictalurus furcatus* and *Pylodictis olivaris*)
- Northern snakehead (*Channa argus*)
- Nutria or coypu (*Myocastor coypus*)
- Wild pigs (*Sus scrofa* and *S. scrofa domesticus*)

WHEN HUNTING INVASIVE ANIMALS . . .
Double-check that there are no invasive species removal programs in your area that involve poisoning the creatures you are considering eating. Check with the municipality or park board office wherever you are hunting and foraging.

INVASIVE GAME CARNITAS TACOS

Chris grew up in Hermosa Beach, California, where the Mexican influence is felt in many ways, especially in delicious cuisine. Living now on Canada's West Coast, he finds it tough to find restaurants to satiate his cravings for genuine Mexican food, so we do Mexican at home. Because carnitas is slow cooked, shredded and then cooked again, it is an excellent way to make tough meat tender. If you have the hunting acumen, this recipe would be perfect for invasive wild game. Two types of invasive wild animals doing damage to native ecosystems, and excellent candidates for removal for food, are wild pigs and nutria. If not, carnitas would tenderize old laying hens (chicken or quail) and older rabbit meat. If you can, definitely make your own corn tortillas (see the sidebar for more details).

CARNITAS

4 lbs (1.8 kg) invasive game or other tough meat
1 small onion, halved
2 bay leaves
3 Tbsp (45 mL) vegetable oil
1 tsp (5 mL) cumin
1 tsp (5 mL) cinnamon
2 tsp (10 mL) chili powder (optional)
4 cloves garlic, minced
1 green bell pepper, chopped
Coarse salt and freshly ground pepper to taste

TACOS

3 cups (710 mL) Creamy Roasted Peppers, Corn and Sorrel, recipe on page 45
1 cup (250 mL) Easy Greek-style Yogurt, recipe on page 240 (or substitute sour cream)
24 small corn tortillas (see sidebar)

1. Start by slow-cooking the meat. Use a slow cooker according to manufacturer's directions, or a large stockpot. Add meat, half of the onion, and bay leaves to pot, then fill with water until meat is just covered. Simmer until meat is tender enough to easily shred with a fork.

2. Dice the other half of the onion. In a large skillet on medium heat, sauté onion in oil until translucent. Add cumin, cinnamon and chili powder and stir for 1 minute. Add garlic and peppers and sauté until peppers begin to soften, about 3 minutes. Shred meat into skillet and brown the meat until it starts to crisp. Add salt and pepper to taste. Set aside.

3. Prepare or reheat roasted pepper, corn and dock mixture.

4. To serve, either provide tortillas, carnitas, roasted corn mixture and sour cream to your guests, or add a handful of carnitas and roasted corn mixture to each tortilla and top with a dollop of yogurt.

SERVES 4 FOR DINNER OR 8 AS AN APPETIZER

HOMEMADE CORN TORTILLAS

A lovely Mexican neighbour of ours showed us how easy it is to make corn tortillas from scratch. You'll need to invest 20 dollars in a tortilla press (which will more than pay for itself in the improved texture and taste of fresh tortillas), as well as source corn tortilla flour, called masa harina, from a local specialty market. We had no problem finding the press and flour in our very un-Mexican neighbour-hood. Follow the directions on the package.

PRESSURE-COOKED
RED CURRY DEER

Some good friends of ours had the opportunity to hunt deer in Haida Gwaii, a stunning remote island off the coast of northern British Columbia. Being conservation biologists, they are very conscious of how their consumption affects the planet, and feel that deer meat is a sustainable protein option in the many areas where these herbivores run rampant. Lucky for us, they had us over to share, and this is the meal we enjoyed.

2 Tbsp (30 mL) olive oil

1 large red bell pepper, cut into 1-inch (2.5-cm) chunks

2 medium onions, quartered

2 large potatoes, roughly diced

2 garlic cloves, minced

3 lbs (1.4 kg) deer meat, cut into 1-inch (2.5-cm) chunks

1 15-oz (425-gr) can coconut milk

¼ cup (60 mL) Thai curry paste

½ Tbsp (7.5 mL) soy sauce

1 Tbsp (15 mL) brown sugar

1 Tbsp (15 mL) fish sauce

2 Tbsp (30 mL) Thai basil

1. Heat olive oil in a pressure cooker on the stovetop over high heat. Sear the peppers and onions until slightly charred. Turn down heat and add potatoes and garlic, sauté for 1 minute. Add chunks of deer meat and brown. Remove the vegetables and meat to make the curry sauce.

2. Add cream from the top of the coconut milk and deglaze the pan (stir all the charred bits into the coconut milk). Add Thai curry paste and stir. Continue stirring for a few minutes while the sauce simmers. Add the rest of the coconut milk, soy sauce, brown sugar, fish sauce and basil and mix well.

3. Add vegetables and deer meat back in, then put the lid on the pressure cooker and cook for 10 minutes.

SERVES 4

SUSTAINABLE FORAGING AT THE FISH OR MEAT MARKET

If you're not likely to go fishing or hunting, there are still lots of opportunities to make ecological choices when looking for fish or meat at your local markets or restaurants. Increasingly, conservation-minded restaurants are putting wild-caught invasives on the menu—take a look online to see if you can find one near you. Wild-caught meat from invasive seafood and game is also sometimes available at butcher shops and other specialty retailers in urban centres or even online. If you don't see this option where you shop, ask for it to create a demand.

BEAUTIFUL BUT DEADLY—ASK FOR INVASIVE LIONFISH

Lionfish (*Pterois miles* and *P. volitans*) are very aggressive invasive species with rapidly increasing population size and range; their rapacious appetite for native marine fish is devastating ecosystems. Well known for their ornate colouration and body type, they are often kept as aquarium fish and this is likely how they were introduced here. They can be collected by spear fishing while scuba diving and make for good eating, but have venomous spines. Great care must be taken while collecting them and extracting the spines, which usually requires special training. Once the spines are removed, however, the meat is worth the effort: tender and flaky, somewhat like halibut. It makes delicious ceviche, and is sumptuous seared, grilled, baked or battered and fried. Substitute lionfish for salmon in Fire-cooked Wild Salmon with Creamy Dock Sauce, page 79, for a delicious and fun outdoor meal.

Opposite: For what we can't forage ourselves, Chris and I seek out expert conservation-minded meat and seafood purveyors like Mike McDermid. After spearheading the Ocean Wise seafood campaign, he and chef Robert Clark opened a sustainable fresh seafood and fish & chips shop called The Fish Counter in Vancouver.

INVASIVE MEAT AND FISH TO EAT

- American bullfrog
- Blue and flathead catfish
- Chinese mitten crab
- European grove and garden snails
- Grass, silver, bighead and black carp
- Green crab
- Lionfish
- Northern snakehead
- Nutria or coypu
- Periwinkle sea snail
- Signal crayfish
- Wild pig

Further references

Eat the Invaders website, eattheinvaders.org
Invasivore website, invasivore.org

SUSTAINABLE WILD SEAFOOD

Sometimes we don't have time to forage for wild and invasive edibles, but when collecting food from a market, you can still keep conservation in mind. This is especially important when purchasing wild seafood because you are buying animals that were once part of an ecosystem. So it's good to be aware of whether the populations of the creature you are buying are healthy—and how the method of capture affects other parts of the ecosystem.

As an example, cod, halibut, rockfish, shrimp, scallops and oysters are often caught by bottom trawling and dredging. These methods drag massive anchors and nets along the bottom of the ocean, like a team of bulldozers in the forest pulling nets behind them to snag every tree, fox, frog, owl, songbird and every other living thing in order to get only one target species, then throwing everything but that one species out, usually dead or seriously injured. There are many ways bottom trawling and dredging cause habitat destruction and reduce biodiversity, and these methods should be avoided.

The pelagic longline is another unselective commercial fishing technique with more animals killed as bycatch than removed as the targeted species. These lines are set over vast areas (up to a hundred miles/160 km) with many unmonitored hooks that can snag any and all creatures that pass by, including sharks, turtles and seabirds. Commonly used to catch swordfish and tuna, this is another method that should be avoided. A better alternative is a longline weighed down close to the ocean floor, called a bottom longline.

Finally, some nets can also be harmful. Gillnets are suspended vertically in the water column, and entangle anything that passes by. This is particularly dangerous for air-breathing animals such as whales, dolphins and sea turtles. Purse seine nets hang from floats in the water and are used to encircle and "purse" a school of fish. Both gillnets and purse seines can have high levels of bycatch, including whales, sharks and turtles. However, salmon fisheries using gillnets and purse seines can be highly selective with low levels of bycatch.

The best alternative to bottom trawling, dredging, longlines and unselective netting is the use of small selective traps and hooks and lines (or trolls). These methods are highly selective with limited bycatch, and involve minimal or no damage to habitats. Crabs, lobsters, shrimp and prawns are often caught with selective pots, while tuna and salmon are often caught with trolls or hooks and lines.

Be careful to avoid farmed salmon, shrimp and prawns; they are often very unsustainably produced using lots of toxic chemicals and are a cause of the destruction of coastal habitats and wild fish populations around the world. However, oysters, clams, mussels and inland trout can and are farmed sustainably with little or no chemical input into natural habitats.

So seek out sustainable sources of seafood to protect our oceans and lakes: if you can, go to a fisherman's wharf to directly ask how the seafood was caught. Also, organizations such as Seafood Watch and Ocean Wise provide updates on good and bad choices in your area and usually offer free downloadable pocket guides or apps that you can bring with you when you go to market. They also provide information about ocean-friendly restaurants.

SAFE SEAFOOD PICKS
- Black cod, Pacific halibut, spot prawns, wild salmon, clams, mussels, oysters, and locally farmed Arctic char, catfish, scallops and rainbow trout.

UNSUSTAINABLE SEAFOOD TO AVOID
- Imported crab, Pacific cod, spiny lobster, orange roughy, rockfish, farmed Atlantic salmon, sharks, imported shrimp, squid, swordfish, most tuna.

BE CAUTIOUS . . .
- Farmed: trout (farmed inland), clams, mussels and oysters are okay; salmon, shrimp and prawns should be avoided
- Prawns and shrimp: eat local; avoid imported
- Salmon: eat wild caught; avoid farmed
- Sardines: eat Pacific sardines; avoid Atlantic
- Squid: eat local; avoid imported
- Tuna: only okay if caught by troll or poles (which is not usually the case)

FIRE-COOKED WILD SALMON WITH CREAMY DOCK SAUCE

Don't be intimidated—this meal is delicious and very easy to prepare in a couple of cast iron pans (one lidded) over an open fire. It will work with whatever sustainable locally available fish you have, whether wild salmon bought off the dock or invasive lionfish sourced from a conservation-minded fish market. For the greens, forage for weeds containing oxalic acid—curly dock, sheep or wood sorrel, purslane, amaranth or lamb's quarters—all of which imbue a lemony tang. Accompany this dish with a side of other simple chopped seasonal greens, such as nettles (spring), beet tops (summer) or kale (fall), steamed with a little water in a lidded pot over the fire and served with butter and lemon. For more on gathering nettles (and how not to get stung when you do it), see page 30.

4 fillets wild salmon, 6–8 oz (170–225 gr) each (or lionfish)
½ cup (120 mL) water
2 Tbsp (30 mL) butter

2 cups (475 mL) curly dock, chopped sorrel or purslane
1 cup (250 mL) 10 percent cream
½ cup (120 mL) sour cream

1. Build a wood fire in a safe place, such as a metal campfire barrel with a grate on top. Wait for it to get hot (look for glowing red embers in the centre) while putting together your ingredients.

2. Place the salmon fillets in a lidded cast iron pan, skin side down. Pour water on top and cover with a lid. Cut butter into a second cast iron pan. Place both pans on the grate over the fire, the fish in the hottest spot. When poached, the salmon should be light pink on the sides and just barely translucent in the centre, about 5 to 6 minutes (this will vary depending how close the grate is to the fire). When butter starts browning, add greens, stir to coat with butter and let wilt slightly. Pour cream and sour cream onto greens and stir. Allow to simmer 1 to 2 minutes, or until thickened. Take everything off the fire, pour the creamy greens onto the fish and serve right from the cast iron skillet. Use oven mitts—the pans will be hot.

3. Alternatively, this can be made on the stovetop—it's just not as fun!

SERVES 4

KEEPING

KEEPING MICROLIVESTOCK

Opening the door to welcome newcomers to my old one-bedroom apartment, I invariably received looks like "oh, no . . . I've entered crazy rabbit lady territory" when they came face to face with the oversized bunny condo on the far side of my living room. Filled with shredded newspaper, branches and weeds, it was reminiscent of a small forest in a box. And when guests found out these animals weren't pets, but instead were destined for my dinner plate, their response either ramped up to a look of horror or an exclamation of "that's awesome!" For those with shocked expressions I spent time explaining my carefully contemplated experimental project, hoping it would give them something to think about.

WHY KEEP YOUR OWN ANIMALS FOR FOOD?

I have long been appalled by the suffering of animals in factory farms, as well as the outrageous environmental impact of industrial meat production, and because of this I didn't eat meat for a decade. Many expert food sustainability organizations, including Slow Food International, say that avoiding factory farmed meat is healthier, causes less animal suffering and is better for the environment.[2] But after 10 years of trying to do the right thing by saying no to that tasty blue cheese burger in favour of a soggy tofu patty, I realized that, ironically, a lot of my proteins were being shipped in from distant places where forests—along with all the creatures in them—were being obliterated to make space to grow soybeans. According to leading environmental organizations like the World Wildlife Fund, clearing land for soy farming is destroying some of the world's most valuable ecosystems, including the Amazon rainforest and the Brazilian Cerrado, and contributing to species extinctions, water pollution and climate change.[3]

As a solution, eating only locally and sustainably grown dry beans and lentils sounds great, but this wasn't a viable option for me because they aren't readily available where I live. So my choices seemed limited to depending on protein from miserable and anonymous animals from factory farms or relying on vegetation with a very heavy eco-footprint. There had to be a better option.

After carefully weighing this question, I decided the most ethical and sustainable protein source accessible to me as a city condo dweller was to eat what I could grow in my own very limited space. I admit that a rabbit condo does take up a lot of this square footage and isn't a typical urban decorating accoutrement (although I did stain the wood to

2 Ariana Banfi, Elisa Bianco, Edoardo Maturo, Annamaria Pisapia and Emma Slawinski. "Too Much at Steak: How to Choose Your Meat; Less and Good, Clean and Fair." (Carru, Italy: Slow Food Editore, 2012), 1–33.

3 Joshua Levin and Martha Stevenson, eds. "Soy," in *The 2050 Criteria: Guide to Responsible Investment in Agricultural, Forest, and Seafood Commodities.* (Washington, DC: World Wildlife Fund, 2012), 45–50.

match my art deco cabinet and antique piano; that has to count for something, right?). But, as an avid foodie and passionate supporter of sustainable urban food production and animal welfare, I was willing to experiment. So I threw caution to the wind and celebrated my inner rabbit lady.

Since then I have also embraced raising other types of microlivestock suitable for urbanites in tight spaces, including quail for eggs and meat, freshwater seafood, bees for honey, and even mealworms and crickets to feed the quail and fish . . . and me, when these insects are dried and ground into a high-protein flour used to make Dark and Stormy Chocolate Cupcakes (page 141).

TAKING AN ETHICAL STAND

As an ecologist, I don't oppose humans consuming other creatures for food, provided these animals are respected and allowed to live free of fear and express natural behaviours. Furthermore, I strongly believe that if one is going to eat meat, one should be aware of every part of the raising, slaughtering and butchering that goes into it—and be involved in the entire process at least once. The more engaged we are in how the animals we consume are raised, the more empowered we are to ensure they are chemical-free and humanely treated.

Adorable and fluffy day-old quail chicks become full-fledged egg layers within two months.

RAISING MICROLIVESTOCK IN THE CITY

Hey, while I realize keeping livestock in a city apartment might sound kind of cuckoo, it wasn't that long ago that people lived with pigs mucking about in their yards, chickens roosting on the front stoop and even guinea pigs tucked somewhere in the kitchen—yes, guinea pigs were domesticated as food animals. In our North American culture, people have lost that connection with their food, especially in cities. But now, as urbanites become more aware of the rising negative impacts of large-scale industrial agriculture, and are increasingly concerned with food safety and security, they are gravitating back to raising their own food. It's certainly possible to grow your own protein in urban areas both sustainably and humanely.

Many cities now allow the keeping of laying hens in backyards and some, like Seattle, have gone so far as to legislate for miniature dairy goats, which is really cool. If you have the option to keep hens and mini goats in your backyard, do it! If you don't live in one of these cities, though, or live in an apartment or house with very limited outdoor space, consider other microlivestock as a low maintenance, quiet and highly productive means of growing your own protein—one that can even be managed indoors or on a small patio. City and condominium bylaws may be less likely to restrict these choices, as these birds and animals often fall under pet rather than livestock legislation.

CHECK OUT LOCAL RULES AND REGULATIONS

One of the challenges of being a trailblazer in urban homesteading is becoming familiar with regulations on keeping livestock in the city. Every municipality has different bylaws, and if you live in an apartment building or condo, your building probably has rules as well.

Notably, most of the microlivestock species discussed here haven't been legislated because they are not commonplace in urban settings (yet). Rabbits, quail, insects and aquatics are more likely to fall under "pet" designation, and these rules are usually a lot less restrictive than those for designated "livestock" species such as chickens or goats. So if that's the case, it's appropriate to simply work within the "pet" framework.

Whatever you are raising, be aware of any limits on the number of animals you can keep or how large their housing can be, as well as whether or not you are allowed to slaughter on-site. You most likely won't be permitted to do this if you live in an urban area or apartment (and you almost certainly can't slaughter at home to sell the meat), but animals can be moved to a less urban location where rules are less restrictive. Or, since microlivestock species are small and relatively easy to process, some urban homesteaders opt to discreetly slaughter at home as part of their routine method of cooking.

The best way to become acquainted with city bylaws is through a local homesteading organization—if you're lucky, someone has already done the research for you. If you can't find a group like this where you live, start one! And begin your research by connecting with a local animal control organization, which may have clearly delineated the regulations for each type of animal you are considering.

If that doesn't work, go to your municipal government website. I've found these harder to navigate, and you may be required to read through technical documents on bylaws. If you can, it's often easiest to go directly to the municipal hall to ask questions (but be prepared—your inquiries will be considered unusual, and you may come away with few or no answers). Finally, if you are in a shared building, you'll need to become familiar with any bylaws restricting activities inside your apartment or on your balcony. To do this, contact your building or condo management.

Opposite, clockwise from top: Michelle with a laying quail hen; signage at a local farm; baby turkeys hitch a ride on a dairy goat; Roe steals some veggie scraps headed for the rabbits.

RABBITS

———

RECOMMENDED BREEDS: New Zealand or Californian (*Oryctolagus cuniculus*)
PRODUCTS: Meat, fur
URBAN SPACE REQUIREMENT: Minimum 30 square feet (2.8 square m)
for 2 rabbits or 60 square feet (5.6 square m) for up to 6,
outdoor or indoor
TIME COMMITMENT: 15 minutes per day
FEED: Grass, foraged edible weeds, veggie scraps and alfalfa pellets
ESTIMATED START-UP COST: $220 (see Getting started, page 89)

What is it about rabbits that have food sustainability thinkers like Michael Pollan and Novella Carpenter so excited? For one thing, the environmental impact of rabbits is very low compared to many other meats—scientists calculate their ecological footprint (relative to their weight) as over three times less than beef, for example.[4] Rabbits can be fed on grass cuttings, garden weeds and vegetable scraps from the kitchen. Their clean, odourless manure is worth its weight in gold for fertilizing power. And in urban areas rabbits make sense because they are quiet and don't require a lot of space (though they do need more room and environmental enrichment than typical hutches provide). After only two months of quietly consuming about twenty dollars' worth of rabbit feed along with lots of free weeds and lawn clippings, all the while producing great amendment for your potted plants or garden patch, each rabbit will be ready to become about six delicious dinners.

4 Marco Scotti, Cristina Bondavalli and Antonio Bodini. "Ecological Footprint as a Tool for Local Sustainability: The Municipality of Piancenza (Italy) as a Case Study." Environmental Impact Assessment Review 29 (2009): 39–50.

HUSBANDRY

In nature, rabbits are social prey animals that live in large groups, love to spend time grazing grass and chewing vegetation, and defend themselves from predators by digging underground tunnels. They startle easily and can die from stress and fear. Creating a friendly environment with their habits in mind will really help to keep your rabbits healthy and happy.

I recommend about 30 square feet (2.8 square m) per rabbit, with an enclosed private area for hiding in and a predator-proof run (isolated from dogs or cats and also from small children) in order to give them space to move about and sprawl out. Rabbits also love to dig, and while this can be challenging, a thick bed of straw helps, especially when it comes time for a doe to kindle (give birth): she will tunnel into it to make a deep nest, lining it with soft fur pulled from her belly.

I would estimate feeding your rabbits and cleaning their habitat requires about 15 minutes a day, plus a little time for foraging trips to collect weeds and prunings from the garden or empty lot down the street. Believe it or not, rabbits can even train themselves to use litter boxes, which is very convenient when it comes to cage cleaning time—this is what made me first think it might be possible to raise them in an apartment. Kept clean, their cage does not smell.

Rabbits prefer grass to anything else, so clippings from a non-chemically treated lawn are an excellent source of food. If you have your own lawn, you can allow them to graze using a rabbit tractor (a moveable, covered, predator-proof pen). However you manage it, ensure they always have plenty of fresh or dried grass to munch on, or provide dried hay if you can't access a lawn.

Vegetation that is non-toxic to people is safe for rabbits—just don't give them too much of any one thing (except for grass). Our rabbits love foraged weeds such as dandelions and clover, along with bamboo and invasive Himalayan blackberry branches. Plant-based garden and kitchen scraps are also eagerly nibbled, especially apples, carrots, celery and lettuce. Cabbage, kale, broccoli and cauliflower are fine, too, but limit these crops to half a cup (120 mL) per day per rabbit or less—otherwise they may cause bloat, which can be fatal.

Rabbits are social animals, so when starting out, get at least two. Beginners may decide to purchase kits and raise them to slaughter size rather than breeding their own. Make friends with someone raising rabbits near you by joining local homesteading groups or online forums, and simply purchase kits regularly. Kits from the same litter can be housed together until they are ready to eat. To avoid potential issues with fighting, it is advisable to get kits from the same litter—those from separate broods can sometimes be hostile to each other. Make the rabbit enclosure as large as you possibly can to give them plenty of space and allow for the addition of lots of foraged branches and other goodies. Pruning branches off nearby non-toxic trees (such as maple, alder, willow and bamboo) and shoving the whole thing into the hutch will provide something edible for your rabbits to chew.

If you want to raise your own rabbits from scratch, you'll need to keep one male and at least one female, with each rabbit in a separate enclosure. Remember that rabbits like to live in groups, so when separating them, use a wire mesh wall rather than solid partition in order to allow them to continue to keep each other company.

Rabbits are naturally very prolific breeders, which is one of the reasons they make such good animals to raise for protein. We keep two females and one male, and breed the females only three times per year, which provides plenty of meat for the two of us, while not putting too much stress on the mothers. It's certainly physically possible to breed them more often—many commercial breeders mate their does two to three weeks after they give birth, for eight litters per year per animal. That means the doe is giving birth every month and a half, and I personally feel this is far too hard on her.

To breed, place the female into the male's enclosure

and allow them to go to town (this takes between 10 seconds and 10 minutes). Don't leave them unattended during this time or they may fight. Just 31 days later you will have kits, and 6 to 8 weeks after that you can harvest the meat. Rabbit moms, in my experience, have excellent care instincts and will birth and raise their kits with very minimal assistance. All you need to do is provide a safe place with some deep straw bedding she can build a nest in.

GETTING STARTED

I've outlined my costs for starting out with two rabbit kits to grow to slaughter size, both from the same litter so they can be housed together. Note that you need two litter boxes and two waterers if the two rabbits are to be housed separately. Keep in mind most of these costs are one time only. Building your own hutch is less expensive than buying one, but another economical option is a used urban chicken coop, often available through an online classified site or homesteading forum. Just be sure to disinfect your second-hand cage before setting up your rabbit house.

CLEANING A SECOND-HAND COOP

To prepare a second-hand coop or cage for your rabbits, quail or other microlivestock, you need to ensure it is clean and disinfected. If you are in an apartment, this is easiest to do where people normally wash their cars.

Start by scraping out everything left from the previous inhabitants (a metal trowel or hoe works well for wooden floors and walls, or a hard-bristled scrub brush for wire), rinsing with a hose, and then scraping again to get any leftover softened bits. Next, use a scrub brush, water and disinfectant, making sure to get into all the nooks and crannies. I prefer plain white vinegar, because it works well as a sterilizer and is not harmful to animals or to the environment. Dilute vinegar 1:1 with warm water. Bleach is highly toxic to you, your animals and in the groundwater, but if you do use it, dilute very well (3 Tbsp/45 mL to roughly 1 gallon/4 litres of

Gear	Estimated cost
2 rabbits (meat breed, without pedigree)	$40
Materials for building cage or used chicken coop	$75
Feed for 8 weeks (two 44-lb/20-kg bags)	$25
Weeds and branches	free
Litter box	$10
Waterer	$10
Bedding (shredded paper)	free
Paper shredder	$20
Straw bale	$10
Butchery shears	$30
Total	$220

water), do not use hot water, do wear gloves and ensure the area you've applied it to is completely dry and ventilated before housing animals in the cage. However you disinfect it, if possible, leave the coop or cage out in the sun and fresh air to dry thoroughly.

SLAUGHTER AND PROCESSING THE MEAT

Like the other aspects of raising rabbits, slaughter and processing are brief and uncomplicated. When Chris and I raised our first pair of rabbits, we enlisted the help of my dad, since he has experience keeping and butchering them. And though I trusted his wisdom, I still made him and Chris sit with me while watching online instructional videos about humane rabbit slaughter, in which they indulged me with a minimum of complaint. In the end, of course, we went with my dad's original, practical suggestions, but I felt better educated and more comfortable with what we were about to do. Using tools available from kitchen supply stores, including small scissors, a sharp knife and butchery shears, we set up shop in his backyard and had the meat ready to cook and the cleanup complete in less than an hour.

There are several methods of humane dispatch for rabbits, but the one we've found to be fastest and most foolproof is cervical dislocation. This involves putting the rabbit on the ground, either outdoors or in, and giving him a tasty treat. We always take a moment to thank the rabbit and appreciate his contribution to us in the form of food. While in our experience no rabbit has tried to run away while we were doing this, staying in an enclosed space may be a good idea, just in case. While he is eating, gently place the wooden handle of a broom or garden hoe against the back of his neck just behind the ears, step on the handle from behind him on each side of his head, and then swiftly and firmly grab the back legs and pull them up towards your chest. This should only take about 30 seconds and does not require great strength. You will hear the dislocation and the rabbit will be killed immediately with a minimum of discomfort or fear. The rabbit's legs will kick for another minute, but don't worry—this is only the result of automatic muscle spasms. There should be little blood at this point.

Promptly tie string to both back legs and hang the rabbit from a hook or fence post over a large bucket to catch draining blood. If you are worried about spatter, stretch out a tarp under the bucket. This isn't really necessary, though, as the fresh blood is very easy to rinse off with soap and water.

Now, with a very sharp knife or butchery shears, quickly remove the head and keep the body over the bucket to catch the blood. If you are outside, you can let the blood drain and rinse with a hose afterwards. Do this part as swiftly as you can so less blood accumulates in the body cavity (although if blood does start to clot in the body you can rinse it out later and it won't affect the taste of the meat).

If you are very intrepid, you can save the blood to make sausage, but I haven't gone quite that far yet. There will only be about half a cup (120 mL) of blood per rabbit (I'm estimating; I've never measured it). Next, cut off the front feet at the ankle.

You can remove the pelt all in one piece by using very sharp scissors to carefully cut a band around the back legs at the ankle, then a "V" into the groin. Hold the tail, anus and urethra and cut off together. You should now be able to peel the pelt from the body (and I suggest you don't waste this precious resource—see the next section for what to do with it). Next, break open the hips. Using small scissors to avoid going deep, slice open the body cavity lengthwise from near the anus all the way to the rib cage, being careful not to perforate any of the internal organs. The bladder and digestive tract should easily come out of the body at this point. Remove them and set aside. The liver, kidneys and heart should be kept to eat (they are delicious and very healthy—see Rabbit Pâté with Oyster Mushrooms, page 97), but be sure to remove the gallbladder from the liver; it's the inedible greenish sac of fluid containing very bitter bile. Remove the lungs, trachea, connective tissue and any clotted blood. If you have a dog, fresh lungs are a well-loved and healthy treat. Finally, cut the back feet off.

If you can, bury the bladder, digestive tract, trachea and connective tissue deep in a garden or compost pile where they can break down into rich nutrients for plants. If you don't have the outdoor space, add them to the municipal compost if they accept meat. Just note that these body parts are particularly pungent, so you might want to time this process with compost pickup day. If you don't plan to do anything with the pelt, feet or head, you can compost them the same way. Rinse out the carcass under running water and freeze in an airtight container or cook.

USING EVERY RESOURCE

Some people who raise or hunt rabbits for meat simply compost the hides and fur, but to me this is a waste of a beautiful and useful material. Personally, I think farming animals purely for fur to use as a fashion accessory is morally undesirable (to put it nicely). However, if you have that luscious fur as a by-product of your ethical protein production, why not make it into warm mittens or boot liners, or even a conspicuous collar to start conversations about the sustainable stuff you're doing?

There are several uncomplicated methods to prepare the fur that don't require harsh chemicals. An ancient and very straightforward process simply involves scraping the pelt, applying fat (eggs, oil or brains), and stretching and drying it. If you want to try your hand at brain tanning, which I've seen several workshops on, keep the heads of the rabbits as well. Your imagination is the only limit to what you can make with these exquisite pelts!

Another option, especially if you enjoy knitting or felting, is to consider keeping angora rabbits: simply cut the fibre from the pelt and spin it into fuzzy and soft angora yarn.

You can also keep the feet from your rabbit livestock to make charms and accessories to share with friends. Rinse any blood and tissue from the feet and let them air-dry overnight. Next, place in a container, such as a zippered freezer bag, in borax powder (about ⅓ cup/80 mL per 4 rabbit feet) for 1 or 2 weeks, or until they are completely dried out. Brush the powder off and fashion each foot into a keychain or charm—you'll find lots of ideas on how to do this with a quick web search.

Further reference

Deerskins into Buckskins: How to Tan with Brains, Soap or Eggs by Matt Richards

A simple wooden hand spinner is all that's needed to turn super-fine angora rabbit fibre into yarn for knitting, or create soft and supple furs from the pelts of short-haired breeds.

RABBIT STOCK

Stock is invaluable in the kitchen and a fabulous way to make good use of the bones left over from butchery. Throw in whole bones and joints, which add flavour and depth to the stock—you can filter out unwanted bits and keep any meat left on the bones once you've made it. Store stock for months in small batches in the freezer for when you need it. This rabbit stock is a very flavourful alternative to the vegetable or chicken stock often called for in soup and risotto recipes. If you don't have time to make stock following butchery, freeze the carcass to add to the stockpot later.

1 rabbit carcass (bones with some
   meat left on from butchery)
1 onion, halved

1 bay leaf
Coarse salt to taste

1. Fill a stockpot with enough water to just cover the rabbit bones. Add the onion halves and bay leaf. Simmer on the stovetop until the remaining meat falls off the bones, about 1 hour.

2. Remove from heat and allow to cool enough to pull the meat off the bones. Strain the solids out of the stock and add the meat back. Use immediately or freeze.

MAKES ABOUT 12 CUPS (2.8 L)

RUSTIC ROASTED RABBIT

As part of our gift to dear friends getting married on remote and beautiful Hornby Island (a four-ferry trip from our place), we hauled over a cooler full of rabbit meat and all the other ingredients needed to create a family feast the day before the wedding. Having spent most of that day sampling the excellent selection of wineries on the island, Chris and I, with two other close friends (who were very good sports), rushed around the tiny kitchen in our B&B like something out of a Food Network reality show. Somehow, we managed to pull off this roasted rabbit (which is actually really easy), along with two huge vats of Coconut Curry Rabbit (page 96) and two loaves of Chris's Rustic Rosemary Sourdough Bread (page 214). We enjoyed local Pinot Noir grapes (of the fermented variety) with it.

1 rabbit (about 3–3½ lbs/1.4–1.6 kg), loins and legs separated
½ Tbsp (7.5 mL) olive oil
½ Tbsp (7.5 mL) finely chopped fresh rosemary
½ Tbsp (7.5 mL) finely chopped fresh sage
½ Tbsp (7.5 mL) finely chopped fresh thyme
¼ tsp (1 mL) coarse salt
1 lemon

1. Preheat oven to 350F (180 mL).

2. Brush olive oil on rabbit pieces, both top and bottom. Mix herbs and salt together and rub on rabbit meat, both top and bottom, as well as inside the body cavity.

3. Place slices of lemon on baking pan, and rabbit pieces on top. Roast until the internal temperature reaches 165F (74C), about 15 minutes.

SERVES 4

COCONUT CURRY RABBIT

This is probably the dish we make most often at our place. It's hearty and tasty, and works just as well for the two of us (with yummy leftovers) as it does for larger groups. I've suggested kale, because that's what we most commonly throw in, but any foraged or perennial edible green works. This goes well with a pot of jasmine rice.

1–1½ lbs (455–680 gr) Yukon Gold or similar potatoes
2 rabbit loins
1 Tbsp (15 mL) coconut oil
1 medium onion, chopped
4 cloves garlic, minced
1 Tbsp (15 mL) fresh ginger, grated
1 tsp (5 mL) curry powder
1 tsp (5 mL) coriander
1 tsp (5 mL) cardamom
1 tsp (5 mL) turmeric
1 tsp (5 mL) cumin
1 15-oz (445-mL) can coconut milk
1 cup (250 mL) chopped cauliflower
1 cup (250 mL) peas, fresh or thawed
2 cups (475 mL) chopped kale, ribs removed

1. Clean potatoes (leaving the skins on) and chop potatoes and rabbit into 1-inch (2.5-cm) cubes.

2. Sauté garlic, onions and ginger in coconut oil over medium heat until onions are translucent. Add spices to pan and sauté for another 2 minutes, or until fragrant.

3. Add rabbit loins and cook until browned, about 7 minutes. Add coconut milk, turn heat down, and simmer for 5 minutes. Add potato and cook another 8 minutes, then add cauliflower, peas and kale and cook 5 minutes more.

SERVES 6

RABBIT PÂTÉ WITH OYSTER MUSHROOMS

My grandparents always kept pigs on their little home-stead, and I grew up having "liver spread" sandwiches. I now know this as pâté, and have come to realize that my grandma's recipe stands up to the best pâtés I have tried. Here is my variation from homegrown mushrooms and rabbit meat—no pig parts required. And if you grew the rabbits yourself and fed them healthy food, no need to worry about toxic chemical buildup in their livers.

2 cups (475 mL) rabbit livers (from 4–5 rabbits)
2 Tbsp (30 mL) + 1 cup (250 mL) butter, divided
1 small onion, minced
½ cup (120 mL) chopped oyster mushrooms
½ tsp (2.5 mL) ground allspice
¼ tsp (1 mL) ground cloves
¼ cup (60 mL) dry port
2 Tbsp (30 mL) flour
1½ cups (350 mL) whole milk
½ cup (120 mL) 35 percent cream
2 eggs
¾ tsp (3.7 mL) freshly ground pepper
1 Tbsp (15 mL) coarse salt

1. Preheat oven to 300F (150C). Cut the rabbit livers into 1-inch (2.5-cm) cubes.

2. In a saucepan over medium heat, sauté onions in 1 tablespoon (15 mL) of the butter until the onions are translucent. Add livers and mushrooms and sauté until liver is just browned on the outside (about 2 minutes). Purée the mixture with 1 cup (250 mL) butter, allspice and cloves in a food processor. Pour into large bowl.

3. Deglaze the pan with the port, and simmer until reduced to 2 or 3 tablespoons (30–45 mL). Add the port reduction to bowl with liver purée.

4. Over medium heat, melt remaining tablespoon (15 mL) butter in the pan, then stir in flour and cook for 1 minute. Add milk and cream and stir continuously until thickened, about 2 minutes. Pour into bowl, mix, and allow to cool slightly.

5. In a small bowl, whisk eggs with salt and pepper. Fold into pâté mixture to mix everything completely.

6. Pour the mixture into ceramic terrines or oven-safe glass jars (my grandma used her old-fashioned loaf pan). Place the terrines or jars into a shallow pan filled with boiling water (don't let water go over tops of jars—about halfway is fine), and place the pan in the oven. The water should be at a very low simmer while cooking. Bake for 1 hour to 1 hour 15 minutes (or less if using very small vessels) until the top of the pâté has browned.

7. Store the pâté in the refrigerator for up to 2 weeks, or in the freezer for 6 months or more.

MAKES 3 CUPS (710 mL)

QUAIL

———

RECOMMENDED BREED: Japanese quail (*Coturnix japonica*)
PRODUCTS: Eggs, meat, feathers
URBAN SPACE REQUIREMENT: 6 square feet (0.6 square m) for 6 to 7 birds in an
outdoor or indoor coop
TIME COMMITMENT: 15 minutes per day
FEED: Game bird crumble and homegrown mealworms
ESTIMATED START-UP COST: $165 (see Getting started, page 102)

When my municipality finally passed a bylaw allowing backyard chickens, I was elated. It was such a great move towards self-sufficiency and food security in the city, especially in today's climate of disconnection and corporate control when it comes to food. The only problem was that I didn't have a backyard! Despite this, I couldn't stop imagining morning treks to a little coop, the gentle clucks of hens, warm eggs collected from soft straw nests. I thought about birds foraging contentedly, about being able to turn my kitchen scraps into food. And, of course, about fresh eggs, produced in the healthiest and most ethical way possible, all just outside my door. Sigh.

Happily, I found an alternative for apartment dwellers and others with limited space—Japanese quail. In comparison to a chicken, the quail produces larger eggs proportional to its size, lays more often and requires less food for the same amount of output.

A quail's eggs are larger than its head and generally 7 percent of its body weight. This is amazing when you think about it—that would be like a woman having a very large baby every single day (human babies are typically 5 percent of their mother's body weight). While the eggs might seem small compared to those of a chicken, a small balcony-sized hutch is enough space for the equivalent output of about one to two chicken eggs a day—plenty for most single or coupled apartment dwellers. Plus, if you're an intrepid homesteader, quail are very fast growers and make excellent roasts. Given lots of fresh straw, leaves and a bit of soil, quail can happily keep you in fresh, local, ethical eggs and meat, even in a city apartment.

HUSBANDRY

Quail are ground-dwelling birds from the pheasant family—they spend their days foraging for seeds and insects in fallen leaves and staying hidden from predators in dense vegetation, preferring to scuttle away on foot rather than fly, something they can do but not much better than chickens. Provide domesticated quail with an enclosed cage equipped with straw litter to hide in, pans of soil for dust bathing and fresh leaves that they can clean bugs off of and they will be perfectly happy.

Luckily for apartment dwellers and others living in smaller settings, quail take very well to confined living spaces. A typical small outdoor rabbit hutch (say 2 x 3 feet/60 x 90 cm) can work very well and will fit on most apartment balconies. Or house quail in an indoor rabbit cage in a spare room, a corner of the living room or in the basement—you'll just have to clean an inside cage more often to keep it smelling fresh. The quail themselves are very quiet, mostly making contented chirps when given fresh straw, soil or leaves to play in. Males do "crow," but nothing like the raucous cry of the chicken rooster; instead it's a soft sound similar to paper ripping and not much louder than your speaking voice.

Find a hutch or cage with a ¼-inch (0.6-cm) to ½-inch (1.25-cm) wire mesh bottom, which allows droppings and spilled food to fall through onto a tray you can easily remove and clean. I would recommend slightly angling the wire bottom of the hutch so the eggs gently roll to one edge for easy collection. If you're not building your own cage, do this by adding shims an inch (2.5 cm) high under the legs on one side of the hutch.

The droppings are dry and can be scraped off the tray with a garden trowel. Along with any spilled food, they make good garden amendment if you have somewhere to let them age several months before applying around edible crops. If not, they can be composted in municipal collection. Fairly clean used straw makes good mulch for patio containers or garden beds, or can be tossed into worm composting bins. Soiled, smelly and wet straw is best composted in a bin or in municipal collection.

For half a dozen quail, clean an outdoor cage once every week or so to keep it fresh; if indoors twice a week is recommended. Use vinegar and water (1:1 ratio) to wipe up messy spots and periodically freshen the whole cage. While a vinegar solution shouldn't hurt them, it's best to avoid splashing your birds.

If you can't access fresh straw (a good place to ask for it is at the farmers' market—some growers pack with straw), use shredded newspapers. You will need to clean them out more often because they will get soggy. Use shallow dishes of soil from the garden, or organic potting soil, for the dust baths. While any type of leaves may be fine since the quail won't eat them, non-toxic options are always safest—anything from the garden is okay, or forage for maple, alder, willow, bamboo and edible weeds. Quail especially love whole plants with lots of soil on the roots.

Always place the cage away from drafts and avoid placing it at high elevations, as this can be stressful to its occupants. On high-rise apartment balconies, set the cage in a low and secure spot where your quail won't feel exposed to dizzying heights, and use a screen to block high winds.

Make sure your birds always have access to fresh water, and feed them a crumble made for laying birds. I keep the feed dish topped up at all times, since quail won't overeat and get fat like some other animals will. Consider keeping two or more dishes of water and food if you have more than four or five birds to prevent any bullies from excluding the more submissive birds.

How many quail you keep will depend on your own preferences, but a starting range for urban quail keepers might be about one bird per square foot (commercial production calls for six or more, which I believe is far too crowded). Unlike chickens, you do need to mix in some males with the females in order to ensure good egg production, so think about keeping one quail rooster for every four to five hens. So in a typical rabbit hutch, you could keep about six quail—one male and five females. That would result in up to five quail eggs a day (at peak production), the equivalent of two chicken eggs. If you've got a backyard, double the space for twice the birds and twice the eggs.

Note that it is normal for quail to lay almost every day throughout the spring and summer, but once the days start getting short in the fall their laying will tail off. This gives their bodies time to rest and recuperate from their amazing production, so they are ready to start laying again in the spring.

If you want to go the meat route, you can fit more meat quail into the same area than laying quail, since they will be growing to full size. In the same rabbit hutch space (6 square feet/0.6 square m) you could grow 12 quail in only two short months. Just be sure to give them plenty of straw or shredded paper to hide in, especially towards the end when they are larger.

When you purchase poultry to raise yourself, you will generally start with day-old chicks. Place the tiny (and so cute!) quail chicks in a plastic storage tote lined with paper towels under a brooding light and decide how close to position it by watching to see if they huddle close to the light or back away from it; the chicks should be evenly spaced throughout the brooder. Pull back the light slowly over a week or so until they get adult feathers and are ready to move

into their hutch or coop. Provide water and crumbled feed in shallow dishes, such as the lids to yogurt containers.

Adult quail hens won't set their eggs, so if you want to breed quail yourself, you'll have to collect the eggs each day to hatch in an incubator. This takes 16 to 18 days. We've had fairly low success rates, with less than a quarter hatching, using a second-hand self-turning Styrofoam incubator bought for $50, but the chicks that did hatch were just fine. The most finicky part is keeping enough humidity (75 percent) in the incubator. For the last 3 days, increase humidity to 90 percent and do not turn the eggs. Once the chicks hatch and fluff out (this takes a few hours), put them under the brooding light as with the day-old chicks.

A SMALL QUAIL CONUNDRUM

Quail can be aggressive towards each other, using their beaks to pull out feathers, bruise and even break the skin of other birds they are sharing space with. We have noticed this especially in the spring when their hormones are running high.

The best way to reduce hostile behaviour is to minimize stress by making sure the birds aren't too crowded, that there is adequate water and food and that they have lots of places to hide and dust bathe. Adding straw or shredded paper and fluffing it up each morning gives them comfy places to escape from potential bullies.

A last resort is to use nail clippers to trim the very tip (1 mm or so) of the beak of overly aggressive birds. Be careful not to cut any blood vessels. The beak will grow back but the quail may be less antagonistic by that time, or you can keep the beak trimmed if necessary.

GETTING STARTED

The easiest and least expensive way to get started with quail is to purchase day-old chicks from someone growing them locally, and find a used rabbit hutch or urban chicken coop (see the sidebar on Cleaning a Second-hand Coop, page 89). I found a local chick grower and a used coop online.

(see the sidebar on Cleaning a Second-hand Coop, page 89)

DIY QUAIL BUDGET

Gear	Estimated cost
10 day-old quail chicks	$25
Brooding tote	$5
Brooding light and bulb	$40
Used rabbit hutch or chicken coop	$50
Feed for 8 weeks (one 44-lb/20-kg bag)	$15
Feeder	$5
Waterer	$5
Bedding (shredded paper or straw)	free
Paper shredder	$20
Weeds, branches and bugs	free
Soil for dust bathing	free
Total	$165

SLAUGHTER AND PROCESSING THE MEAT

Quail are exceptionally easy to slaughter and prepare, taking maybe 15 minutes from cage to oven per bird. If you're okay with catching a fish and preparing it for the pan, you'll be fine with quail.

Chris and I have spent a lot of time researching, considering and trying humane slaughter methods for our birds (quail, chickens and turkeys). There are two main methods we've tried.

One involves hanging the bird upside down (as this calms them), then grasping the head and severing it quickly with a very sharp knife. The muscles spasm for some time and blood tends to spatter, but death is very swift.

The other involves hanging the bird upside down (or sitting with it on your lap with its head hanging down) and using a sharp knife to cut the veins and arteries in the neck, avoiding the trachea (as cutting the trachea causes the bird to feel suffocation and struggle, and this experience must be very unpleasant for it). The bird then bleeds out slowly over a couple of minutes but doesn't struggle much, and the post-death muscle spasms are less pronounced.

Personally, I prefer the first method. While messier and involving a lot of flapping (which I know may put some people off), the bird dies more quickly and I believe is the most humane way.

With quail, because they're so small, dispatch is very easy and can be done over a sink for ease of cleaning. If you have two people available, this is easy to do, as one person can hold the bird upside down over the sink while the other severs the head. If only one person is available, pin the bird with your forearm at the edge of the sink, holding the head in your fingers, say your thanks to the bird, and quickly cut through the neck with the other hand.

Pluck the feathers out with your fingers and cut off the feet and wings with scissors or a sharp knife. You can also simply peel off the skin and feathers together instead of plucking by hand. Next, cut open the body cavity from vent to rib cage, being careful not to slice too deeply and pierce any internal organs (which you can see once you make a small incision). Scoop out the digestive tract with your fingers and set aside. Keep the heart and liver to eat. Remove the lungs, reproductive organs (these are on the inside in both male and female birds and you'll be surprised by how large they are), trachea and connective tissue.

Compost anything you can't eat by either digging it deeply into garden beds or a compost pile, or through municipal pickup that accepts meat products. The digestive tract will be smelly, so you might want to coordinate slaughter day with municipal compost pickup. Rinse out the carcass under running water and freeze in an airtight container or cook.

USING EVERY RESOURCE

I keep the quail feathers for handmade jewelry and housewares, and also preserve feet and wings for décor—they look really cool when dried. Like rabbit feet, simply rinse quail feet (but not the wings) and leave them to air-dry, then place in borax powder. Pin the wings (using map pins) to cardboard if you want them to dry open, or simply dredge the meaty parts through the borax powder (about 2 Tbsp/30 mL for each set of wings and feet). Leave the wings and feet to dry in the powder for two weeks, then brush them off.

We adapted this urban chicken coop for keeping our laying quail, but a recycled rabbit hutch would work just as well in a smaller space.

PICKLED QUAIL EGGS

Pickled quail eggs are perfect for a relaxing evening of shared conversation with friends over beer. One rainy fall day, we paired these tangy eggs with a craft-brewed pumpkin ale, nutty crackers and cranberry duck pâté. Or you can skewer them onto an olive pick for a tasty cocktail garnish. They are so delicious that it's hard to sit back while the eggs pickle in the brine—but it's worth the wait!

2 dozen quail eggs, hard-boiled and peeled (see sidebar)
12 cloves garlic, peeled
1¼ cup (300 mL) apple cider vinegar
½ cup (120 mL) white vinegar
½ cup (120 mL) white wine (Riesling is my pick!)
1 tsp (5 mL) coarse salt
1 bay leaf
10 cloves
½ tsp (2.5 mL) turmeric
½ tsp (2.5 mL) paprika
½ tsp (2.5 mL) whole peppercorns

1. Place hard-boiled, peeled quail eggs and peeled garlic cloves in a 4-cup (1-L) glass canning jar, leaving at least 1 inch (2.5 cm) of space at the top. Bring vinegars and white wine to a simmer on the stovetop in a stainless steel pot. Add salt and spices and simmer for 5 minutes.

2. Warm the canning jar by running the outside under hot water for 30 seconds to prevent the glass from cracking. Pour hot liquid into jar over eggs and garlic so eggs are completely submerged. Screw on lid and allow the eggs to season for 1 to 2 weeks in the refrigerator before eating. Pickled eggs will keep in the refrigerator for up to 3 months.

MAKES 2 DOZEN PICKLED QUAIL EGGS

HARD-BOILED QUAIL EGGS

Fresh hard-boiled eggs can be hard to peel, especially quail eggs. For best results, follow these directions.

Make a pinhole in the large end of the raw egg (this is where the air sac is located). Place eggs in a single layer in a saucepan and cover with about 1 inch (2.5 cm) of cold water. Place the lid on the pan and bring to a boil. Remove from heat and let sit with the cover on for 10 minutes. Remove the eggs from the hot water (leaving water in pot) and put in a bath of ice water for 1 minute.

While the eggs are in the ice bath, reheat the water to a simmer. After 1 minute of cold, place the eggs in simmering water for only 10 seconds. This will heat up and expand the shell away from the cold egg inside. Crack the shell from the large end where the pinhole was made. Gently roll the egg between your hands to crack and loosen the shell all over before starting to peel under cold, running water.

BLOODY NERO COCKTAIL WITH PICKLED QUAIL EGGS

I know some of you Scotch fans out there will be aghast at the idea of mixing it with anything, let alone Clamato juice. But I myself am a single malt fan, and while I always enjoy a wee dram on a blustery evening, I also can't get enough of single malt cocktails (try the Penicillin cocktail with Laphroaig whisky if you like your Islays—mmmm!). This Bloody Nero is our punchy homestead take on the Bloody Mary or Canadian Caesar. It isn't for the faint of heart, but really does a body good. Especially for certain Sunday brunches.

Lime wedge

Coarse salt with a dash of smoked salt, for rim of glass

2 oz (60 mL) scotch (blended is okay here)

1 cup (250 mL) Clamato or tomato juice

2 dashes Worcestershire sauce

3 Pickled Quail Eggs (see sidebar, page 105)

1 pickled garlic scape

1. Rim a double cocktail glass with juice from lime wedge, then roll in mixed salts.

2. Fill half the glass with ice, then add Scotch and fill with Clamato juice. Season with Worcestershire.

3. Place pickled eggs on a cocktail skewer across top of glass.

MAKES 1 COCKTAIL

SMOKED WILD SALMON DEVILLED QUAIL EGGS

Devilled quail eggs are perfect for a summer picnic or garden potluck . . . these succulent bite-sized morsels pair well with sunshine and dry Riesling. For tips on boiling and peeling quail eggs, see the Hard-boiled Quail Eggs sidebar on page 105.

2 dozen quail eggs, hard-boiled and peeled

¼ cup (60 mL) sour cream

1 oz (30 gr) chèvre

1 Tbsp (15 mL) mayonnaise

½ Tbsp (7.5 mL) fresh lemon juice

2 oz (60 gr) Salmon Smoked Outdoors with Black Tea and Honey (page 209), finely chopped (or substitute store-bought smoked wild sockeye salmon)

½ tsp (2.5 mL) coarse salt

¼ tsp (1 mL) freshly ground pepper

1 Tbsp (15 mL) finely chopped fresh chives

1. Slice eggs in half lengthwise. Carefully remove yolks and place in mixing bowl. Place whites with cut sides up and sprinkle with salt.

2. Add the sour cream, chèvre, mayonnaise, lemon juice, smoked salmon, salt and pepper to the yolks and mash together with a fork.

3. Fill the egg whites carefully with the yolk mixture using a plastic bag with one of the bottom corners cut off. Refrigerate for 30 minutes to allow the flavours to mix, then garnish with chives.

MAKES 48 BITE-SIZED TREATS

QUAIL STUFFED THREE WAYS

Stuffed quail makes an impressive appetizer for a dinner party, especially when you clean and pluck them together right before dinner! Getting your guests involved is a good introduction for meat-eaters to see what goes into the process of butchery. Especially those real testosterone types. While quail are small, they are very flavourful and especially elegant when stuffed and served on a bed of slightly bitter greens, such as arugula, dandelion or chicory.

4 quail (partially deboned or whole)

2 Tbsp (30 mL) good-quality olive oil, divided

1 cup (250 mL) good white wine

¼ cup (60 mL) arugula

¼ cup (60 mL) kale

½ Tbsp (7.5 mL) balsamic vinegar

Choice of stuffing (options on page 115)

1. Preheat the oven to 450F (230C). Prepare the stuffing of your choice, and stuff the quail. In a large skillet, heat 1 tablespoon (15 mL) of the olive oil over high heat. Add quail and sear until browned all over.

2. Transfer quail to a shallow roasting pan. Add any additional ingredients from the stuffing recipe. Roast the stuffed birds on the top rack of the oven for 5 minutes. Turn down heat to 350F (180C) and roast for an additional 10 minutes or until a thermometer inserted into the breast reads 130F (55C). Remove the quail from the oven and let rest for another 3 minutes.

3. At the same time, deglaze the skillet you used to sear the quail by simmering white wine in the skillet and scraping to loosen any browned bits. Add juices from the roasting pan, and reduce the sauce if needed by simmering for a couple of minutes.

4. Toss arugula and kale with the remaining tablespoon (15 mL) olive oil and the balsamic vinegar. Slice each quail right down the centre, place on a bed of greens, and drizzle with sauce. Garnish with any additional stuffing ingredients.

CONTINUED ON NEXT PAGES

1. GOOSE PROSCIUTTO-WRAPPED PEARS

3 ripe Anjou pears, chopped
7 oz (200 gr) Dry-cured Goose Prosciutto (page 211),
    thinly sliced
½ tsp (2.5 mL) ground cardamom
⅛ tsp (0.6 mL) cinnamon

1. Wrap chunks of pear with prosciutto and sprinkle with spices. Stuff the quail with prosciutto-wrapped pears and roast any leftover pear chunks in pan alongside quail.

2. RABBIT PÂTÉ WITH APPLES, WALNUTS & MUSHROOMS

1 Tbsp (15 mL) butter
7 oz (200 gr) Rabbit Pâté with Oyster Mushrooms,
    recipe on page 97
1 local sweet apple, chopped
Half a small onion, chopped
1 cup (250 mL) wild or homegrown mushrooms
½ cup (120) chopped walnuts
2 tsp (10 mL) chopped fresh thyme

1. In a large sauté pan, melt butter over medium heat. Brown pâté, then add apple, onions and mushrooms, and sauté until soft. Add walnuts and thyme and mix. Remove from heat, then coarsely blend in a food processor. Stuff the quail with pâté, then use the sauté pan to sear the birds.

3. FORAGED FRUIT, ORANGE & GINGER

¼ cup (60 mL) dried foraged berries, such as
    autumnberry, blueberry, huckleberry, salal or
    wolfberry
½ cup (120 mL) orange juice
2 cloves
¼ cup (60 mL) chopped dried apricots
1 Tbsp (15 mL) grated fresh ginger
½ cup (120 mL) chopped hazelnuts
Coarse salt and freshly ground pepper

1. Simmer dried berries, orange juice and cloves in a saucepan for 5 minutes. Discard cloves. Strain berries from orange juice, setting juice aside. Mix berries with apricots, ginger and hazelnuts and use mixture to stuff quail.

2. Rub quail with salt and pepper and baste birds with orange juice during roasting.

SERVES 4 AS AN APPETIZER

FRESHWATER
SEAFOOD — AQUAPONICS

———

RECOMMENDED TYPES: Fish, crayfish, prawns, mussels, snails
PRODUCTS: Meat, shells
URBAN SPACE REQUIREMENT: Medium, indoor possible
TIME COMMITMENT: 5 minutes per day
FEED: Commercial fish food, homegrown algae, worms and mealworms
ESTIMATED START-UP COST: $480 (see Getting started, page 117)

One excellent option for growing food in limited space and without soil is aquaponics: water is the medium that transfers nutrients derived from fish waste into food for plants, with plants filtering the water that recirculates back to the fish.

Requiring a sturdy tank to hold the fish, aquarium supplies to pump and circulate water and a veggie bed containing a hydroponic growing medium such as clay balls or gravel, aquaponics systems are a bit more complicated than a simple patio pond. However, they allow you to grow many common garden herbs and veggies—such as basil, lettuce, kale, tomatoes and squash—with no soil at all, while also providing homegrown fish protein.

The fish tank and vegetable grow bed are connected together through the water that is pumped up from the fish tank to the grow bed, draining from the grow bed back to the fish tank.

See Aquaponic Plants, page 120, for more information on what to grow in an aquaponics grow bed.

HUSBANDRY

Grow bed

Developing and managing a functioning aquatic ecosystem is essential for maintaining an aquaponics system. The nutrient cycling works through the action of many vital microorganisms, which transform the fish waste products into useable food for the plants. These little critters grow on the surfaces in your system and the pebbles in the veggie grow bed are a great place for them. Worms (regular red wriggler compost worms) also love the grow bed medium, and can help to break down the solid waste from the fish, keeping the grow bed from becoming compacted.

Fish tank

Ecosystem thinking helps when designing the fish tank as well. The fish will benefit from being provided with shelter, either created from materials such as netting or segments of pipe on the bottom of the tank, or from floating plants (use edibles—see page 155). If you have a larger tank, consider growing several varieties of aquatic animals that use different parts of the tank. For example, crustaceans such as freshwater crayfish live on the bottom, fish like tilapia hang out in the middle, while snails stick with the edible plants on the surface. You can also grow food for the fish to eat instead of purchasing commercial products. See Concepts for Raising Microlivestock Sustainably and Ethically, page 142.

One aquaponics innovation I saw was a cold-water system that produced coho salmon, freshwater crayfish, wasabi and tomatoes, all of which were sold to local high-end restaurants. The water was cycled into tanks for the salmon, then crayfish, then wasabi, being filtered and drained of nutrients along the way, finally ending with tomatoes and clean water. Best of all, the salmon were fed with scraps from nearby sustainable fisheries processors.

What you grow will depend on which type of system you want to have. In outdoor ambient Canadian and northern US climates, cold-water systems allow you to grow trout, salmon and crayfish, but require highly filtered and oxygenated water.

For warm-water systems in most parts of Canada and the US, you'll need to heat the water or keep the system indoors. The optimum temperature will depend on the species of fish you decide to raise—for example, tilapia needs about 84F (29C). Warm-water systems may be easier for beginners, as the types of fish you can grow tend to be less sensitive, and you can get away with less aeration and filtering of the water. What you can grow is also more varied, and includes carp, perch, bluegill and catfish, in addition to tilapia. There are also varieties of crayfish that like warm water, along with freshwater prawns. Both crayfish and prawns can live in the bottom of any fish tank with rocks or PVC pipe providing habitat. Freshwater snails can live throughout the tank as well, and can be harvested for such dishes as Wild Greens Pasta with Periwinkle Sea Snails, page 60, or Crispy Pan-fried Escargot and Arugula Salad, page 70. They can also be used as food for other microlivestock you are growing, such as quail and fish.

GETTING STARTED

The infrastructure for an aquaponics system is more complicated than for rabbits or quail. If you have no experience with plumbing, it would help to consult with someone familiar with pond building or aquariums. When designing and managing your system, think through the relationships between your fish, plants and nitrifying bacteria, and about how the recirculating water needs to be moved, filtered and aerated.

Building your own system is the least expensive option, and allows you to choose the size and design that best fits your space and needs. However, purchasing a pre-made kit is another strategy, and you may be able to have an aquarium or aquaponics consultant come to help you set it up, depending on what is available in your area.

Gently used foodsafe shipping containers make great tanks and are available through classified websites. The top quarter of the tank is flipped over to be used as a grow bed and placed on top of the bottom fish tank. An IBC (Intermediate Bulk Container) is

about 3 feet cubed and 250 gallons in volume (1 m cubed and 1,000 L), which is just over 2,000 lbs (950 kg) in weight. This size is ideal for a limited outdoor space, such as a small backyard, a ground-level patio or perhaps a small area on the grounds of an apartment building if you have been given permission.

Smaller systems are certainly possible for those with higher-floor balconies that have weight limitations (check with your building management). While they may not be suitable to growing fish for food, goldfish are great candidates for providing nutrients to edible plants.

Whatever the size, the ideal density at which you stock the fish will depend on how much you want to commit to maintaining water quality and aeration. The more fish, the more work. The densities I have suggested are fairly low, making aquaponics easier for beginners and more comfortable for the fish.

Gear	Estimated cost
Growing medium (such as clay balls made for hydroponics)	$150
Red wriggler worms	free
Seedlings	$20
Water pump	$50
Drain, tubing and fittings	$50
IBC food shipping container	$75
25 tilapia fingerlings (1 fish per 8 gallons/30 L)	$40
5 crayfish (5 per 10 square feet/1 square m of bottom surface area)	$15
40 freshwater snails	$20
Rocks and PVC pipe scrap	free
Air pump	$20
Air stones	$10
Water heater	$30
Total	$480

SLAUGHTER AND PROCESSING THE MEAT

To harvest your aquaponics fish, crayfish, prawns, mussels and snails, you can either do it all in one go, or you can net, trap and angle.

If you want to harvest your fish all at once, simply drain most of the water from the fish tank and remove the fish. The water can be used to fertilize containers or any other plants. This will remove your source of dissolved nutrients, however, which may starve your nitrifying bacteria and reduce food available for your plants, so keep that in mind. It may be difficult to resume the balance of your aquatic ecosystem. Reserve some of the water to inoculate fresh water when you add it.

Further references

Getting Food from Water: Guide to Backyard Aquaculture by Gene Logsdon

Aquaponic Gardening: A Step-By-Step Guide to Raising Vegetables and Fish Together by Sylvia Bernstein

Opposite, clockwise from top left: an old bathtub can easily become an aquaponics grow bed; a repurposed 30-gallon food shipping barrel converts to a culinary herb grow bed with a goldfish tank beneath to provide nutrients; a backyard pond can be used to grow fish and other seafood while floating pots of edible plants provide shelter and shade; a standard 275-gallon IBC food shipping tote is the ideal option for a patio or backyard aquaponics system to grow fish and other seafood and vegetables. (*Photos Chris Mull*)

To selectively harvest your freshwater seafood, simply use whichever methods you would use to capture their wild counterparts. For fish, nets and lines can work. For crayfish and prawns, use baited traps. For mussels, you can dig using a long-handled dip net, and snails can be removed by hand as well.

For the fish, once removed from the water, you'll need to dispatch them right away since they cannot breathe air and will feel like they are suffocating. Immediately knock the fish out with a swift and sure blow to the head with a blunt object, possibly a rolling pin, against a clean kitchen counter or the outside ground. If you're really uncoordinated like I am, this can sometimes be hard to do on a slimy, flopping fish. Another option is the method called ikejime, or spiking, which involves using a sharp point, such as a sharpened screwdriver, to pierce the brain just behind the eye, killing the fish immediately. Look up the exact location to insert the ikejime tool for the species of fish you have (there are diagrams available online).

Immediately bleed the fish after knocking it unconscious or killing it. Using a sharp knife, cut the fish from the underside towards the spine where the head meets the body to sever the main artery. Hang or place the fish upside down in the sink or a bucket to allow the blood to drain out. This blood can be used to fertilize the garden—or let it clot, then feed it to any prawns you have in your aquaponics system.

Once you've gathered your crayfish, prawns, mussels or snails, they can be kept in a bucket of water reserved from the tank, or tap water the same temperature as your system, for up to 1 hour until you are ready to cook them. The Royal Society for the Prevention of Cruelty to Animals says the humane way to dispatch shellfish is to stun them with an electrical pulse before killing, using a specialized machine,[5] but that isn't feasible for most people at home. Instead, before dispatching crayfish, prawns, mussels or snails, I stun them by placing them in the refrigerator for an hour to slow their metabolism and senses. Then I use a sharp ikejime spike to quickly pierce the area between the eyes of the crayfish and prawns, then pierce again through the chest from the underside. This should kill the animal quickly. Next, firmly grasp and twist off the head. Mussels and snails can be boiled whole—while this may not be the most humane way to kill these shellfish, it is the standard method and is likely the only feasible way to do it in the home kitchen. Do ensure the water is boiling hard before you place the cold-stunned mussels and snails in, so that the process takes only a few seconds.

USING EVERY RESOURCE

The shells of freshwater snails are beautiful and can be used in crafts. After removing the meat, brush them out to remove any debris and soak overnight in 1 cup (120 mL) of water with 1 teaspoon (5 mL) of baking soda or vinegar mixed in. Then scrub again, rinse and allow to air dry.

Or, to keep things in the kitchen, bones and shells leftover from processing and cooking your aquatic animals can be used to make excellent seafood stock and Crustacean Bisque (recipe next page).

AQUAPONIC PLANTS

Leafy annual garden plants, culinary herbs, edible flowers and microgreens thrive in the vegetable grow bed of an aquaponics system, while water-loving plants like watercress and water spinach can grow in floating baskets (bought from pond-supply stores) over the fish tank (see page 157 for a list of shallow-rooted and floating edible pond plants).

Fruiting annual garden plants can be grown too, but they're a little trickier, requiring a system with good nutrient flow (from the fish) and a well-established ecology of microorganisms to buffer and break down the fish waste into useable food for the plants. Once you have successfully grown a few leafy vegetables in your system, try fruiting vegetables next.

5 "Humane Electrical Stun/killing of Crustacea." Royal Society for the Prevention of Cruelty to Animals, accessed November 2014, http://www.rspca.org.uk.

CRUSTACEAN BISQUE

This is adapted from one of my favourite recipes in one of my favourite cookbooks, Barefoot Contessa at Home by Ina Garten. For those not able to grow aquaponic crayfish and prawns, this recipe works equally well with foraged or sustainably harvested crab, prawns and lobster from your local market. You'll need to allow a good hour for the stock to simmer before moving on to make the bisque. Serve with fresh buttered Rustic Rosemary Sourdough Bread (page 214) on a cool evening by the fireplace. A dram of cognac to accompany the meal is optional but highly recommended.

STOCK
1½ cups (350 mL) crustacean shells (from about 1 lb/455 gr of crustaceans)
2 Tbsp (30 mL) olive oil
2 medium onions, chopped
3 carrots, chopped
3 celery stalks, chopped
3 cloves garlic, minced
1 cup (250 mL) dry white wine
1 Tbsp (15 mL) coarse salt
1 tsp (5 mL) fresh ground black pepper
2 bay leaves

1. Rinse whole crustaceans under cold water and remove shells. Set meat aside.

2. In a stockpot over medium heat, sauté the crustacean shells, onions, carrots, celery and garlic in oil until lightly browned (about 15 minutes). Add 6 cups (1.5 L) of water, wine, salt, pepper and bay leaves. Bring to a boil, then reduce heat and simmer for an hour.

3. Strain through a colander.

4. Use immediately to make crustacean bisque, or stock can be frozen for later use.

BISQUE
3 Tbsp (45 mL) olive oil
2 cups (475 mL) chopped onions
3 cloves garlic, minced
1 lb (455 gr) crustacean meat (from freshwater prawns or crayfish, Dungeness crab, spot prawns or Atlantic lobster)
½ cup (120 mL) cognac
¼ cup (60 mL) butter
¼ cup (60 mL) flour
2 cups (475 mL) 10 percent cream
4 cups (1 L) seafood stock
Coarse salt to taste
Freshly ground pepper to taste

5. In a Dutch oven or large pot over medium heat, sauté onions and garlic in olive oil until translucent. Turn the heat to low, add the crustacean meat and cook for 2 minutes. Add the cognac and cook for another 3 minutes. Transfer the mixture to a food processor and process for a coarse purée.

6. In the same pot, make a roux by melting the butter, then adding the flour and cooking over low heat for 1 minute, stirring constantly. Add the cream and whisk for another couple of minutes. Then add the puréed crustacean mixture and seafood stock, and heat through. Season with salt and pepper to taste.

SERVES 4 FOR DINNER

JAPANESE KNOTWEED CHUTNEY ON PAN-SEARED TROUT

A freshwater fish, trout can be sustainably farmed inland or grown at home in a cold-water aquaponics system, which takes pressure off wild populations and doesn't pose the risk to marine environments that open-net pen salmon farming does. Similar to rhubarb, Japanese knotweed is an invasive plant with such an aggressive growth habitat it can do serious damage to properties and native flora. The newly sprouted stems (gathered before they become woody) are both sweet and tart, and make tasty chutney to pair with fatty fish like trout, but would also work with other aquaponic fish, such as tilapia or perch. A big batch of this chutney can be made in one go in the spring when tender knotweed stems are available, then frozen into single-dinner servings.

CHUTNEY
¼ cup (60 mL) Dijon mustard
1½ cups (350 mL) peeled and diced knotweed stems
3 Tbsp (45 mL) apple cider vinegar
½ cup (120 mL) brown sugar
¼ cup (60 mL) water
3 garlic cloves, crushed
1 small onion, diced
1 Tbsp (15 mL) tamari
¼ cup (60 mL) of your favourite homemade jelly
3 Tbsp (45 mL) Worcestershire sauce

FISH
2 8-oz (225-gr) trout fillets
2 Tbsp (30 mL) olive oil
Coarse salt to taste
Freshly ground pepper to taste

1. Combine all chutney ingredients in a saucepan. Simmer over medium heat until knotweed softens, about 10 minutes. Blend coarsely in a food processor. Set aside.

2. Rinse the fillets and pat dry. Heat a large cast iron skillet to medium-high or high heat. Add olive oil and sear the fillets for 2 to 3 minutes on each side, or until outside is crispy and inside is opaque. Season with salt and pepper. Plate the fillets and top with sauce.

SERVES 4 WITH SIDES

Opposite: Invasive Japanese knotweed is all-too-easy to find and removing it helps conserve local ecosystems. Best of all, it tastes and cooks just like a familiar spring favourite—rhubarb!

HONEYBEES

———

RECOMMENDED BREEDS: Italian, German, Russian, Carniolan, Caucasian, Buckfast (*Apis mellifera*)

PRODUCTS: Honey, honeycomb, bee pollen, royal jelly

URBAN SPACE REQUIREMENT: About 2 x 2 feet/60 x 60 cm (commercial-style hive) or 2 x 4 feet/60 x 120 cm (top bar hive)

TIME COMMITMENT: 5 to 10 minutes every other week

FEED: Organically grown flowers in your area

ESTIMATED START-UP COST: $270 (see Getting started, page 128)

Bees are fascinating and hard-working creatures that not only do the indispensable job of ensuring we continue to have food and natural landscapes, but also produce amazing food with many health benefits—honey and bee pollen.

Bees travel from flower to flower and, in the act, pollinate plants. They eat the flower nectar, used to make honey, and collect pollen (plant sperm) in little baskets on their legs to take back to the hive for their colony to store. Fanning the flower nectar to remove moisture from it, bees make honey inside the hive, using it to feed themselves and their babies when no nectar is available, particularly through winter. The honey provides carbohydrates while the pollen is a protein source for the hive and baby bees.

Wax, produced from glands on the worker bees' abdomens, is used to create a frame (honeycomb) with cells to store honey and house baby bees. The queen bee's job is to lay eggs in these cells, with the worker bees assigned to collect nectar and pollen to feed the queen, babies and younger worker bees. While each worker lives only a few weeks, the queen bee can survive for several years. The number of worker bees is largest in the height of the flowering season in late spring and early summer, maximizing the hive's ability to collect and store nectar and honey. In the fall, the queen reduces her egg-laying to lessen the consumption of honey and pollen stores, reducing the hive to just enough bees to keep it warm through the cold months.

Not only is it possible to keep bees in urban areas, this may in fact be vital to bee conservation. Honeybee populations all across North America are under serious threat due to a number of causes, the most serious of which is likely pesticides used in industrial agriculture. Urban areas actually create havens free from agricultural pesticides, so it's critical to bee populations to have hives in urban settings. Do your part in honeybee conservation by keeping your own. And the honey's pretty good, too!

HUSBANDRY

While there is a world of information on beekeeping out there, which can seem daunting, keeping bees can be very low maintenance because they source their own food. In fact, bees can fly amazing distances to find flowers in bloom—up to 4 miles (6.5 km)—and the inhabitants of a single colony can potentially cover 50,000 acres (20,200 ha).

You must make certain the bees you keep will have access to flowers throughout the spring, summer and into fall. Although an apple orchard will ensure they are fed for a few weeks, the period before and after its blossoming is just as important. In urban areas, gardeners tend to focus on sequential blooming in landscaping, so bees are often able to forage successfully without pause. If you have space to plant in a backyard or on a balcony or rooftop, plan a bee garden with consecutive blossoming from spring to fall. Pollinators particularly like culinary herbs—such as basil, lavender, rosemary, oregano and thyme—and these make excellent edible landscaping as well. The Umbelliferae (Apiaceae) family, with its large umbrella-shaped inflorescence—including fennel, dill, parsley, cilantro and carrots—is also a favourite of bees and other pollinators; just be sure to limit your harvest of these edibles to allow lots of flowering. Bees also love borage and comfrey, both of which have edible flowers and make excellent soil amendments when composted.

Do keep an eye on the hive, especially through the first growing season, to make sure its inhabitants are increasing their honey stores. If you find the honey is staying steady or reducing at any point in the growing season, this might indicate the bees can't find enough pollen. You may need to supplement their food, and if possible plan to grow plants that bloom during that time of the season for next year. Bees can be supplemented with commercially prepared sugar and protein patties, but this should be avoided unless absolutely necessary because they don't contain all the nutrients needed to stay healthy.

Once you've decided to keep bees, and planned and planted your bee garden if you can, you'll have to decide what type of hive you want. The conventional commercial hives are called Langstroth hives and are the typical square hives you usually see. They are easy to stack and transport (hence their popularity in commercial use), and also easy to obtain. Within the hive, each level (called a super) is filled with hanging frames, similar to hanging files in a filing cabinet drawer. The frames are like the file folders, and are printed with a honeycomb pattern where the bees create honeycomb to store honey and secure their babies. To work with the hives or collect honey, you simply take the lid off the top super and remove the hanging frames one by one.

Another type of hive is called a top bar hive, which commonly looks like a tiny long barn on stilts but can also be built out of hollowed-out logs like wild bees would use. Inside, it contains wooden bars from which bees attach and build honeycomb. These tend to be more popular with urban homesteaders because they are easy to build and maintain yourself, they disturb bees less during maintenance because the hive doesn't need to be disassembled, and they allow bees and beekeepers to mimic nature better than Langstroth hives. Some natural beekeepers believe allowing the bees to create their own comb size (not possible with Langstroth hive frames) reduces stress and may even deter mites.

In either case, locate the hive somewhere protected from high wind, in dappled sunlight and where there is good drainage so the hive doesn't become flooded. Urban rooftops can be a good option, but a windscreen is recommended in any elevated and exposed location. Ground-level areas in a backyard, on a patio, beside an apartment building, or especially in a community garden (always away from heavy foot traffic), will make bees perfectly happy. Your neighbours might be a different story, so engage them in any decision-making about starting a hive. I do have to say that educating people about bees really helps—most think bees are out to sting them, but that really isn't true. None of our 5,000-plus bees have ever stung a single person (that we know of).

Provide your bees with a source of water if a natural one isn't readily available throughout the year. Place a shallow pan a few feet from the hive. Fill with water and add some protruding rocks to ensure safe landing areas (this is key because without rocks to clamber onto bees can drown), and check daily to ensure the pan does not dry out.

When handling your bees, remain calm, move slowly and avoid blocking their flight path to the entrance of the hive. Many people use a hood or full suit when doing anything with their bees, but Chris and I found that beekeeping gloves were all we needed and neither of us has ever been stung by our bees. You will also need a prying tool because the propolis (building material bees produce) will have

adhered the pieces of the hive together. For larger jobs, like first moving the bees into the hive, we also used a smoker. This is a very simple tool formed from a can and bellows, which you can use to smoulder grass or wood chips and blow smoke into the hive. The smoke makes the bees think there may be a fire, so they concentrate on filling up with honey inside the hive in case they have to move it, which means they aren't flying around in a panic and getting in the way. However, if you are calm and move slowly, we have found that we don't even need a smoker.

The best time of year to get your bees is late winter or early spring. This will give them time to collect lots of nectar and pollen spring through summer. Commercial and conventional beekeepers collect honey in the late summer because this is when stores are largest, before bees start using it to feed on through the cold season. Generally, commercial beekeepers take all the honey and then feed the bees sugar through fall and winter. Natural beekeepers object to this method, as it is not nearly as healthy for bees as allowing them to eat what nature provides to sustain them. So, for healthier bees, let them thrive on their own honey through the winter and you can collect the excess in the spring when they once again have access to flowers and nectar. See page 128 for information about how to extract honey from a hive.

To prepare your bees for winter, check the brood and honey stores to ensure they have ample to get them through. Some people insulate their hives, especially in areas with very cold temperatures, but this is debated because it can cause moisture buildup inside the hive. In fact, bees can survive in weather well below freezing by clustering together. They do benefit from being protected from cold winter winds, which you can do by stacking straw bales or sheets of plywood near the hive, while still allowing some air flow to reduce condensation (a few inches away).

By far, the most important consideration through winter is moisture—condensation from the heat of the bee cluster can collect on the ceiling of the hive if it is flat, as with Langstroth hives. This then cools and drips onto the bees, which can be fatal. The best way to avoid this is to mimic nature and allow the bees to behave as they would in the wild. Wild honeybees would colonize a hollowed-out log and seal any drafts using propolis in the winter, leaving only one opening at the bottom of the hive. This allows the inhabitants to maintain temperature and moisture by fanning at the opening to create air ventilation. You can allow the bees to do this in a top bar hive, especially one made from thick wood, which naturally insulates the hive.

For a Langstroth hive, the standard practice is to use a thin shim (Popsicle or paint-stirring sticks work) to prop the lid of the top super so that any condensation runs down the side of the hive instead of dripping on the bees. While this is not ideal because the bees can't seal the hive with propolis and will expend more energy keeping warm, it is the standard way to deal with moisture in a Langstroth hive.

With any type of hive, reduce the size of the entrance opening to ⅜ inch (9 mm) to make it easier for the bees to defend themselves from invading insects and mice. If it snows, leave the snow on the hive, since it acts as a good insulator, but ensure the entrance isn't blocked. Don't warm the hive in cold weather because the bees will think spring has arrived and will start becoming more active and eating more honey.

Outside of these considerations, check on the bees every week or two from spring to fall to ensure the hive is healthy and hasn't become infected with mites, moths, mould, viruses or other diseases. You want your bees to look lively, and don't want to see dead bees, webs or black growth. Make careful observations of what you see when your hive is looking sick, and consult online natural beekeeper forums or your local beekeeping club for diagnosis and advice. Commercial and conventional beekeepers use preventative pesticides to reduce the likelihood of infection, but over time these tend to reduce the bees' resilience to disease and there is also debate about safety for human health. Natural beekeepers believe the key to vigorous hives is mimicking nature in the construction and maintenance of the hive itself by simulating a natural tree cavity, keeping bees that were bred locally and thus adapted to their conditions, feeding natural food (honey) rather than sugar or corn syrup, and avoiding medications and pesticides.

Getting started

Find a beekeeper near you who breeds nucleus colonies (nucs), which are the queen and workers that make up a hive. First, set up the hive in the right location, then move your new bees in.

Gear	Estimated cost
Hive nuc (queen and workers)	$150
Materials to build hive (top bar)	$50
Beekeeping gloves	$30
Hive tool (prying bar)	$10
Bee smoker (optional)	$30
2 clean food safe 5-gallon (20-L) buckets	free (used)
Total	$270

Processing the honey and beeswax

Honey extraction and beeswax preparation are the only real processing required with beekeeping. First, you need to remove the honeycomb from the hive and extract the honey from the comb. With a Langstroth hive, remove the frames and scrape the cap off the comb with a honey extraction tool. With a top bar hive, break off the honeycomb by hand.

A honey extraction machine is a common way to get the honey from the frames and comb, and works using centrifugal force much like a separator or that ride at the fair that spins you until you vomit. However, these machines are expensive, so unless you have a neighbour who doesn't mind sharing one, a less expensive option is simply to strain the honey out using gravity. While this takes longer, all that's required are two clean five-gallon (19 L) buckets. Drill small holes in the bottom of one bucket and place it inside the second. Scrape all the honey and comb off the frame and place in the top bucket, then crush with a potato masher or large muddler. The more it is crushed the more readily the honey will emerge. Cover the top bucket to discourage insects, and wait several hours or overnight for the honey to drip out. Strain the honey through cheesecloth to remove any debris, and store in clean glass jars with airtight lids in a cool dark place for up to a year.

USING EVERY RESOURCE

The leftover comb from honey extractions is mostly made of beeswax, which is a wonderful product for making candles, soap and body care items like lip balm and hand salve. Rendering beeswax from the honeycomb is quite straightforward: Fill a large pot you don't mind getting wax on halfway with water and place it on the stove on medium-low heat. Wrap the honeycomb (debris and dead bees are okay) in cheesecloth pulled into a bag shape and secured at the top with an elastic band. Place the bag into the water. The wax will begin to melt and seep out, leaving the debris inside the cheesecloth bag. Once it has melted out (in about 10 to 20 minutes), squeeze out any remaining wax with kitchen tongs. Turn off the heat to allow the wax floating on the surface of the water to cool and solidify (this may take several hours). Once it has cooled, simply pop the wax round from the sides of the pot and allow it to air dry.

Further reference

The Practical Beekeeper: Beekeeping Naturally by
  Michael Bush

Commercial-style hives like these ones are easy to source when starting out. Or consider a more humane and natural beekeeping approach—build a top bar hive or use a hollowed out log to simulate a tree cavity.

HONEYED COCONUT GRANOLA
(WITH HOMEMADE YOGURT)

A tasty and nutritious way to start your day, this granola goes well with Easy Greek-style Yogurt (page 240). Forage and dry autumnberry, blueberry, huckleberry, blackberry, wolfberry and prickly pear cactus fruits and use whichever nuts are locally available. Top the granola and yogurt with fresh blackberry, kudzu and maple flowers, and whatever fresh fruit and berries are available at the time.

½ cup (120 mL) coarsely chopped almonds

½ cup (120 mL) coarsely chopped walnuts

½ cup (120 mL) coarsely chopped cashews

4 cups (1 L) rolled oats

2 cups (475 mL) shredded coconut

½ cup (120 mL) vegetable oil

½ cup (120 mL) honey, heated until very liquid

4 cups (1 L) finely chopped dried fruit

1. Preheat the oven to 350F (180C). Place the chopped nuts 1 layer thick on a baking dish and toast until golden brown.

2. In a large bowl, toss the oats, coconut and toasted nuts with the oil and honey. Pour onto a baking dish to about ½ inch (1.25 cm) thick. Bake in oven, stirring occasionally, until golden brown, about 45 minutes. Remove from oven and allow to cool. Stir in dried fruit.

3. For breakfast, spoon ½ cup (120 mL) of yogurt and ½ cup (120 mL) of granola into a bowl. Top with fresh fruit if available. Drizzle honey on top.

4. Store extra granola in a large, clean glass jar in a cool, dark place (like a cupboard) for up to 6 months.

MAKES 12 CUPS (2.8 L) OF GRANOLA

Opposite: Bees make great urban homesteading livestock because they find their own food! Here a honeybee feeds on invasive purple loosestrife, which is also edible for people and delicious in recipes like Creamy Braised Purple Loosestrife and Mushroom Risotto (page 154).

WILD ROSEHIP &
SPICE-INFUSED HONEY

In fall, we make infused honey to package up as winter gifts. While you can use virtually any spices you like for infusion, here's one combination we recommend for a delicious result.

¼ cup (60 mL) wild rosehips, dried (see Drying, page 198)
1 inch (2.5 cm) dried cinnamon stick
1 inch (2.5 cm) dried vanilla bean
½ tsp (2.5 mL) cardamom seeds

3 cloves
2 Tbsp (30 mL) dried lavender flowers and leaves
½ cup (120 mL) honey

1. Fill a clean 1-cup (250-mL) glass jar with the dried rosehips and spices. Pour the honey over top and mix with a spoon. Clean any honey from the outside of the jar and tightly close lid. Leave on the counter or a windowsill and turn upside down once or twice a day for 2 weeks.

2. After 2 weeks, the honey will be ready. Strain out the solids or leave them in for visual interest.

3. Will store in a cool, dark place for a year or more.

MAKES ½ CUP (120 ML) HONEY

Opposite: Honeybees are fascinating social creatures that work together to build combs, collect nectar and pollen, and raise their young. Along the way, they create honey, bee pollen and beeswax, all delightful additions to the urban homesteader's pantry.

EATING INSECTS

——

RECOMMENDED TYPES: Mealworms (*Tenebrio molitor*) and crickets (various, including *Acheta domestica* and *Gryllus assimilis*)

PRODUCTS: Livestock feed, and meat and flour for humans

URBAN SPACE REQUIREMENT: Up to 2 x 2 feet (60 x 60 cm), indoor or outdoor for mealworms, indoor best for crickets

TIME REQUIREMENT: 10 minutes 3 times per week

FEED: Chicken food pellets, leftover grain, vegetables and fruit

ESTIMATED START-UP COST: $50 (see Getting started, page 137)

I recently got into a very long discussion string on a popular media website with conservation-scientist colleagues about how much water it takes to raise animal protein, since access to fresh water is a huge concern for conservation and agriculture alike. According to the Food and Agriculture Organization (FAO) of the United Nations, global demand for livestock products will double within the next 50 years[6].

6 Arnold van Huis, Joost van Itterbeeck, Harmke Klunder, Esther Mertens, Afton Halloran, Giulia Muir and Paul Vantomme. "Environmental opportunities of insect rearing for food and feed," in *Edible insects: Future prospects for food and feed security.* (Rome: Food and Agriculture Organization of the United Nations, 2013), 59–66.

And if we keep demanding the type of livestock products we do now—beef, in particular—we are going to run into major trouble finding enough fresh water to meet these demands. It takes more than 5,800 gallons (22,000 L) of water to produce just over 2 lbs (910 gr) of beef, and it's 20 times more consumptive to grow beef than plant-based proteins[7].

Compare that to chicken eggs, which require less than half the water to provide nearly the same calorie and protein content. So what is the best, most sustainable alternative protein to beef? Chickens and, even more so, rabbits and quail are good contenders because of their superior feed-conversion efficiencies (how much food they need to produce each pound of meat), as well as the ease of raising them on a small, sustainable scale. Other ideas are eating more seaweed, legumes and fungi.

But I have yet another suggestion for an alternative, one that is by far the most sustainable source of animal protein available and perhaps the future of food amidst our planet's declining resources—eating insects. Yep, bugs. They require significantly less space, energy and water than other animals, have higher feed-conversion efficiencies, can be reared on food waste, and present fewer animal-welfare concerns than keeping mammals and birds. According to the FAO, compared to what is required to produce mealworm protein, twice as much land is needed to yield a similar weight in chicken eggs and ten times the space is required for the same amount of beef.[8] In addition, mealworms are higher in calcium and iron than even red meat, so think about that, health nuts!

Now before you get grossed out, there are many ways to use insects to produce food that don't involve sautéing mealworms or deep-frying grasshoppers. Yet, despite the many benefits of growing insects for

sustenance, as well as rising concerns over the unsustainability of most animal agriculture, the yuck factor is a big barrier to bug cuisine. Most people in Western nations can't yet fathom the idea of eating mealworms, crickets and grasshoppers. But never fear! You can still be involved in the most environmentally friendly animal protein around without having to crunch into bugs.

Flour can be easily made at home from dehydrated insects and mixed with grain flour for use in most baking (maybe not fluffy croissants, but for bread, cakes and cookies, it works just fine). This slightly nutty, high-protein flour is rising in popularity, and commercial insect flour producers and baking companies are now popping up across North America.

Live mealworms and crickets can also be fed to your quail and aquaponics fish, providing them a natural and sustainable food you can produce yourself—which in effect becomes another way for you to use insects as part of your own nourishment.

Further reference

The Eat-a-Bug Cookbook by David George Gordon

MEALWORMS

Very high in nutrients, mealworms are the larval form of a type of darkling beetle and often used in biological research because they're so easy to grow. In three inexpensive plastic totes, you can keep a colony of mealworms to feed on leftover grains, such as oatmeal, bread starter, dough, dried spent grains from beer making and spilled or leftover chicken or quail feed. A colony of adult beetles produces the larvae (mealworms), which you can eat yourself or use as feed for other microlivestock, such as quail and aquaponics fish.

HUSBANDRY

The size of the containers depends on how many mealworms you want to produce. I use 2-gallon (8-L) plastic pantry totes and started with 200 mealworms. Begin with 3 containers and label them

7 Mesfin M. Mekonnen and Arjen Y. Hoekstra. "A Global Assessment of the Water Footprint of Farm Animal Products." *Ecosystems* 15 (2012): 401–415.

8 Arnold van Huis, Joost van Itterbeeck, Harmke Klunder, Esther Mertens, Afton Halloran, Giulia Muir and Paul Vantomme. "Environmental opportunities of insect rearing for food and feed," in *Edible insects: Future prospects for food and feed security*. (Rome: Food and Agriculture Organization of the United Nations, 2013), 59–66.

"Larvae," "Pupae" and "Adults." Drill 15 to 30 holes (⅛ inch/0.13 cm) through the lids or sides near the lid to allow air flow. Fill the "Larvae" container with about 1 inch (2.5 cm) of dry grains and/or chicken or quail food pellets. Add a cut carrot or potato to the "Larvae" container to provide moisture.

A local pet or aquarium supply store can provide your starter mealworms. Add them to the "Larvae" container, covering them with a few scraps of cardboard or newspaper to keep their environment dark. Keep the container in a warm, dark place. Check on your colony once or twice a week, replace mouldy vegetables with fresh, and gently stir up the bedding to prevent mould growth.

If the larvae are happy, in two to four weeks they will start to develop into their next life stage, pupae. The pupae will be very light in colour and lack the segmented appearance of the larvae. Prepare the pupae container by layering about ½ inch (1.25 cm) of bedding (shredded paper or the same feed/bedding as the "Larvae" container) and adding a cut carrot or potato to provide moisture. The pupae do not eat in this life stage. When you start noticing pupae in the "Larvae" container, move them into the "Pupae" container (you can gently use tweezers to do this).

After a week or two of gradually darkening in colour, the pupae should begin to hatch into adults. As soon as you see them, move the adults with your hands or tweezers or they may eat the pupae before they hatch. Place the adult beetles into the "Adults" container, which you have prepared like the "Larvae" container with feed/bedding and veggies for moisture. Keep an eye on the "Adults" container for eggs, which the females will lay in the bedding. When the eggs hatch in a few days to a couple of weeks, move the larvae back into the "Larvae" container (and, again, do this promptly, as the adults may eat the larvae).

Once you have your first generation completed, the process of moving each stage between containers will be ongoing, but only needs to be done once or twice per week. Harvest the larvae as you need them for your own food or for your livestock, leaving some to pupate into adults.

CRICKETS

As many reptile enthusiasts will tell you, growing crickets is a cinch. Like mealworms, they can easily be reared in plastic totes, but do require supplemental heat. Crickets are a healthy food for your quail, or grind some up to make flour for baking.

HUSBANDRY

High-sided totes are a good choice because crickets use the vertical space as habitat. To house a colony of 500 crickets, you'll need 3 totes (14-gallon/50-L). Label your totes "Eggs," "Juveniles" and "Adults." Drill 15 to 30 holes (⅛ inch/0.13 cm) through the lids, covering the inside of each lid with metal screening because crickets can chew plastic.

Next, layer the floor of the "Adults" container with bedding—vermiculite is a common choice because it reduces moisture and odour; the bedding will need to be replaced every few months. Place a couple plastic containers filled with organic soil in the bedding—small disposable plant pots or ½-cup (120-mL) glass jars work—which are what the females will lay eggs in. Add lots of cut carrots and/or potatoes for moisture. Place a dish or two of feed in the container: use plant-based kitchen scraps (fruits, vegetables, grains, bread), spilled or leftover chicken or quail feed, or even dry dog or cat food.

Refresh any vegetable scraps before they rot. Layer a few scraps of cardboard in the tote for the crickets to climb on—egg cartons work well. Finally, provide heat with a space heater or heat light (a brooding light works when you're not using it for your birds) to maintain a temperature of about 85F (30C). As crickets do chirp, you may prefer to set them up where you won't hear them all night.

Obtain crickets from a pet or aquarium supply store, starting with about 50, and place into the "Adults" container. About 3 times a week, check on them and mist the bedding and soil containers with water so the eggs and insects don't dry out. After about 2 weeks of adequate feed, moisture and heat, the crickets should lay eggs in the soil you've provided. Once you see the eggs, which look like small grains of rice, move the containers of soil into the "Eggs" tote and add new pots of fresh soil into the "Adults" tote.

Seal the "Eggs" tote containing the impregnated soil containers, keeping it in an enclosed space heated to about 85F (30C). Mist every few days. Set up the "Juveniles" container similar to the "Adults" container, with bedding, feed and moisture. After a couple of weeks, small crickets should emerge from the eggs. Capture them with your hands or a small aquarium net to transfer to the "Juveniles" container. Mist every few days.

After about a week, you can move the juveniles to the "Adults" container. Continue misting, replacing food scraps and transferring between containers every few days. While both juvenile and adult crickets are edible, adults provide a larger portion of food. Crickets can be processed into food for humans or fed to quail (depending on your quail coop and whether it is cricket escape-proof.)

Getting started

The number of insects to start with depends on the size of your totes. Here are estimates for a small system for mealworms and crickets.

Gear	Estimated cost
Mealworms	
200 mealworms	$20
Three 2-gallon (8-L) plastic totes	$25
Leftover grains	free
Supplemental chicken or quail feed	$10
Cardboard or newspaper scraps	free
Total	$55

Gear	Estimated cost
Crickets	
50 crickets	$10
Three 14-gallon (50-L) plastic totes	$30
Plant-based kitchen scraps	free
Supplemental chicken or quail feed	$10
Cardboard egg cartons	free
Total	$50

SLAUGHTER AND PROCESSING

Many people simply place the crickets or mealworms into a sealed container and put them in the freezer for two days to kill them. However, this may not be the most humane method, and others prefer to first place them in a sealed container in the fridge to slow down their metabolism, then place them in boiling water for a minute. This choice is up to you, but I prefer to stun them in the fridge for an hour and then boil them, because this is a quicker death.

OTHER USEFUL INSECTS: RED WRIGGLER WORMS AND BLACK SOLDIER FLIES

Although they don't make great meals for people, the birds and fish among your microlivestock happily eat red wriggler worms and the larvae of black soldier flies.

Red wriggler worms

An excellent homesteading addition, red wrigglers will break down your vegetable-based food waste, producing nutrient-rich castings for container plants or garden soil. Use a 5-gallon (19-L) plastic tote with 10 or more $\frac{1}{8}$-inch (0.13-cm) holes drilled through the lid for air circulation and the bottom for drainage. Place it on an upside-down tote lid as an under tray to collect precious nutrient-rich "worm tea" to nourish your garden or container plants.

Add a few cups of organic potting soil, ½ cup (120 mL) or so of red wriggler worms (get these from a friend's compost pile), top with straw or shredded paper, and water generously (like you would a houseplant). Add kitchen scraps every few days, including any fruit and veggie leftovers and coffee grounds, but avoiding cooked food, grains, citrus and onions. Harvest the worms to feed your quail and fish.

Black soldier flies

The larvae of this fly grow on any type of food waste, especially the cooked food, meat and dairy scraps that can't go in your compost or worm bins. Easy to culture, they simply require a ventilated tote and steady supply of food and moisture. Collecting the larvae is a bit more complicated since the adults can fly and so you don't want to open the container. But there are many clever DIY designs available online, or you can simply purchase a kit. Quail and fish will love the black soldier fly larvae.

INSECT FLOUR

Eating bugs—grody! But they are oh so sustainable and nutritious, too. Be the pioneer to get over our cultural bias, and make insect flour. You won't detect a buggy taste, I promise. Believe me, my mom didn't . . . Sorry, Mom!

**1 cup (250 mL) boiled crickets or
  mealworms**

1. Preheat oven to 200F (95C). Arrange crickets or mealworms on a baking sheet in a single layer. Dry in the oven for about 1 hour or until they are completely dry and will crush easily with a spoon. Remove from oven and let cool.

2. For crickets, remove legs and antennae by rolling each cricket between your hands. Use a mortar and pestle or flour grinder to grind the dried crickets or mealworms into flour.

3. Before using, blend the insect flour with other types of flour, including wheat, rye, barley, oat, spelt, rice or quinoa, at a ratio of about 1 part insect flour to 3 parts grain flour. For example, ¼ cup (60 ml) of insect flour to ¾ cup (180 mL) all-purpose flour.

MAKES 1 CUP (250 ML) OF INSECT FLOUR

ADDING INSECT FLOUR TO BAKING

When baking biscuits, cookies, cakes and more, you can substitute a quarter of your baking flour of choice with cricket or mealworm flour. For example, for 1 cup (250 mL) flour, use ¼ cup (60 mL) insect flour and ¾ cup (180 mL) baking flour.

DARK & STORMY CHOCOLATE CUPCAKES WITH CRICKET FLOUR

These cupcakes are adapted from one of the many beautiful and moody chocolate recipes in Mast Brothers Chocolate: A Family Cookbook. *The ginger and rum combo is a play on the Dark 'n Stormy cocktail concocted by Gosling's Rum just after World War I. While the Mast brothers don't call for cricket flour, this adaptation shows that most baking works just fine with insect flour mixed in.*

CUPCAKES
½ cup (120 mL) sugar
½ cup (120 mL) molasses
½ cup (120 mL) butter
2 Tbsp (30 mL) coconut oil
¼ cup (60 mL) Insect Flour, recipe on page 139
1 cup (250 mL) flour (I like organic spelt, but try
    whatever you like)
2 Tbsp (30 mL) grated ginger
1 tsp (5 mL) cinnamon
½ tsp (2.5 mL) cardamom
½ tsp (2.5mL) sea salt
¼ cup (60 mL) water
½ cup (120 mL) dark rum
2 eggs
2 tsp (10 mL) lime zest
1 tsp (5 mL) baking soda
½ cup (120 mL) finely chopped good-quality dark
    chocolate

GANACHE TOPPING
1 cup (250 mL) heavy cream
1½ cup (350 mL) finely chopped good-quality dark
    chocolate

1. Preheat oven to 350F (180C) and butter a muffin tin or line with paper liners.

2. In a large bowl, mix sugar, molasses, butter and coconut oil. In a separate bowl combine insect flour, flour, ginger, cinnamon, cardamom and sea salt, then stir into the wet mixture. Add water, rum, eggs, lime zest and baking soda, then fold in chocolate just until combined.

3. Pour the batter into the muffin cups to about halfway. Bake for 15 minutes or until a toothpick inserted into the centre comes out clean. Remove from tin and place on a cooling rack to cool completely before frosting.

4. While the cupcakes are cooling, make the ganache topping. Bring cream to a boil in a saucepan, then pour over chopped chocolate in a heatproof bowl and let sit for 5 minutes. Stir gently until smooth and glossy, then spoon onto tops of cooled cupcakes.

MAKES 12 CUPCAKES

CONCEPTS FOR RAISING MICROLIVESTOCK SUSTAINABLY AND ETHICALLY

- Mimic natural ecosystems
- Allow and encourage your animals to express their natural, instinctive behaviours
- Recycle nutrients
- Use waste as a resource
- Reduce reliance on nutrients from outside your homestead ecosystem
- Let your livestock forage for themselves: use rabbit and quail tractors
- Forage for chemical-free weeds and grass in your neighbourhood
- Grow food for your livestock: mealworms, crickets, black soldier flies, worms, azolla, algae

GROW YOUR OWN CHICKEN FEED

Although I think raising chickens could be a great DIY cooperative project for apartment dwellers on the grounds of their building, this usually isn't an option for high-rise inhabitants. But for those who have access to backyard space and are living in cities that allow hens, chickens are an excellent way to use kitchen scraps to produce food.

Chickens are omnivorous and will eat almost anything. While you can't feed cooked food, dairy or meats to your compost or worm bin, you can feed them to chickens. And they will gobble down pretty much any food waste, including kombucha scobys you can't find homes for, whey from cheese making, spent grains from beer making, even take-out leftovers. They also like worms when the worm bin is getting crowded, as well as home-grown mealworms, crickets and fly larvae and the azolla that is overgrowing your patio pond.

Animal	Natural Diet	Homegrown Feed	Supplemental Feed
Rabbit	Herbivorous: mainly grass	Grass, weeds collected from neighbourhood, fresh vegetable kitchen scraps	Commercial alfalfa pellets
Quail	Granivorous: seeds	Worms, mealworms, crickets, black soldier fly larvae	Commercial quail crumble
Salmon and trout	Carnivorous: other fish and insects	Fresh meat and seafood waste, worms, mealworms, crickets, black soldier fly larvae	Commercial fish pellets
Tilapia, carp, perch, bluegill, catfish	Omnivorous: pond plants, insects, other fish	Algae, azolla, kitchen meat and vegetable scraps, snails, worms, mealworms, crickets, black soldier fly larvae	Commercial fish pellets
Crayfish	Mainly herbivorous: plants and algae	Algae, azolla, vegetable scraps, fish waste and edible plants in aquaponics system	Commercial sinking algae wafers
Freshwater prawns	Mainly herbivorous: plants and algae	Algae, azolla, vegetable scraps, fish waste and edible plants in aquaponics system	Commercial sinking algae wafers
Freshwater mussels	Filter feeders: suspended plankton	Fish waste	None required
Freshwater snails	Herbivorous	Algae, azolla and other edible plants growing in the system	None required
Bees	Nectivorous: nectar and pollen from flowers	Flowers in bee garden with successional blooming	Flowers available in a large radius around the hive
Mealworms	Granivorous: mostly grains	Leftover grains, bread, dried spent beer-making grains	Commercial chicken or quail feed
Crickets	Omnivorous: plants, fungi and other insects	Leftover fruit, vegetables and grains	Commercial chicken or quail feed

PULLED POULTRY ENCHILADAS

This is a delicious way to make the most of the older laying hens you would like to remove from your flock. The trick to eating older birds is simply to brine them first, then slow cook them. This recipe is amazing (of course it is—it's from Chris), and works equally well with quail or even rabbit.

PULLED CHICKEN
½ cup (120 mL) pickling salt
8 cups (2 L) water
1 chicken (about 3–4 lbs/1.4–1.8 kg)
3 Tbsp (45 mL) vegetable oil
1 small onion, halved
2 bay leaves
½ tsp (2.5 mL) cumin
½ tsp (2.5 mL) cinnamon
2 tsp (10 mL) chili powder (optional)
3 cloves garlic, minced
1 green bell pepper, chopped
1 corn cob, kernels sliced off
Coarse salt and freshly ground pepper to taste

ENCHILADA SAUCE
1 small onion, chopped
4 cloves garlic, minced
1 Tbsp (15 mL) olive oil
1 Tbsp (15 mL) butter
2 Tbsp (30 mL) flour
1 cup (250 mL) canned crushed tomatoes
½ tsp (2.5 mL) cumin
1 tsp (5 mL) dried oregano
½ tsp (2.5 mL) chili powder
Coarse salt to taste
Freshly ground pepper to taste

TO ASSEMBLE
1 cup (250 mL) Farmer's Cheese (page 249) or
    cheddar, shredded
10 small corn tortillas

1. In a large non-reactive pot, add the salt and water and stir until dissolved to make the brine. Add the chicken and weigh it down with a dinner plate so it stays submerged. Leave the meat in the brine for 2 to 12 hours in the refrigerator, depending how old the bird is (the older the bird, the tougher it will be, so the longer you should brine).

2. Preheat oven to 375F (190C). Prepare the pulled chicken. Use a slow cooker or a large stockpot. Add meat, half of the small onion, and bay leaves to pot, then fill with water until meat is just covered. Simmer until meat is tender enough to easily shred with a fork.

3. Chop remaining half onion. In a large skillet over medium heat, sauté onion in oil until translucent. Add cumin, cinnamon and chili powder and stir for 1 minute. Add garlic, green pepper and corn, and sauté until pepper begins to soften (about 3 minutes). Shred meat into skillet and brown the meat until it starts to crisp. Add salt and pepper to taste and set aside.

4. Prepare the sauce. In a small saucepan over medium heat, sauté onion and garlic in butter and oil until translucent. Make a roux by adding flour and cooking for 1 minute, stirring constantly. Add the crushed tomatoes, cumin, oregano and chili powder, and simmer for 10 minutes.

5. Place a handful of pulled chicken in the centre of each tortilla, roll the tortillas (leaving ends open), and place side by side in a 9 x 13–inch (22.5 x 32-cm) baking dish. Cover tortillas with enchilada sauce, then top with shredded cheese.

6. Bake for 15 to 20 minutes until cheese is melted and top is slightly browned.

SERVES 4 FOR DINNER

WHEN YOU CAN'T KEEP YOUR OWN

While I hope I've made a good case for keeping your own animals, even in urban settings, if you're going to consume animal proteins, I realize there are those of us who can't DIY. But—take heart—there are still local sustainable options.

Visiting a farmers' market will often lead you straight to local growers and artisans making yummy meat and dairy products. Another option is to purchase a CSA (community supported agriculture) box from a local, ethical meat producer. This model requires payment at the start of the season for the farmer to use to purchase the necessary inputs, and provides you with a regular supply of local, ethical meat, often delivered into the city or even to your door.

Buying directly from the farmer is a great option because it allows you to use your purchasing power to vote for what you believe in—sustainable and ethical farming by local producers.

Even if you are unable to rear them yourself, rabbit scores high from a sustainability standpoint and is often locally produced in decent conditions, though this meat can be difficult to source in some North American markets. Ducks and geese are other good choices because they are easy to keep happy and can be successfully integrated into a sustainable farm ecosystem, with their environmental impact generally on the low side.

Beef and pigs generally have the heaviest ecological footprints. Ask around though—occasionally you will locate a conscientious urban farmer who is recycling food "waste" (like perfectly good organic fruit slightly too ripe to be shipped to grocery stores) into pig food and allowing his or her animals to slop in the mud, run afield, and happily express all their piggy instincts.

Another promising option for the urban dweller, especially those wishing to find a source of raw milk to make delicious dairy products at home (see page 237), is a cow or goat share. In many areas, onerous health regulations prevent local farmers from selling raw milk to the public. With a cow or goat share, you become part owner of the animal and reap the benefits of its fresh raw milk production, while not breaking any rules.

GROWING

GROWING FOOD IN THE CITY

While not everyone in urban areas is lucky enough to have ample space to garden, it's still possible for those with very limited soil, or even none, to grow food. Whether you have a backyard, some available area around your apartment building, patio, balcony, solarium or even just a spare indoor closet, there is a way to raise your own edible plants and mushrooms.

Growing projects	Indoors	Solarium	Balcony	Patio	Apartment Grounds	Backyard
Sprouts	✔	✔				
Microgreens	✔	✔	✔	✔	✔	✔
Mushrooms	✔	✔	✔	✔	✔	✔
Edible patio ponds		✔	✔	✔	✔	✔
Aquaponics	✔	✔	✔*	✔	✔	✔
Food forest		✔	✔	✔	✔	✔
Edible landscaping			✔	✔	✔	✔

*See Weighty Decisions, (page 155)

SPROUTS AND MICROGREENS

Many seeds can be quickly and efficiently grown into delicious sprouts and microgreens for fresh, organic, nutrient-packed goodness available to you any time of the year in any urban home.

Grow these healthy sprouts or microgreens to add new vitality to your meals. Use sprouted greens to tuck into wraps and sandwiches or toss over hot soups and stir-fries for a splash of fresh texture, flavour and colour. Or choose beans and grains to boost the bulk and heartiness of cold or hot meals, and even to give your baking a delicious bump up in nutrition.

Add Freshness

- Alfalfa
- Broccoli
- Carrot
- Clover
- Lettuce
- Kale
- Spinach

Enhance Flavour

- Basil
- Garlic
- Mustard
- Onions
- Radish

Up the Colour

- Beets
- Swiss chard

Increase Heartiness

- Buckwheat
- Lentils
- Mung beans
- Peas
- Pumpkin
- Soy beans
- Sunflower
- Quinoa
- Wheat

Boost Baking

- Buckwheat
- Pumpkin
- Quinoa
- Sunflower
- Wheat

SPROUTS

No matter where you live, you can grow sprouts—you don't need access to outdoor space or even a windowsill, as sprouts will grow in a dark cupboard.

Get growing

All you need is a jar and some seeds. A 2-cup (475-mL) wide-mouth jar and a couple of tablespoons (30 mL) of seeds is a good start.

Soak the seeds overnight in a cup. Drain and transfer to the jar, covering it with an old nylon stocking or cheesecloth secured around the top with an elastic band.

Rinse with room temperature water twice a day, draining after rinsing.

After a few days to a week, just when they start to sprout tiny leaves, you will have perfect little sprouts ready to eat.

MICROGREENS

Microgreens require a little bit of soil and light so the first pair of leaves on the sprout unfurls and turns green (the green leaf is what distinguishes sprouts from microgreens). A very sunny windowsill works well, or you can use a compact grow light anywhere indoors, including a dark closet.

Get growing

You'll need a shallow, well-draining container of soil (2 to 3 inches/5 to 7.5 cm deep) with an under tray. A reused plastic annual pot from the nursery or a plastic clamshell from the grocery store both work well.

Sprinkle the seeds fairly densely in the container (as far apart as the size of the seeds) and cover with a layer of soil about ⅛ to ¼ inch deep (0.13 to 0.6 cm). After sowing seeds, water with a mister. Keep the soil as moist as a wrung-out sponge by misting two or three times a day. Once the first leaf pair (cotyledon) has opened, your microgreens are ready to eat. There are two easy ways to harvest—you can pull them from the soil, rinse the roots and eat the whole plant, or cut just above the level of the soil and start again. Keep several containers going at once and stagger the seeding in each for successive harvests.

TREE COLLARD, MINT & MICROGREEN SALAD WITH PEANUT DRESSING

Planning to make this recipe with rice wine vinegar, I realized halfway through that I didn't have any, so reached instead for coconut white balsamic purchased from a local olive-oil company. And, wow, coconut really goes with peanut butter! I've since discovered this dressing works well with any kind of vinegar—just use what you have and add a teaspoon (5 mL) of coconut oil too if you have it.

DRESSING

3 Tbsp (45 mL) natural peanut butter

3 Tbsp (45 mL) coconut white balsamic vinegar (or any homemade vinegar)

1 Tbsp (15 mL) soy sauce

1 Tbsp (15 mL) minced fresh garlic

1 Tbsp (15 mL) minced fresh ginger

1 tsp (5 mL) sesame or coconut oil

SALAD

4 cups (1 L) finely chopped tree collards or perennial kale

1 cup (250 mL) minced mild-flavoured mint leaves (reduce to ¼ cup/60 mL for spearmint or peppermint)

1 cup (250 mL) microgreens, such as kale, broccoli or spinach

1 cup (250 mL) chopped almonds

½ cup (120 mL) chopped mint flowers, if available

1. In a food processor or blender, blend the dressing ingredients until they are fully mixed. If using coconut oil, heat slightly to liquefy before adding.

2. Toss the tree collards, mint and microgreens with half the dressing. Reserve a handful of microgreens for garnish. Taste and add more if needed.

3. Top with chopped reserved microgreens, almonds and mint flowers.

SERVES 4 AS A SIDE SALAD

CULINARY MUSHROOMS

Growing your own mushrooms is one of the best secrets for urban homesteaders with very limited space. Mushrooms don't need light, although they do require moisture, so growing them in the bottom of a closet or cupboard that you can keep damp works best. Under the kitchen sink is a great spot—or you can even put them outside on your balcony if the weather is not too cold.

GROWING MUSHROOMS INDOORS

To grow mushrooms, all you need to do is culture the mushroom mycelium—the white hair-like structures that grow in soil—and wait for the healthy mycelium to send out fruits, which are the mushrooms you eat.

Indoor Picks

- Button
- Crimini
- Lion's mane
- Oyster
- Shiitake
- Portobello

Get growing

It's easy and quite inexpensive to purchase a full mushroom-growing kit from a local homesteading store or online when you are first starting out. This will set you up with the mushroom spawn (sawdust with mushroom spores or mycelia), as well as the container and growing medium for whichever mushroom you choose.

Most mushrooms can be grown in plastic bags or buckets filled with straw, sawdust, coffee grounds or composted manure. If you purchase a kit, the growing medium will already be inoculated with the spawn. Usually all you have to do is pierce the bag to allow the mushrooms somewhere to sprout, then place it in a cool, dark place and keep it moist while waiting for the mushrooms (the mycelial fruits) to grow. To keep the growing medium moist, cover it with a damp cloth. Keep a spray bottle of water nearby and mist the growing medium every day or two, replacing the damp cloth each time.

After about a week, you should notice mushroom fruits starting to sprout, and in another week or so they will be ready to start harvesting. They will continue to sprout for up to three months. Continue to mist the growing medium and keep covered with a clean damp cloth.

If you purchase the spawn and growing medium separately, ask at the store or check online to make sure you get the right medium for the mushroom you would like to grow. You will need to inoculate the growing medium with the mushroom spawn yourself by warming up the growing medium and stirring the spawn into it. Once this is done, place the inoculated medium into the bag or bucket and follow the same steps as above.

Opposite: Portobello and shiitake mushrooms can be grown in a damp cupboard in only a few short weeks.

GROWING MUSHROOMS OUTDOORS

These same methods can be used to grow mushrooms outdoors, using a plastic bag or bucket of growing medium, a log or even a compost pile.

Outdoor Options

- Maitake
- Lion's mane
- Oyster
- Reishi
- Shiitake
- Wine caps

Get growing

Inside or out, mushrooms like to be moist at all times. They also prefer the weather to be fairly warm, so you are looking for an outside temperature of about 55F (13C).

As with indoor mushroom growing, buckets and bags also work outside. If you have the space outside, you can grow your mushrooms on a hardwood log (alder, maple or oak) using sawdust plugs inoculated with mushroom spawn (supplied by a homesteading store or ordered online). Fresh logs work best because the introduced mushroom spawn will not need to compete with existing fungus or other microorganisms, and you can be more certain of growing what you have inoculated with.

Use a log about 3 feet (90 cm) long and 4 to 10 inches (10 to 25 cm) in diameter. Drill holes the size of the plugs (usually about ½ inch/1.25 cm wide and 2 inches/5 cm deep), spaced about 4 inches (10 cm) apart. Place the plugs into the holes and tap in with a hammer. Use melted beeswax to seal the holes.

Keep the inoculated log moist and off the ground (to prevent rot). The mushroom mycelia may take several months to colonize the log, but the mycelia should fruit for several years if kept moist in spring and fall. If you have a garden or compost pile, try inoculating a corner of it with shade-loving varieties like wine caps. Keep the area covered with about 2 inches (5 cm) of compost and keep it moist, and you could have mushrooms sprouting within a few weeks.

CREAMY BRAISED PURPLE LOOSESTRIFE & MUSHROOM RISOTTO

Risotto is a wonderful way to enjoy the deep, earthy taste of mushrooms combined with the green taste of purple loosestrife. A very invasive plant in wetlands across North America, purple loosestrife is in fact edible and the leaves cook much like spinach. Serve this hearty recipe with a fresh kale salad and bottle of Pinot Noir, Cabernet Sauvignon or even a sparkling white.

3 cups (710 mL) chopped purple loosestrife leaves
2 Tbsp (30 mL) olive oil
8 Tbsp (120 mL) butter, divided
1 medium onion, chopped
2 cloves garlic, minced
Coarse salt and freshly ground pepper to taste
½ cup (120 mL) water
1 lb (455 gr) fresh mushrooms
7–9 cups (1.7–2.1 L) Rabbit Stock, recipe on page 93 (or substitute quail or chicken stock), divided
2½ cups (600 mL) arborio rice
½ cup (120 mL) dry white wine
½ cup (120 mL) dry vermouth
¼ cup (60 mL) shredded Farmer's Cheese, recipe on page 249 (or substitute Parmesan)

1. Prepare the loosestrife by removing any woody stems from the leaves and rinsing.

2. In a large pot or Dutch oven, heat the olive oil and 2 tablespoons (30 mL) of the butter over medium heat. Add onion and garlic and cook until translucent. Stir in loosestrife and season with salt and pepper. Add water and bring to a boil. Reduce heat and simmer 3 minutes.

3. Meanwhile, in a large skillet, sauté mushrooms in butter over medium heat until tender and beginning to brown, about 3 to 4 minutes. Set aside.

4. Once loosestrife is tender, add 3 cups (710 mL) stock and bring to a simmer. Add rice and stir for 3 to 4 minutes. Add white wine and vermouth and stir until liquid is absorbed, about 1 minute. Continue to add stock ½ cup (120 mL) at a time, stirring until absorbed each time, until rice is tender but firm and risotto is creamy, about 10 to 15 minutes (add the sautéed mushrooms halfway through cooking). Stir in cheese, reserving some for garnish.

5. Transfer to serving bowl and top with shredded cheese.

SERVES 4 FOR DINNER

EDIBLE POND PLANTS

Many edible plants will happily grow in a small tub of water on your patio, or even in an indoor condo solarium. I'm always delighted to show people the beautiful red and green foliage in my "pocket pond," pointing out that each plant is edible.

GROWING WATER PLANTS FOR FOOD

In only 30 gallons (just over 130 L) of water and within about a radius of 1.5 feet (46 cm), I easily grow 12 types of edible plants. Many plants naturally live in aquatic ecosystems, either rooted in the soil underwater or floating on top. If we choose the right plants (the ones that like water), and think about how they like to grow (in soil or floating, submerged or emergent), it's easy to mimic a pond ecosystem and grow water plants for food.

Weighty Decisions

First, consider weight restrictions. Water is heavy, so if you are thinking about setting it on a raised balcony, ensure your pond won't pose a safety threat. Water weighs about 8.5 lbs (almost 4 kg) per gallon, on top of the weight of the container and everything else in it, so keep this in mind when choosing how large the pond should be and check with your building management, if applicable.

CHOOSING A POND CONTAINER

Visit a local nursery that specializes in pond supplies. A 30 to 40-gallon (or roughly 150-L) pond around 10 to 12 inches (25 to 30 cm) high is a good start for most small patios or balconies. Even ponds this small will weigh up to 350 lbs (about 160 kg) or so. Look for food-safe materials. You can also repurpose plastic food shipping barrels (usually 55 gallons) by cutting the bottom 12 inches (30 cm) off, or use an old enamel bathtub if you have the space and weight capacity.

EDIBLE POND PLANTS

Hopefully, your local pond expert will be able to tell you which of the aquatic plants they sell are edible, but they may not know, so show up with your own list of possibilities. Choose a variety of growing types—deep emergent, shallow emergent, floating emergent, submerged and floating. This helps make the best use of vertical space, and also improves water quality by increasing oxygenation (through the submerged plants) and reducing algae growth on the surface (through the floating plants).

Water Plant Growth Types

- **Deep emergent:** rooted in soil 6 to 24 inches (15 to 60 cm) underwater
- **Shallow emergent:** rooted in soil 3 to 4 inches (7.5 to 10 cm) underwater
- **Floating emergent:** rooted in soil just under surface of water
- **Submerged:** rooted in soil and submerged below water's surface
- **Floating:** not rooted in soil, floating on surface

WATER AERATION ADDITIONS

Grow submerged plants to improve water aeration—this is essential if you have fish. Many edible plants can be used for this, though they are less choice to eat and can be a bit stringy and tough. These include coontail or hornwort (*Ceratophyllum demersum*), eelgrass (*Vallisneria americana*), sago pondweed (*Stuckenia pectinata*) and whorled water milfoil or parrotfeather (*Myriophyllum verticillatum*).

WHY CONSIDER FISH?

Your pond supplier is also likely to sell goldfish or mosquito fish. The value of including fish in your pocket pond is twofold. First, they eat mosquito larvae; second, they excrete nutrients that feed plants. In the first growing season, plants do not require supplemental feeding—the soil in their pots (along with nutrients floating in the water) is adequate—so you may not need to keep fish. However, to boost their growth or keep plants into the next growing season, the addition of fish to the pond ecosystem is beneficial. For more on keeping fish, see page 116.

SETTING UP YOUR ECOSYSTEM

When you get home, place your pond where you want it to go—once it's filled, you won't be able to move it. Most pond plants like full sun, but if you have fish and live in a hot climate, ensure the pond has midday shade to keep the water cool. If placing your pond in an area where wildlife like raccoons or herons may have access to it, consider covering the top of the pond with strong wire to protect the fish while allowing the plants to grow through the wire. You may also want to choose more camouflaged fish, such as mosquito fish rather than goldfish. With a variety of pond plants and bricks under the water (as described below), your fish should have comfortable places to hide from predators.

Get Growing

Start by placing bricks in the bottom of the pond to create varying bottom levels. Place the deep emergent plants (in their mesh pots) on the very bottom of the tub, then shallow emergent plants on the bricks. Submerged plants can go directly on the bottom too. Fill the pond with water to about an inch from the top, then add floating plants. By planting a combination of species that includes edible shoots, leaves and roots, you will be able to harvest fresh produce from spring to fall.

Maintenance

Plan to check your pond every week or so. Add more water when needed. If you are keeping goldfish or mosquito fish, you may need to feed them—ask about feed requirements at your pond supplier. Keep an eye on the plants in case they are blown over by wind. If you are keeping fish, watch the temperature of the water in summer, and keep the pond shaded through the heat of the day. The deeper the pond, the cooler it will remain, but you may also want to add cold water. If you have fish, allow tap water to sit for several hours to dissipate the chlorine before adding to the pond.

Harvesting

The parts you can eat differ by plant. Some provide edible leaves that can be harvested throughout the growing season. Vigorous floating plants can be plucked whole at any time. Plants with starchy tubers can be harvested after the vegetation dies back in the fall. If you want to overwinter plants with edible roots, divide them and place some in your indoor pond to overwinter for the next growing season. See our chart on page 157 for more on what parts of each water plant are edible and for a few cautions.

Overwintering

If you live somewhere that gets cold in the winter, you will need to move your pond indoors to overwinter it. Many of the edible pond plants are tropical, so they don't tolerate low temperatures. If you live somewhere warmer, keep an eye on the plants over the winter and protect them with a covering of burlap during colder weather, or bring inside.

Common name	Botanical name	Growth type	Edible parts	Cooking suggestions
Achira	*Canna edulis*	Floating emergent	Roots, young leaves, shoots	Cook starchy roots like potatoes; prepare shoots like leeks; eat leaves like spinach
Arrowhead/wapato	*Sagittaria latifolia*	Deep emergent	Nutty tubers	Cook like potatoes
Azolla*	*Azolla* spp.	Floating	Whole plant	Mild flavour—use in soups and casseroles
Cattail	*Typha* spp.	Deep emergent	Shoots, roots, pollen	Prepare shoots like leeks; use roots like water chestnut; use pollen to make flour
Duckweed*	*Lemna* spp.	Floating	Whole plant	Mild flavour—use in soups and casseroles
Japanese sweet flag/ licorice flag*	*Acorus gramineus*	Shallow emergent	Roots	Culinary herb (licorice or cinnamon)—soak roots in water overnight to remove bitterness
Rice	*Oryza glaberrima* and *O. sativa*	Shallow emergent	Seeds (but not many produced per plant)	Remove grain and steam
Society garlic	*Tulbaghia violacea*	Shallow emergent	Leaves, flowers	Use like ramps or chives
Taro**	*Colocasia esculenta*	Shallow emergent	Roots, leaves	Starchy, sweet roots—cook roasted or sliced crosswise for chips
Tsi*	*Houttuynia cordata*	Shallow emergent	Leaves, roots	Culinary herb (mint with a slightly fishy flavour)—use to flavour cooked dishes
Water celery*	*Oenanthe javanica*	Floating emergent	Leaves and stems	Leaves are like celery—add to soups or casseroles, or blend into smoothies
Water chestnut/ water caltrop	*Eleocharis dulcis*	Shallow emergent	Roots	Crisp, sweet roots for stir-fries and soups
Water lotus	*Nelumbo nucifera*	Deep emergent	Roots	Large, crisp roots—good roasted or sliced crosswise for chips
Watermeal*	*Wolffia* spp.	Floating	Whole plant	Tastes like sweet cabbage—use in salads, soups and casseroles
Water mimosa*	*Neptunia oleracea*	Floating	Leaves	Tastes like cabbage—use in salads, soups and casseroles
Water spinach*	*Ipomoea aquatica*	Floating emergent	Leaves	Like spinach—use in salads, soups, casseroles
Watercress	*Nasturtium officinale*	Floating emergent	Leaves	Lightly spicy—use in sandwiches, salads, soups

* *Vigorous grower and invasive in wild ecosystems—be careful to keep contained*

** *Leaves contain toxins—to remove them, the leaves must be boiled for at least 10 minutes before eating*

SMOKED CHILI WATER LOTUS & TARO ROOT CHIPS WITH LEMONY HERB DIP

Lotus and taro roots are crisp, starchy and slightly sweet, and pair well with lemony foraged greens containing oxalic acid—curly dock, sorrel, purslane, lamb's quarters and amaranth. An underwater rhizome, the lotus root is riddled with air pockets that create a beautiful pattern when cut in cross-section, so these chips are not only tasty but pretty too.

DIP
1 clove garlic, finely chopped
¼ cup (60 mL) finely chopped fresh dock (ribs removed), purslane, sorrel, lamb's quarters or amaranth leaves, chopped
¼ cup (60 mL) chopped fresh mint
1 cup (250 mL) Easy Greek-style Yogurt, recipe on page 240 (or store-bought)
1 cup (250 mL) sour cream
Coarse salt to taste
Freshly ground pepper to taste

CHIPS
1 lotus root, peeled and sliced ¼–½ inch (0.6–1.25 cm) thick
1 taro root, peeled and sliced ¼–½ inch (0.6–1.25 cm) thick
1 Tbsp (15 mL) lemon juice
Smoked salt to taste
Chili powder to taste
2 Tbsp (30 mL) olive oil

1. Mix garlic, greens, mint, yogurt and sour cream together in a bowl. Season with salt and pepper. Chill for a couple of hours before serving.

2. Preheat oven to 450F (230C). Boil sliced roots in water and lemon juice for 10 minutes to soften, then drain and pat dry or use a salad spinner to remove excess water. Toss in salt, chili powder and oil, making sure to completely coat the slices. Spread one layer thick on a baking sheet. Bake for 10 minutes, flip over and then another 5 or 10 minutes until tender on the inside and crispy on the outside.

SERVES 6 AS AN APPETIZER

Opposite, clockwise from top left: Placing bricks into a patio pond creates different water depths for plants; the finished pond with submerged and floating edibles; achira, taro, rice and society garlic are all edible aquatic plants.

CHILLED AZOLLA & WATERCRESS SOUP

This soup makes a refreshing spring or summer lunch. Enjoy it sitting on your patio beside your edibles pond. You'll almost be able to see the azolla growing while you're eating; that's how prolific it is! If you don't have a pond, use any spinach-like greens you can forage; if it's available, lamb's quarters are a wonderful weedy addition, or use amaranth, chickweed, curly dock, purple loosestrife or stinging nettle. You can also substitute the potato with perennial sunchokes or foraged wapato roots.

2 cups (475 mL) chopped azolla
2 Tbsp (30 mL) butter
½ cup (120 mL) chopped leeks
1 medium potato, diced
3 cups (710 mL) Rabbit Stock, recipe on page 93
    (quail or chicken stock works as well)
2 cups (475 mL) chopped watercress
Up to 1 cup (250 mL) foraged or perennial greens
    (optional)
½ cup (120 mL) Easy Greek-style Yogurt, recipe on
    page 240 (or use store-bought)
Salt and pepper to taste
4 Hard-boiled Quail Eggs, sliced in half (see sidebar
    on page 105)

1. Prepare the azolla by rinsing thoroughly under cold water to remove any debris or algae. Discard long roots or fibrous parts.

2. In a stockpot or Dutch oven, melt butter over medium heat. Add leeks and potato and sauté until leeks are translucent. Add stock and simmer until vegetables are tender, about 10 minutes. Stir in azolla, watercress, and greens (if using) and cook until wilted, about 1 minute. Turn off heat and stir in yogurt.

3. Once cooled, season with salt and pepper to taste. Purée in blender, then transfer to a container for refrigeration. Chill until cold or overnight.

4. Ladle into bowls and serve each garnished with two quail egg halves.

SERVES 4

Opposite: Growing ultra-fast, azolla is a super-nutritious floating aquatic plant that can be grown in a patio pocket pond or even cultivated in a bowl on a sunny windowsill.

HOMEMADE WASABI PEAS

I have always enjoyed the singed-sinus and burning-scalp sensations of wasabi. If you can grow your own wasabi or find someone raising it locally, this recipe is a fresh take on a favourite Japanese snack. Be careful when handling fresh wasabi . . . treat it like a hot pepper and avoid touching your eyes before thoroughly scrubbing your hands.

3 cups (710 mL) fresh peas
   (thawed frozen peas also work)
2 Tbsp (30 mL) olive oil
1 Tbsp (15 mL) sesame oil
Coarse salt
¼ cup (60 mL) fresh grated
   wasabi

2 Tbsp (30 mL) tahini
1 Tbsp (15 mL) rice wine vinegar
1 tsp (5 mL) Dijon mustard
1 clove garlic, minced

1. Preheat the oven to 200F (95C).

2. Toss peas in olive and sesame oil. Spread on rimmed baking sheet, one layer thick. Sprinkle lightly with salt. Bake for 2 to 3 hours, tossing occasionally, until peas are dry. Pour dried peas into a bowl.

3. Meanwhile, finely grate the wasabi root (like you would grate ginger), and mix with tahini, rice wine vinegar, Dijon mustard and garlic.

4. Toss peas with wasabi mixture and stir to coat each pea. Pour them back onto the cookie sheet in a single layer and return them to oven. Bake for another 10 minutes until the coating is dry.

MAKES 3 CUPS (710 ML)

URBAN FOOD FORESTS

As a big fan of coffee, I became very interested in how it was grown and spent time in South America doing research on coffee growing for my master's degree in conservation biology. I wanted to know the difference between regular and shade-grown coffee—what each type of farm looked like and what it meant for local wildlife and people.

In Ecuador I came across people growing food within forests, and saw the benefits to the farmers and the ecosystem. While most coffee farms were vast plantations of only coffee, providing very little wildlife habitat and no security for farmers in case the coffee crops failed, there were other farmers growing "agroforests" of various food crops mixed in with natural cloud-forest plants. As in nature, these food forests have a diverse combination of plants with a mixed structure of heights and growth types. These systems provide complex habitat for wildlife (including the bats, beetles and tarantulas I shared my treehouse with), as well as diverse crops for the farmer, so if one fails there are others to depend on.

One family I stayed with mixed plantings of coffee with cocoa, four kinds of citrus, seven kinds of bananas, mangos, avocados, papaya, guava and bamboo, along with many natural forest trees and plants that provided building materials, fuel and medicine, keeping a natural cloud-forest ecosystem intact (including endless orchids and stunning hummingbirds, to my delight).

STACKING UP URBAN EDIBLES

The food forests I studied provided several major advantages that can be translated to urban areas.

First, they allow the natural ecology of a place to flourish by providing habitat for beneficial insects and birds that help reduce pest populations. This cuts down on the time and inputs spent dealing with crop pests.

Second, they provide diverse crops, which is a healthier and more robust way to plant than a monoculture and can ensure a variety of food is available throughout the growing season.

Finally, they make excellent use of space. Rather than sprawling sameness, food plants of differing heights are stacked together. Trees are used to provide structure for vines to climb up, while perennial shrubs are planted below with more shade-tolerant annuals—and all are edible! This means these systems can be incredibly productive in a smaller space, and the dissimilar plants grouped together can benefit each other.

For example, in a large patio container, a dwarf apple tree can provide structure for a bean vine to climb up; this bean vine fixes nitrogen from the air and adds it to the soil; a chive below attracts beneficial insects that feed on the pests on all of these plants; meanwhile, nasturtiums act as living mulch to improve water and nutrient retention. And all are stacked within a footprint the diameter of the dwarf apple, while looking beautiful and producing apples, beans, chive greens and nasturtium flowers.

Planting for Good Group Dynamics

It may seem counterintuitive, because "food forest" sounds like it requires a lot of room, but using this concept can be even more important in urban areas, where space is very limited. Thinking about food plants as an ecosystem and working within the framework of a food forest is a good idea for anyone interested in homesteading and sustainability. Even if you have no ground to plant in, you can use containers, vertical plantings, perennials and mulching to create your own food ecosystem and gain these advantages:

- Better use of limited area by accessing vertical space
- Combining the functions of different plants to benefit each other
- Highly productive gardening: more food in less space
- Diversity for healthy variety
- Easily available fresh, chemical-free food

NURTURE THE SOIL

As important as the complex plant relationships in your food forest, your growing medium—the soil—has an intricate and wonderful ecology of microorganisms that will treat you to amazing production if you nurture it. Feed your edible ecosystem's living soil by adding organic matter (compost, worm castings or rabbit manure). Recycle kitchen waste by feeding it to worms, then amend the soil of your edible plants with the nutrient-rich castings (see page 138 for more on raising red wriggler worms).

Protect your living soil by minimizing disturbance (no tilling). Instead of raking or pulling out weeds, which disrupts organisms and causes weed seeds to germinate, use organic or living mulch to cover the ground and smother weeds. In addition to helping retain moisture in the earth, mulch reduces erosion, and this is important when you have limited soil in containers. Bare soil allows nutrients to leach out when containers are watered or when it rains.

LIST OF FOOD FOREST PLANTS

Plants for an Urban Food Forest	How to Fit into the Edible Landscaping Ecosystem	Functions and Benefits
Bamboo	In containers adjacent to food ecosystem	Attractive and functional windbreak on high balconies, edible
Carrots, chicory, cilantro, dandelion, dwarf dill, garlic, mint, oregano, parsley, parsnips, thyme	Edible landscaping, in container with or beside fruit/nut trees	Repel pests, attract beneficial insects, ornamental, edible
Climbing beans or peas	In containers beside fruit/nut trees or railings they can climb	Nitrogen fixation, edible
Clover	In container with fruit/nut trees, edible landscaping	Nitrogen fixation, edible
Dwarf fruit or nut tree	As central element in edible landscaping	Structure for vines, shade for ground cover, edible
Fruiting shrub	As mid-height element in edible landscaping	Provide mid-height habitat for wildlife, living fence, edible
Hops	Climbing vine	Vertical climber, edible
Lavender, rosemary, sage	Edible landscaping, in container or beside fruit/nut trees	Attract beneficial insects, use as windbreak, edible
Strawberries	Ground cover, in container with or beside fruit/nut trees	Living mulch, attract beneficial insects, ornamental, edible

Mulch with dry kitchen waste like corn husks, or with shredded newspaper or fairly clean straw from your microlivestock. Leaf prunings make great mulch, especially from nitrogen-fixing plants like beans and peas. If you are growing annuals in a garden, it is very important to mulch during the non-growing season to build the soil and prevent erosion. Use a nitrogen-fixing living mulch, or cover crop, like alfalfa or clover, then cut it down to mulch the soil before the growing season starts. Or cover your beds with a layer of rabbit manure and soiled straw in the fall to slowly break down until the growing season starts again.

CONCEPTS FOR SUSTAINABLE URBAN EDIBLE ECOSYSTEMS

- Nurture soil ecology to improve growth
- Mimic nature by recycling nutrients
- Use waste as a resource to reduce reliance on outside inputs like fertilizers (even organic ones)
- Use kitchen and plant waste to feed worms, then use worm castings to feed garden or container plants
- Use dry kitchen and plant waste as mulch in garden and containers
- Reduce disturbance to soil by layering organic additions on top, mulching and planting perennials
- Provide habitat for beneficial insects to reduce pest populations

PLANTS FOR PATIO CONTAINERS

For homesteaders in city spaces, accessing sunlight and, most importantly, space, can be the biggest challenges when it comes to growing food. I always choose apartments with a south-facing balcony to get the most sunlight on my "food forest" containers, and look forward every year to new varieties of vegetables specifically bred for pots.

Nowadays, there are container-happy varieties of almost all the common garden veggies and herbs, as well as dwarf fruit and nut trees and berry bushes. Just make sure they start with adequate drainage and very good soil that you amend regularly with worm castings, water from your aquaponics system, compost or organic fertilizer. Ensure your balcony containers get lots of light and adequate water, and that they are protected from high winds.

Annuals

- Arugula
- Basil
- Beans
- Beets
- Broccoli
- Cabbage
- Carrots
- Cauliflower
- Chard
- Cilantro
- Cucumber—climber
- Dwarf dill
- Dwarf melon—climber
- Eggplant
- Garlic
- Kale
- Kohlrabi
- Leeks
- Lettuce
- Nasturtium
- Onions
- Parsley
- Peas
- Peppers
- Potatoes
- Radishes
- Squash—climber
- Tomatoes

Perennial Herbs

- Chive
- Lavender
- Mint
- Oregano
- Rosemary
- Sage
- Thyme

Dwarf Fruit and Nut Trees

- Almond
- Apple
- Apricot
- Cherry
- Citrus
- Fig
- Olive
- Nectarine
- Peach
- Pear
- Plum

Dwarf Berry Bushes

- Blueberry
- Currant
- Raspberry
- Strawberry (as an edible living mulch)

EDIBLE VINES TO GROW UP

Okay, so by integrating plants at different levels in your patio containers (or in the ground), you are moving towards better use of space and starting to create a more complex food ecosystem. What's the next step? Vertical plantings!

Vines can be a great edible addition for those with limited space, because they don't take up a lot of room in the ground. Use your tall to mid-level plants to provide structure for climbers, or train the vines along your balcony railing.

Annual Vines

- Beans
- Cucumber
- Melons
- Peas
- Squash

Perennial Vines

- Grapes
- Hops
- Kiwi (dwarf)

PATIO CONTAINER PEACH & CARDAMOM CRISP

When I was little, I used to forage in my grandma's mini-orchard, garden and nearby woods to collect whatever fruit was in season, triumphantly returning to the house with a basketful to make into something tasty. My grandma, being the patient woman she was, would always rally, and together we would start creating in the kitchen. One of our favourites was this quick and easy crisp, made with peaches or whatever is in season in your patio containers or the urban foraging landscape—apples, plums, strawberries, blueberries, blackberries, rhubarb and especially the invasive Japanese knotweed. Even now, this is my go-to dessert for unexpected guests.

3 cups (710 mL) peeled and diced peaches (or other seasonal fruit)
1 Tbsp (15 mL) tapioca (substitute flour if using apples)
¼ cup (60 mL) orange juice
1 tsp (5 mL) orange zest

¼ cup (60 mL) flour
½ cup (120 mL) brown sugar
1 cup (250 mL) oats
¼ tsp (1 mL) cinnamon
¼ tsp (1 mL) cardamom
¼ cup (60 mL) cold butter

1. Preheat oven to 375F (190C).

2. Mix diced peaches or other fruit, tapioca, orange juice and orange zest in a bowl. Pour into a 6-inch (15-cm) square baking dish.

3. Combine flour, sugar, oats, cinnamon and cardamom in a bowl. Cut in butter until pea-sized.

4. Evenly spread topping over fruit.

5. Bake for 40 minutes until fruit is bubbling.

SERVES 6

SEA SALT, TOASTED ALMOND & DARK CHOCOLATE SPREAD

This simple yet decadent spread is delicious on toasted Rustic Rosemary Sourdough Bread (page 214). I would pair this with a Vancouver Rain Latte (page 39) for a bad-girl breakfast, but that part is up to you. Use the best dark chocolate you can find.

2 cups (475 mL) almonds (or hazelnuts), shells and husks removed

2 cups (475 mL) finely chopped good-quality dark chocolate

2 Tbsp (30 mL) coconut oil

1 tsp (5 mL) sea salt

¼ cup (60 mL) sugar (optional)

½ cup (120 mL) 35 percent cream

1. Preheat oven to 350F (180C). Spread nuts on baking tray one layer thick. Toast, tossing once or twice until brown, about 10 minutes. Purée the toasted nuts in a food processor or blender until smooth and creamy. Add dark chocolate, coconut oil, salt and sugar, and purée together. Pour into medium-sized heatproof bowl. Set aside.

2. In a small saucepan over medium heat, bring cream to a boil. Pour over nut and chocolate mixture and let sit for 5 minutes. Mix completely, then spoon into clean mason jars. This spread will store in the refrigerator for a month.

MAKES 2 CUPS (475 ML)

FIG & FENNEL CLAFOUTIS

A dwarf fig tree makes an excellent patio container food plant, if you're lucky enough to have enough room and sunlight for one. If not, be like me and make friends with someone with a fig tree. My hilarious friend Sharon Hanna (the "Queen of Kale" and author of The Book of Kale) has a beautiful food garden on her urban lot, complete with several fruit trees. I picked her figs at the height of ripeness and we ate them with fresh goat cheese in the sunshine. Luckily, there were more than enough for me to take some home, so I also made fig clafoutis with some foraged fennel for brunch. Always a big hit when served to guests, you can also use dried figs for this recipe, so pick a bunch in season or purchase some from a local grower to dry for use throughout the year.

½ cup (120 mL) finely chopped almonds
20 figs, fresh or dried
1 vanilla bean
4 eggs
1 tsp (5 mL) lemon zest
½ cup (120 mL) sugar
¾ cup (180 mL) heavy cream
¾ cup (180 mL) whole milk
¼ tsp (1 mL) almond extract
6 Tbsp (90 mL) flour
Pinch of salt
3 Tbsp (45 mL) butter
¼ cup (60 mL) honey
¼ cup (60 mL) finely chopped fresh fennel leaves
Sour cream for garnish
2–3 fennel flower heads for garnish, if available

1. Toast the almonds on a baking tray under the broiler for a couple of minutes—watch to ensure they don't burn. Preheat the oven to 400F (205C).

2. Cut the stems off the figs and quarter them lengthwise. Slice the vanilla bean lengthwise and scrape out the seeds. Set aside.

3. In a bowl, whisk the eggs until frothy, then whisk in lemon zest, sugar, cream, milk and almond extract. Add the flour and salt and stir until incorporated. Let rest 15 minutes.

4. Meanwhile, heat a large cast iron skillet over medium-high heat. Melt butter with honey and vanilla seeds and pod. Add the figs and fennel leaves. Stir to coat figs and mix in fennel. Cook for a couple of minutes until the figs start to soften. Remove the vanilla pod.

5. Pour the batter over the figs and fennel, sprinkle toasted almonds on top, and place the skillet in the oven. Bake about 30 to 40 minutes, until golden and the centre doesn't jiggle when you move the pan.

6. Serve with a dollop of sour cream on each piece, sprinkled with fennel flower pollen.

SERVES 8

GREEN BEAN & ASPARAGUS GRATIN

Here is a gooey, cheesy way to mix your small-space garden vegetables. If you don't have climbing beans or perennial asparagus, no worries—this dish is very versatile. Use other edible pods, stems or even green leaves, such as kale or chard, or try perennial tree collards, lamb's quarters or good King Henry. See page 247 for tips on making breadcrumbs from leftover homemade bread.

2 cups (475 mL) chopped scarlet runner beans
4 cups (950 mL) chopped asparagus spears
1 Tbsp (15 mL) whole grain mustard
2 cups (475 mL) 35 percent heavy cream
Pinch of salt
Pinch of freshly ground pepper
2 Tbsp (30 mL) butter, divided
1 small onion, chopped
2 Tbsp (30 mL) flour
½ cup (120 mL) grated Gruyère

TOPPING
½ cup (120 mL) grated 30-minute Mozzarella, recipe on page 246 (or store-bought)
¼ cup (60 mL) grated Parmesan
¼ cup (60 mL) breadcrumbs

1. Preheat the oven to 350F (180C).

2. Remove and discard any woody parts of the beans and asparagus spears and chop. Spread in a baking dish.

3. Mix mustard, cream, salt and pepper in a small bowl. In a saucepan over medium heat, sauté the onion in 1 tablespoon (15 mL) of the butter until translucent. Add the remaining tablespoon (15 mL) butter and the flour. Stir to mix and allow to bubble in pan for 1 minute. Pour the cream mixture into the pan. Bring to a simmer and stir for 1 minute. Add the Gruyère cheese and stir until melted.

4. Pour over the asparagus spears. Bake for 20 minutes uncovered.

5. Mix the Mozzarella, Parmesan and breadcrumbs. Remove the baking dish from the oven after 20 minutes and top with the breadcrumb mixture. Replace in the oven for another 15 minutes until the top has a light, golden crust.

SERVES 4 AS A SIDE

CREATE A VERTICAL PLANTING STRUCTURE

Basically any annual garden veggies and most small herbs can be grown in a vertical planting structure that can also provide support for climbing vines. Tie landscaping cloth bags or reused soda bottles to railings to use as planters, or fill a hanging fabric shoe rack with small herbs. Get creative: containers nailed inside a repurposed wooden packing crate and attached to the wall, or vertical lengths of PVC pipe with 2-inch (5-cm) holes drilled and stuffed with soil are just a couple of many ways to house edible plants.

Vertical Plantings
- Arugula
- Basil
- Chives
- Cilantro
- Lettuce
- Oregano
- Parsley
- Sage
- Strawberries
- Thyme

THE PERKS OF PERENNIALS

The process of sowing seed, digging weeds and tearing out annual vegetables and tender herbs every year is not good for fostering healthy soil ecology. It also creates the extra work of replanting every spring and means that your containers or garden are bare during the non-growing season. Perennial plants—which do not need to be replaced every year, as opposed to annuals or biennials, which die every year or two—are often more abundant and better producers than annuals.

Perennials include many of the plants we've been discussing, including fruit and nut trees, berry bushes and numerous vines and herbs. There are many advantages to adding perennials to your urban food forest:

- Less work—no annual replanting, less weeding
- Minimal soil disturbance reduces weed growth
- Presence of foliage for shade also reduces weed growth
- Improved soil ecology—less erosion, reduced tillage, natural mulch from dead leaves
- Abundant yields
- Edible products when annual plants aren't in season
- Habitat for beneficial insects and birds when annual plants are in season, reducing pest problems in the edible garden
- Excellent for edible landscaping, providing shade, structure, permanent living fences and/or ground cover

In short, using perennials as the backbone of your patio or garden and filling in with a few annuals can greatly increase yield, the length of harvest and the health of your food ecosystem, while reducing the amount of effort you have to put in.

As we have discussed, perennial fruit and nut trees, berry shrubs and fruiting vines can be stacked vertically to make the best use of limited urban space. But most of these are fruit—so what about vegetables?

PERENNIAL VEGETABLES

Many North American gardeners aren't aware of the possibilities that perennial vegetables offer. There are at least two perennial vegetables most people are familiar with: asparagus and rhubarb (we'll call rhubarb a vegetable because even though it's cooked in desserts, we are eating the stem of the plant, not the fruit). There are also artichokes and horseradish, which are perennial in warmer zones.

But are there others? Can we start vegetables once and harvest from them for many years? Actually, there are tons of perennial plants that provide vegetable crops. It does depend on where you are—a perennial plant's endurance is determined by its tolerance of the temperature where it is planted; in challenging zones, it will behave as an annual and die in the winter. If you live in a cooler climate, you may want to consider overwintering cold-sensitive perennial edibles indoors and placing them outside again when the weather warms up. However, there are also many perennial vegetables for colder climates—check which hardiness zone you live in to determine which perennial vegetables will flourish in your region.

Many native perennial greens (see pages 31–35) can also be cultivated in food forests, as well these more unusual edibles:

Crosnes or Chinese artichoke (*Stachys affinis*)

Roots. Hardy to Zone 5. Actually from the mint family, crosnes tubers are sweet and can be used in recipes in place of yams and sometimes squash. Planted as a ground cover, its foliage will protect soil from erosion and form a living mulch. Like other members of the mint clan, crosnes tend to spread aggressively, so are best kept in containers.

Groundnut (*Apios americana*)

Roots. Hardy to Zone 3. Native to eastern North America, these plants have been cultivated here for centuries. Forming potato-like tubers that can be harvested year-round, groundnuts can grow under fruit and nut trees or mid-height shrubs. Like other members of the pea family, these plants fix nitrogen, so their vigorous foliage can be cut and used as mulch to amend container soil. The flowers and "peas" (seeds inside the bean-like pods) are also edible, but the tubers develop best if the vegetation is kept clipped back to 6 feet (1.8 m) tall. Groundnut can spread aggressively, so keep this in mind.

Good King Henry (*Chenopodium bonus-henricus*)

Shoots, leaves, seeds. Hardy to Zone 4. Originally a European vegetable, this versatile plant is in the amaranth family along with lamb's quarters and quinoa. Easy to grow in large containers, it can be harvested for shoots (like asparagus), foliage (like spinach) or seeds (like grain). Good King Henry tolerates shade, so it does well planted under edible trees, berries and vines. Leaves tend to be bitter raw, so are best in cooked dishes in place of spinach or kale.

Perennial kale, "Western Front" (*Brassica napus*) and branching bush (*B. oleracea ramosa*)

Leaves. Hardy to Zone 4. In the cabbage clan, these hardy kales can be overwintered even in cold regions, with some protection from wind and intense cold (such as burlap covers). Leaves can be harvested throughout the year, but their flavour is best early in the season or after a freeze.

Sea kale (*Crambe maritima*)

Shoots, flower heads, leaves. Hardy to Zone 4. Also in the cabbage family, sea kale is native to the coasts in Europe, where it is both foraged and grown as a garden vegetable. The shoots are the choice part of this edible, and can be covered with mulch in early spring to keep their nutty flavour mild. Harvest at 6 to 9 inches (15 to 23 cm) long. The flowers can be eaten like broccoli and the more tender leaves of non-flowering plants cooked like spinach or kale.

Sunchoke or Jerusalem artichoke (*Helianthus tuberosus*)

Roots. Hardy to Zone 5. In the aster family, sunchokes are related to dandelions and sunflowers, but are known for their starchy roots tasting of water chestnuts rather than their slightly bitter leaves or their seeds. Easy to grow, they produce large yields of crisp and sweet tubers throughout the year (unless the ground is frozen). Simply leave them in your container or garden plot until you are ready to cook. They grow to 12 feet (3.7 m), so they may not be suitable for all balconies. Be warned that they tend to spread and are prolific once established, so may be best grown in containers. Their flowers attract beneficial insects and pollinators. Although not as starchy, they can be cooked like potatoes or in place of squash in some recipes.

Tree collards or walking stick kale (*Brassica oleracea acephala*)

Leaves. Hardy to Zone 8. Not to be confused with annual collard greens (which are also in the cabbage family), tree collards are short-lived (3 to 5 years) perennial shrubs that grow around 6 to 10 feet (1.8 to 3 m) tall. The leaves are green, soft and look like kale, and can be harvested continually. Most tree collards prefer milder climates and do well in coastal regions.

Turkish rocket (*Bunias orientalis*)

Leaves, flower heads. Hardy to Zone 4. Somewhat like arugula in flavour, with the pungent spiciness of mustards, this perennial is actually in the cabbage family. Young leaves and flower heads are edible and can be cooked like spicy kale or broccoli.

Further reference

Perennial Vegetables: From Artichokes to Zuiki Taro, a Gardener's Guide to Over 100 Delicious, Easy-to-Grow Edibles by Eric Toensmeier

Sunchokes are hardy perennial vegetables that will prolifically produce sweet and crisp potato-like tubers year after year.

RABBIT & KALE STEW

My mom and I came up with this recipe, adapted from a much-loved pot pie she's been making for our family for over 30 years. The first time we created this was after dispatching our first meat rabbits at my parents' house with the help of my experienced and patient dad. In the end, we had a hearty meal from homegrown perennial kale and the healthy meat of rabbits we knew had lived a happy life and were humanely treated. We celebrated the success of our urban rabbit farming and my parents' 40th wedding anniversary with a lovely evening of rabbit stew, red wine and family reminiscing.

1 rabbit (about 3–4 lbs/1.4–1.8 kg dressed)
1 Tbsp (15 mL) salt
2 stalks celery, chopped
2 bay leaves
2 large onions
5 carrots, chopped
1 bunch kale, chopped
¼ cup (60 mL) butter
¼ cup (60 mL) flour
½ tsp (2.5 mL) salt
1 tsp (5 mL) Worcestershire sauce

1. Put rabbit meat, salt, celery, bay leaves and one whole onion in a large stew pot and fill with water to barely cover meat. Simmer until meat falls off the bone, about 1 hour and 30 minutes.

2. Remove pot from heat, allow to cool slightly and strain solid ingredients from stock. Set aside 2 cups (475 mL) of stock for the stew and save the rest for other uses. Let the meat cool, then remove all bones. Compost remaining solids.

3. Chop second onion. Add meat back to stock, along with chopped onion and carrots. Simmer another 20 minutes until carrots are tender, adding the chopped kale for the last 5 minutes.

4. To thicken the sauce, make a roux: Heat the butter and flour in a saucepan on medium heat for 2 to 3 minutes. Stir in the 2 cups (475 mL) of stock, salt and Worcestershire and simmer for another few minutes, until thickened. Add sauce to the stew pot and simmer another 2 minutes to blend and heat through.

5. Serve with Rustic Rosemary Sourdough Bread (page 214) and butter, and pair with a full-bodied red, such as a Bordeaux-style blend or a dark and brooding Malbec.

SERVES 8

ROASTED SUNCHOKES WITH HONEY BALSAMIC GLAZE

Sunchokes—also called Jerusalem artichokes—are amazingly versatile edible tubers that work very well as a substitute for potatoes in many dishes. The wonderful water chestnut-like texture and slight sweetness of sunchokes really shine in this recipe. If you don't have sunchokes handy (yet), use groundnuts or potatoes.

2 Tbsp (30 mL) olive oil
1 Tbsp (15 mL) honey
1 Tbsp (15 mL) balsamic vinegar
1 lb (455 gr) sunchokes, cubed
Coarse salt to taste

Fresh ground pepper to taste
4 Tbsp (60 mL) sour cream
4 tsp (20 mL) finely chopped
  chives, garlic or onions

1. Preheat oven to 450F (230C).

2. In a small bowl, whisk the olive oil, honey and balsamic vinegar.

3. Toss the sunchokes into a roasting pan with the mixture, and sprinkle with salt and pepper to taste.

4. Roast for 15 minutes, pull out and toss, then roast for 10 more minutes until the sunchokes are tender with the skin slightly browned.

5. Plate with a dollop of sour cream and garnish with chopped onions, garlic or chives.

SERVES 4 AS A SIDE

GINGERED PERENNIAL ROOT VEGETABLE SOUP

I love making soup with ginger. Crosnes and ground-nuts—somewhere in between potatoes, water chestnuts and turnips—have a crisp starchiness that works well in both savoury and sweeter dishes, and this soup plays with that, adding the bite and spice of ginger and yellow curry. Many perennial tubers can be used in place of the crosnes, including a combination of water chestnuts, water lotus and taro. If you don't have groundnuts, use sunchokes or potatoes.

4 lbs (1.8 kg) crosnes roots
2 lbs (910 gr) groundnut, peeled and halved (or potatoes)
1 small squash (about 1 lb/455 gr), halved
4 cooking apples, quartered
3 Tbsp (45 mL) olive oil, divided
2 Tbsp (30 mL) butter, divided
Coarse salt to taste
Freshly ground pepper to taste
1 medium onion, diced
2 Tbsp (30 mL) yellow curry powder
¼ cup (60 mL) minced ginger
2 cups (475 mL) Rabbit Stock, recipe on page 93 (or substitute chicken stock)
Up to 2 cups (475 mL) dry apple cider

1. Preheat the oven to 400F (205C).

2. Prepare the groundnuts by boiling them in water until soft, about 30 minutes.

3. In a baking dish, place the crosnes, squash halves and apple quarters cut side up and drizzle with 1 tablespoon (15 mL) of the olive oil. Season with coarse salt and freshly ground pepper. Bake until tender, about 25 minutes.

4. Meanwhile, in a large stockpot, heat 2 tablespoons (30 mL) butter and 2 tablespoons (30 mL) olive oil over low heat and sauté the onions, curry powder and ginger until onions are translucent.

5. Once the crosnes, squash and apples are done, scrape the flesh from the skins of the squash and apples. Add the groundnuts, crosnes, squash, apples and rabbit stock to the stockpot. Bring to a boil, cover and cook for 5 minutes. Take off the heat and let cool slightly, then use an immersion blender or food processor to coarsely purée the mixture.

6. Pour the purée back into the pot. Add apple cider until desired consistency and taste is reached, up to 2 cups (475 mL). Season with salt and pepper to taste. Serve with crusty bread or salad.

SERVES 4 FOR DINNER

EDIBLE URBAN LANDSCAPING

Living in an apartment complex in East Vancouver, I proposed adding some landscaping around the building. Some of my neighbours were reluctant to put in "food gardens" because of concerns about them looking messy and attracting pests. However, no one objected to my idea of adding some "edible landscaping."

Except for harvesting the food, it's no more work to tend edible shrubs than non-edible shrubs. And once the plants are in, they replace the need for costly and time-consuming annual flowerbeds. I planted mostly perennial edible greens and herbs, brightened by a few annual edible flowers. Many of my neighbours used the plants, snipping leaves, flowers or small branches here and there as the recipe they were using required. This edible landscaping brought everyone in the building together and gave us something to talk about in our shared space.

Culinary herbs—such as lavender, rosemary, oregano, thyme and sage—are excellent choices for shrub plantings, being aesthetically pleasing, a favourite of bees and other pollinators, and lush throughout most if not all of the year. Hedging options include many edible berries (currants and gooseberries, among others), while edible vines (such as grapes and hops) can beautify fences.

In place of annual flower beds, bushy perennial greens like good King Henry, Turkish rocket, sea kale or lamb's quarters are excellent low-maintenance alternatives, in addition to edible native plants like fiddlehead ferns and oxalis. And if your neighbours really do insist on those colourful annuals, suggest edibles with gorgeously hued foliage, fruit and flowers—such as rainbow chard, curly "Redbor" kale, spotted lettuces, red cabbages, bright peppers, pink-flowered chives, vibrant nasturtiums and golden calendula.

MISO-CREAMED PERENNIAL GREENS

Go ahead and use anything with edible green leaves, such as lamb's quarters, good King Henry, tree collards, Turkish rocket, sea kale, water spinach, even fiddlehead ferns—or a combination of all these healthy greens, depending on what you are able to grow in edible landscaping or an urban food forest, or forage in your neighbourhood.

½ Tbsp (7.5 mL) flour
1 cup (250 mL) Easy Greek-style Yogurt, recipe on page 240 (or store-bought Greek yogurt)
2 Tbsp (30 mL) olive oil

1 onion, diced
2 garlic cloves, minced
½ Tbsp (7.5 mL) miso paste
8 cups (2 L) fresh perennial greens

1. Mix flour with yogurt in a small bowl. Set aside.

2. In a large saucepan, sauté onions in olive oil over medium heat until translucent. Add garlic and sauté another 2 minutes. And miso paste and sauté 1 more minute.

3. Add the greens to the pan, wait for them to wilt, then pour in the yogurt mixture and stir everything together to coat the greens. Cook for 1 minute; do not overcook. Take off the heat and plate immediately.

SERVES 4 AS A SIDE

PRESERVING

PRESERVING AND FERMENTING

No time or room for keeping your own garden or animals? Have no fear—even the busiest and most space-challenged über-urbanite can homestead. Take advantage of what is available locally and seasonally by foraging and visiting farmers' markets in the city, having a CSA harvest box delivered to your door, or day-tripping on weekends to nearby rural areas to load up on whatever fruits, veggies and proteins you like—and then preserve these edibles in the many ways you can enjoy them year round. With the myriad techniques developed to preserve food, from freezing, canning, pickling and brewing to drying, smoking and curing, there is something to suit everyone's taste and timetable.

PRESERVING

There's nothing more satisfying that putting food by for the winter, and with a bit of preserving, you can relish your own homegrown and foraged fruits, vegetables, meat and fish all year long. Start with freezing, canning, infusing and drying, or impress your guests with charcuterie or even some fermenting . . .

FREEZING

It's a treat to enjoy homegrown or local fruits and veggies through the winter and into early spring when seasonally available produce is limited—and one of the quickest and easiest ways to preserve the harvest is to simply freeze it.

To make the best use of limited freezer space, prioritize it for meat and homemade stock, soup, pesto and freezer jam. If you still have room, fresh berries and vegetables like peas and corn kernels can be frozen in airtight containers and thawed for summer-style recipes throughout the year. Wild mushrooms are worth freezing (or drying) if you find them in abundance—sauté in butter until lightly browned, then freeze in recipe-sized containers.

Getting started

Food does best in the freezer in airtight containers. Many people use plastic freezer bags with zippers, but you can also repurpose tetra packs from milk or soup (taped to seal) or glass jars. Liquid expands when it freezes, so if using glass, leave plenty of headroom (room at the top) for this added pressure in order to prevent the jar from cracking. Seal with wax paper and an elastic band.

Opposite: While this may simply look like a whole lot of weeds, we dry a ton of edible-landscaping herbs (like mint, oregano, rosemary and lavender) when in season to use throughout the year in cooking, as well as in tea and infusions, and to flavour kombucha, shrubs, beer and cider.

EASY STRAWBERRY FREEZER JAM

This freezer jam is my dad's specialty in summer and incredibly easy to make. Strawberries are an excellent choice of patio perennials for hanging baskets or vertical beds—or if you can't grow them yourself, stock up in season from a sustainable grower at your local farmers' market. Or substitute up to the full amount of strawberries with foraged fruit such as autumnberry, blueberry, huckleberry or blackberry. If you include pectin-rich fruits, such as Oregon grape, salal or wolfberry, you can add less of the packaged pectin. Because most commercial pectins work by using sugar to solidify the mixture, recipes using pectin usually call for a lot of sugar. Using a brand of pectin labelled "low sugar" allows the use of alternative sweeteners like honey and agave.

8 cups (2 L) strawberries
1½ cup (350 mL) honey
Juice from 1 lemon
1 cup (250 mL) water
2 Tbsp (30 mL) low-sugar pectin, such as Pomona's
    Universal Pectin
4 tsp (20 mL) calcium water (comes with pectin
    package)

1. Remove leaves and stems from strawberries, and mash in a large bowl or pot. Add honey and lemon juice and stir thoroughly.

2. Boil the water, then blend it with the pectin in a blender or food processor for 2 minutes, making sure to vent the hot steam from the lid.

3. Add the pectin mixture and calcium water to the fruit and stir until well mixed. Ladle into ½-cup (125-mL) or 1-cup (250-mL) glass canning jars, leaving ½ inch (1.25 cm) of headspace. Top with parchment or wax paper, and secure with screwband or elastic band. Do not use the metal lid with the screwband if you are planning to store the jam in the freezer, as the jar may crack when the liquid expands as it freezes.

4. Refrigerate jam up to 4 weeks or freeze for up to a year.

MAKES 15 X 1-CUP (250-ML) JARS

CANNING

The next step up from freezing is canning. People have been canning to preserve seasonal bounties for a very long time, and most of us still remember our grandparents' canned plums and peaches, yet somehow it went out of favour. But it's so easy! There are two methods—water-bath and pressure canning.

BOTULISM RISKS

Botulism is a potentially fatal paralytic disease caused by ingesting the toxins produced by the botulism bacteria (yes, the very same botulism toxins injected cosmetically to temporarily paralyze skin and muscles to reduce wrinkles). Botulism bacteria thrive in anaerobic conditions, so are a risk in preserves that are sealed such as through canning. These bacteria are sensitive to acidity, and are held at bay by the acetic acid, lactic acid or citric acid in pickles, jams, jellies and fruit preserves. Canned goods like fish, meat or sauces that don't have high acidity should be protected from botulism bacteria by using high temperature and pressure to destroy any potential harmful microorganisms.

Water-Bath Canning

Preserves with high acid levels, like vinegar pickles, jams, jellies and fruit canned with simple syrup, are good candidates for water-bath canning.

Getting started

A large pot, sturdy tongs (or a jar lifter), and a small metal trivet (or a canning rack). The trivet or canning rack is used to keep the glass jars off the bottom of the pan so they don't heat up too much and break. Make sure your pot is large enough to fit the trivet and your jars, and still have room for 2 inches (5 cm) of water on top (beer-making pots work great).

Procedure

Fill the canner or a large pot with enough water to fully cover the tops of the jars (the extra jars will displace more water) and heat to boiling.

Assemble jars, matching seals and rings. Check that the jars are free of cracks or chips. Wash everything in hot soapy water and rinse well (or run jars through dishwasher). To prevent potential disaster with hot food hitting cold glass (resulting in the glass cracking), place jars in hot water or a warm oven (200 F/95C) until filling. You can also keep the jars warm in the dishwasher until needed. While many older methods suggest boiling the seals, most modern canning seals are designed for single use and do not require this extra step—and overheating can damage them—but check the manufacturer's directions. Rings can also be kept at room temperature, for easier handling.

Fill each jar, leaving ½ inch (1.25 cm) of headspace. Remove air bubbles by running a small rubber or plastic spatula around the inside of the jar (don't use metal, as this may break the glass). Wipe the rim of the jar clean with a clean, damp cloth. Place the seals and lids on the jars, and tighten lids with your fingers (rather than your hands) until you start to feel resistance.

Place the jars into the boiling water one by one, using the tongs or jar lifter. Make sure they don't touch each other or the sides of the pot, so they don't break. Boil for 10 minutes, then turn off heat and let jars sit in the cooling water for another 5 minutes. Remove the jars with the tongs or jar lifter and set them onto a cooling rack or a clean dishtowel (don't put them directly on a cool counter or the glass may break).

Now you have to listen for the sound of the seals. As each jar cools, it will seal and make a pinging sound, so listen for as many pings as you have jars. This should take about 5 minutes. If any of your jars haven't sealed after 1 hour (check by pressing down on the lids), simply put them in the fridge and enjoy the jelly within 3 or 4 weeks, or you can reprocess the jars by repeating the canning procedure with a fresh seal and lid.

OLD-FASHIONED JELLY WITH CURRANTS & HOPS

This jelly is a bit old-fashioned because it doesn't require added pectin, and instead uses natural pectin from the currants. With a fruity tart bite and grassy finish, I like the combination of currants and hops, both perennial edibles that can be grown in urban landscapes, as part of a food forest in pots on a condo patio. The canning method used here is water-bath, fine for highly acidic preserves like fruits and pickles.

4 cups (1 L) currants (stems and flowers are okay)

4 cups (1 L) sugar

½ cup (120 mL) fresh hops (or ¾ cup/180 mL dried)

1. Cook the currants with ¼ cup (60 mL) of water in a lidded pot over medium heat until the fruit is tender, about 10 minutes. Mash the fruit to release the juice and boil hard for 2 minutes. Add the sugar, return to a boil, and boil for 5 minutes.

2. Meanwhile, make a tea from the hops by pouring ½ cup (120 mL) boiling water over them and letting them steep for 5 minutes.

3. Add the hops tea to the jelly and bring back to a boil until the mixture forms a gel. Test by lifting a spoon from the mixture—if the drops are very thick and run together before falling off the spoon, it is ready.

4. Can the jelly using the Water-Bath Canning procedure, page 188.

MAKES 3 TO 4 CUPS (710 ML–1 L) JELLY

Pressure Canning

Using a pressure canner is recommended for low-acid foods such as sauces, meat and fish (see Botulism Risks, page 188), When you're lucky enough to come into a quantity of fresh hunted venison, or sustainably caught fish, a pressure canner can help you preserve it for storage in the cupboard, which is helpful for everyone with limited freezer space. This method isn't difficult, it just requires an extra piece of equipment—the pressure canner.

Getting started

You require clean jars and lids, sturdy tongs (or a jar lifter), and a pressure canner. A pressure cooker will work if you have one, as long as it will accommodate your jars.

Procedure

Place jars in pressure canner, filled with water according to manufacturer's directions for correct operation. Bring water to boil for 5 minutes with pressure valve open, then close valve. Process for 1 hour and 15 minutes at 10 psi, then turn off heat and allow canner to cool and lose pressure. Once the canner is safe to open (completely cooled and no remaining pressure), remove the jars and place on a rack or clean kitchen towel (do not place directly on cool counter or glass may crack).

Listen very carefully for the telltale ping of each jar sealing. As the glass cools down, it creates a vacuum that seals the top of the jar and makes a ping or popping sound. Count the number of pings you hear and compare to the number of jars. If any jars do not seal (check by pressing lids), refrigerate and eat the meat or fish within a few days. The sealed jars may be stored in a cool, dark area (such as a cupboard) for up to 1 year.

CANNED DEER

For anyone who only enjoys venison at restaurants, the idea of canning deer may sound preposterous. But nature sometimes presents a glut of a creature or plant, in which case, being able to preserve food is key to taking advantage of it. And hunting and foraging can actually help to reduce negative ecological pressures humans have imposed. In many developed areas in North America, people have displaced large predators, such as wolves, cougars and coyotes, and their prey populations, including deer, proliferate. This can cause a lot of damage to native ecosystems because more deer eat more plants. Removing deer by hunting can actually help to conserve natural ecology, and it is a more humane option for obtaining meat than factory farming. So go hunt yourself a deer where the population of this forager is getting out of hand—or make friends with someone who hunts and start canning some venison. The method required for meat and fish is pressure canning, which results in a more reliable seal than water-bath canning—see Pressure Canning on page 190.

5 lbs (2.3 kg) venison, cubed
2 Tbsp (30 mL) salt
1 tsp (5 mL) freshly ground pepper
10 cloves garlic, minced

5 medium onions, sliced
¼ cup (60 mL) minced green bell pepper

1. In a large bowl, toss venison cubes with salt, pepper and garlic.

2. Use ten 1-cup (250-mL) jars. In each jar, place half an onion, fill with venison, and top with a sprinkle of bell peppers. Wipe rim with clean, damp cloth. Add seal and lid, and tighten lids with your fingers (rather than your hands) until you start to feel resistance.

3. Can the venison using the Pressure Canning procedure, page 190.

MAKES 10 X 1-CUP (250-ML) JARS

SYRUPS, INFUSIONS, TINCTURES AND TONICS

Another way to preserve the taste of spring and summer is by making syrups, infusions, tinctures and tonics with herbs. The idea behind these preserves is to extract and concentrate the flavour (and/or medicinal components) from the fibrous plant material. This sounds complicated, but really just involves leaving the herb in honey, oil or spirit for a while to let the good stuff seep out, maybe shaking it now and then to help the process. Then you filter out the leaves and flowers (or leave some in if it looks pretty) and voila! Herbal extract. Honey, oil and spirits can be infused with herbs or wild foraged goodies for culinary and medicinal use—use lavender, rosemary, thyme, oregano, sage, chives, rosehips, juniper berries, tree tips and many others.

In herbal medicine, infusions usually mean steeping the herbs (like making tea) but can also refer to any type of herbal extract. Tinctures are herbal extracts involving alcohol, and usually fairly concentrated. These tend to be medicinal, but are also used to make bitters, which are a great addition to cocktails. Tonics generally refer to any type of healthy herbal extract—"tonic" just means it's good for you. Syrups are herbal infusions made with honey or sugar.

Getting started

All you need to make preserved infusions are the botanical flavourings you want to infuse with, the base you want to infuse into (honey, oil or spirits), glass jars with lids, and a strainer.

Infusing Honey

Infusing honey with herbs is extremely easy, and can be done with any flavourful edible you can grow or forage for, including culinary herbs and flowers. Dry all herbs, flowers, leaves, hips or tasty seeds (like fennel) before using to make sure they don't mould.

For a recipe idea, see Wild Rosehip and Spice-Infused Honey, page 133.

Flavouring Spirits

Infusing is a snap, and can be done to create flavoured spirits for cocktails, concentrated tinctures for medicinal use or delicious bitters for drinks. Bitters involve the same process of infusing with fruit and herbs, but result in a much stronger-tasting concoction.

To make bitters, you'll generally need a bittering or flavouring agent and a spirit. For the bittering agent, the urban forager can easily find dandelion or burdock roots. Other options are artichoke leaf, barberry root, Oregon grape root, sarsaparilla and wormwood.

For the aromatic component, just about any flavourful herb or spice will work. Try chamomile, chilies, cinnamon, cloves, coriander, fennel, ginger, hops, juniper berries, lavender, mint, rose, rosemary, sage and thyme. You can even use toasted nuts, coffee beans and cocoa nibs.

For the spirit, something with a high alcohol content will better extract the flavour compounds. Suggestions would be 100 proof vodka, which is easily accessible and imparts little added taste, or 101 proof bourbon or 151 proof rum, which add flavour elements (from the spirit that has been infused with the wood of the barrel it aged in).

Either dried or fresh botanicals can be used. The proportions will depend on how aromatic the bittering and flavouring agents are—the more aromatic, the less you need. In general, if the flavouring is a fresh herb, use one part botanical to two parts spirit: with dried herbs, one part botanical to four parts spirit.

Further reference

The Drunken Botanist by Amy Stewart

Opposite: A summer picnic is the perfect place to test out Rhubarb-infused Gin in Fauxtini Cocktails (page 194).

RHUBARB-INFUSED GIN

Some of the most popular drinks—the screwdriver, greyhound and cosmopolitan come to mind—are simply spirits mixed with fruit juice. And while you can buy pre-made infusions like blueberry vodka and coconut rum, it's a total cinch to dream up combinations at home, and cooler to use your own homegrown or foraged fruits. Or even vegetables . . . try celery or kale for savoury cocktail concoctions. Here's one favourite of ours, perfect for an end-of-the-day pick-me-up after some foraging or gardening. Substitute invasive Japanese knotweed shoots (see page 33) in springtime if you find any.

1½ cup (350 mL) thickly sliced rhubarb
2 cups (475 mL) small batch gin

1. Place rhubarb in a clean quart (1-L) glass jar with a tight-fitting lid and cover with gin. Keep the gin bottle for later. Put the jar on the countertop, and shake it once or twice a day.

2. After 3 days, try it to see if the taste is strong enough. If not, infuse for longer and continue shaking it. Once it's got the right flavour for your taste (up to 1 week, or even longer if desired), strain out the solids and replace the liquid in the gin bottle. Replace the lid and keep in a cool, dark place.

MAKES 2 CUPS (475 ML)

RHUBARB GIN FAUXTINI COCKTAIL

Lemon wedge for rim
Sugar for rim
1½ oz (45 mL) rhubarb gin
¼ oz (7 mL) dry vermouth
¼ oz (7 mL) sweet vermouth
1 oz (30 mL) fresh-squeezed berry juice (from homegrown strawberries or currants, or foraged blueberry, blackberry or wolfberry)
Ice

1. Sugar rim a glass by running a lemon wedge over the rim, then pressing it in sugar.

2. In a cocktail shaker, shake the rhubarb gin, vermouths and berry juice with ice until cold. Pour the cocktail into the glass.

MAKES 1 COCKTAIL

BURDOCK LAVENDER BITTERS

There are a ton of variations you can use to make bitters. This is one combination that uses a pesky weed—burdock, the source of those big fuzzy burrs sticking to your dog's fur; see page 31—along with lavender, that fragrant, bee-beloved culinary herb fantastic for edible landscaping.

2 Tbsp (30 mL) sliced dried burdock root (or 3 Tbsp/45 mL fresh)
2 Tbsp (30 mL) dried lavender (or 3 Tbsp/45 mL fresh)
1 tsp (5 mL) vanilla bean, dried (about 1 inch/2.5 cm of one vanilla bean)
8 oz (240 mL) 100 proof vodka, divided

1. Start with 2 small, clean ½-cup (125-mL) glass jars. Place the burdock root in 1 jar and the lavender and vanilla bean in the other. Add 4 oz (120 mL) vodka to each, cover with tight-fitting lids and label with the date and ingredients.

Leave the jars in a visible location, and shake once a day for about 5 or 6 days.

2. After 5 or 6 days, start tasting the tinctures by adding a couple of drops to a small glass of water. When the infusion is strong enough for your liking, strain out the solids.

3. To make the bitters, combine 5 parts lavender and vanilla tincture to 1 part burdock-root tincture in an apothecary jar with a dropper lid. Leave for about 1 week to let the flavours mingle. Reserve the remaining tinctures for making more bitters. Start tasting after 4 or 5 days.

4. Store the tinctures and bitters in a cool, dark place for a year or more.

MAKES UP TO 4 OZ (118 ML) OF BITTERS

BEE'S KNEES COCKTAIL WITH HOMEMADE BITTERS

Cross a Bee's Knees cocktail with an Aviation and add a splash of lavender bitters and this is what you get.

¼ cup (60 mL) honey
Lemon slice for rim (optional)
Fine sugar for rim (optional)
1–2 dashes Burdock Lavender Bitters, recipe above
2 oz (60 mL) dry gin
½ oz (15 mL) crème de violette
1 oz (30 mL) lemon juice
Edible purple flower for garnish (optional)

1. Prepare a honey syrup by dissolving honey into ¼ cup (60 mL) of boiling water and allowing to cool (keep this refrigerated when not being used).

2. Sugar the rim, if desired. Add ½ oz (15 mL) honey syrup and all other ingredients into a cocktail shaker. Shake well and strain into a chilled cocktail or martini glass. Garnish with an edible flower, if desired.

MAKES 1 COCKTAIL

Oil Infusions

Infused oil is a great addition to both the kitchen and medicine cabinet (as in the case of oregano oil). Packed with aromatics, infused oil is easy to make and use. There are two methods you can use to infuse oil. One uses heat to quickly transfer the flavours of the botanicals into the oil; the other lets the mixture rest and slowly infuse for a more complex flavour. Both work for any type of botanical.

QUICK HERB-INFUSED OLIVE OIL

Easily grown on a patio or even a windowsill, these herbs are often combined in a bouquet garni used by chefs to enhance sauces, stocks, soups and stews. Harvest your fresh herbs and dry them well just before making the infusion (see Drying, page 198). This infused oil can be used for sautéing onions or drizzling over pizza dough prior to cooking.

2 bay leaves
¼ cup (60 mL) dried thyme
¼ cup (60 mL) dried sage
¼ cup (60 mL) dried rosemary
¼ cup (60 mL) dried savory
¼ cup (60 mL) dried tarragon
2 cups (475 mL) good-quality extra-virgin olive oil

1. Start by releasing the aromatic oils from the herbs by rolling them between your hands.

2. Place the herbs in a non-reactive pot, such as stainless steel or enamel, and pour the oil over top. Heat on low for 10 minutes. Do not simmer. Turn off heat, cover, and let infuse for 1 hour.

3. Strain solids out and pour oil into clean glass bottles. Bottles with corks and spouts work great for storing this oil because they minimize air circulation (which reduces the shelf life of oil) and are easy to use in the kitchen. Store in a cool, dry place for up to 3 months.

MAKES 2 CUPS (475 ML)

SLOW PINE-INFUSED AVOCADO OIL

Tree tip-infused oil is more of an unusual taste than your typical herb infusion, imbuing a woodsy but mostly citrusy tang, and can add an element of intrigue to many common recipes. Try drizzling this oil on salad or over a toasted baguette when making canapés. Plan to dry your tree tips at least a full day ahead of making this infusion.

1 cup (250 mL) pine tips
1 cup (250 mL) avocado oil

1. Dry pine tips on a parchment-lined sheet for 24 hours. Stuff a clean 2-cup (475-mL) glass jar with pine tips and cover in avocado oil. Clean any oil off the outside of the jar with a damp, clean cloth. Screw on seal and lid. Keep in a cool location or the refrigerator, and tip the oil upside down and back once or twice a day.

2. After a week, strain into a clean glass bottle. Bottles with corks and spouts work great because they minimize air circulation (which reduces the shelf life of oil) and are easy to use in the kitchen. This oil will keep for up to 3 months in a cool, dark place.

MAKES 1 CUP (250 ML)

DRYING

Late summer and fall is a busy time for the intrepid homesteader while we preserve the abundant local fruits and vegetables for later enjoyment.

Traditionally, many fruits were dried in the sun, such as tomatoes, cherries, apples, pears, apricots, plums, bananas and berries, and then stored plain, in oil or in simple syrup. You can use the sun if you live somewhere hot and dry, the oven if you have the time and room, or a food dehydrator. For all methods, prepare your produce by washing it and removing stems, leaves and pits or seeds. For larger fruit, cut in halves, quarters or slices to reduce the time it takes to dry them.

Sun Drying

The sun can be used when the temperature is high and humidity low (though sun drying doesn't work very well where it rains often or is very humid, such as where I live in the Pacific Northwest). I don't recommend this method for any meat or fish, but it can work for thinly sliced fruits and vegetables, herbs, tea ingredients and tree tips.

Oven Drying

When sun drying isn't an option, the oven is a simple way to simulate solar energy. Oven drying works for any type of herb, fruit or vegetable, or even to make jerky. Use an oven-safe rack, because it will allow better airflow to all parts of the items.

Electric Dehydrating

The electric food dehydrator is the most convenient choice if you plan to do a lot of drying because it doesn't use up oven space and you can set and leave it. Most models allow you to adjust the temperature and airflow based on what you are drying, and come with a guideline for how long to dry different items. I would recommend using an electric dehydrator if you are planning on drying meats to make jerky, because it's less messy and fussy than using an oven (where you need to flip it) and also because you won't have to tie up your oven for the extended periods needed for dehydrating.

SUN-DRIED TOMATOES WITH ROSEMARY IN OLIVE OIL

Sun drying concentrates the essence of tomatoes and their sweetness pairs perfectly with the pungency of rosemary.

10 lbs (4.5 kg) tomatoes (Roma or cherry work best)
4 sprigs rosemary
½ cup (120 mL) vinegar (any kind)
2 cups (475 mL) good-quality extra-virgin olive oil

1. Cut tomatoes in half. Place cut-side up on drying tray with rosemary sprigs. Lay in single layer on a baking dish, and cover with breathable cloth (such as cheesecloth) to prevent insects from getting at them. Place in full sun with good air circulation (on a patio railing works well). Taste periodically until fully dried, which may take a few hours to a few days, depending on temperature, humidity and thickness.

2. Dip dried tomatoes in vinegar, then fill 4 clean ½-cup (120-mL) glass jars with a quarter of the dried tomatoes and sprig of rosemary in each. Fill with olive oil. Top with seals and lids and store in a cool, dark place or refrigerator for up to 3 months.

MAKES 4 X ½ CUP (120-ML) JARS

SEASONAL FRUIT LEATHER

Making this fruit leather fills the kitchen with the sweet smell of your summer or fall harvest simmering on the stove. Store these tasty, nutritious treats all the way into winter—if you can resist them for that long.

8 cups (2 L) fruit, such as berries, apples, pears, peaches, plums
1 cup (250 mL) water
Sugar to taste
Lemon juice to taste
Spices, such as cinnamon or vanilla

1. Rinse the fruit and remove any branches and leaves. Chop and remove pits and seeds.

2. In a large saucepan over medium heat, bring fruit and water to a simmer. Reduce heat, cover and let simmer 10 to 15 minutes, until the fruit has softened. Uncover and mash the fruit in the pan. Taste and add sugar and lemon juice if necessary. Add sugar 1 Tbsp (15 mL) at a time and lemon juice 1 tsp (5 mL) at a time. Add any spices that go well with the fruit you are using. Simmer until fruit mixture has started to thicken (about 5 to 10 minutes).

3. Purée the mixture in a food processor. Taste again and adjust sugar, lemon juice or spices.

Pour the mixture into a large baking sheet with a rim to a thickness of ⅛ to ¼ inch (0.13–0.6 cm).

4. Preheat the oven to its lowest setting (around 140F/60C). Place the baking sheet in the oven. For conventional ovens, prop the door open an inch (2.5 cm) or so to allow airflow. If you have a convection oven, use the convection setting as it will dry the fruit leather faster. No need to prop open if you have a convection oven, which will circulate air inside by itself.

5. Let the fruit leather dry in the oven until it no longer runs when you lift the pan and a knife doesn't slide into it easily. This will take anywhere from 8 to 24 hours.

6. Peel the fruit leather off the baking sheet. Cut into strips and roll up in parchment paper.

7. Store in airtight containers (such as glass jars) in the cupboard for several weeks or in the freezer for a year or more.

MAKES ABOUT 24 STRIPS

See following pages for photographs.

TERIYAKI PINEAPPLE
RABBIT JERKY

Like deer meat, rabbit is perfect for drying because it is quite lean. There are an infinite number of tastes you can infuse into your jerky—from classic spicy smoke to honey garlic to curry—and this is one of our favourites.

2 cups (475 mL) rabbit (or deer) meat
¾ cup (180 mL) pineapple juice
¼ cup (60 mL) teriyaki sauce
1 garlic clove, minced
1 Tbsp (15 mL) minced ginger

2 tsp (10 mL) garlic powder
2 tsp (10 mL) powdered ginger
1 tsp (5 mL) coarse salt
½ tsp (2.5 mL) freshly ground pepper

1. Cut rabbit meat into 1-inch (2.5-cm) wide strips, across the grain.

2. Mix pineapple juice, teriyaki sauce, garlic and ginger. Pour over the meat and marinate it overnight in the refrigerator.

3. In a small bowl, mix powdered garlic and ginger, salt and pepper. Remove meat from marinade and sprinkle with spice mixture.

4. Lay pieces on dehydrator trays with spaces between. Follow manufacturer's directions for jerky. If using the oven, turn to lowest setting. Make sure to turn the pieces frequently on the baking tray to ensure even drying (or use a metal screen instead of a tray).

5. Dry until completely dehydrated, about 24 hours in a dehydrator or oven. Store in an airtight container in the fridge for up to 8 weeks, or in the freezer for up to 6 months.

MAKES 2 CUPS (475 ML)

CHARCUTERIE

Originally, charcuterie was developed as a way to preserve meat before refrigeration was available. Today, delicacies like bacon, prosciutto and salumi (Italian cold cuts), ham, sausage, terrine, pâté, rillettes and confit are still prepared in traditional ways because they are relished for the flavours the preservation processes imbue.

The best types of meat for charcuterie are high in fat. Rabbit and deer are lean meats, but with the addition of extra fat they make excellent pâtés and terrines. Pig meat is the usual choice for charcuterie, but waterfowl like ducks and geese also have suitable fat content. In urban areas, try to source duck or goose from local farmers who will tell you or—even better—show you how the animal was raised and slaughtered, and may also provide some additional fat for making your homestead meat products.

Type of meat	Recommended preservation methods	Special equipment required
Rabbit	Jerky, pâté	None
Quail or chicken	Confit, pâté, stovetop smoked	None
Duck or goose	Prosciutto/salumi, stovetop smoked, confit, pâté	Hanging closet
Deer and nutria	Canned, jerky	Pressure canner
Wild pig (or ethically sourced, locally grown pork)	Prosciutto/salumi, stovetop smoked, pâté	Hanging closet
Fish	Outdoor smoked, canned, pickled and canned	Smoker, pressure canner

Forcemeat: Terrine, Pâté, Rillettes, Confit and Sausage

Some cuts of meat are preserved as is, such as bacon, prosciutto and ham, while others are ground or puréed first and mixed with additional fat. These meat and fat mixes are called forcemeat and include sausage, terrine, pâté, rillettes and confit.

Meats with low fat content, such as fish, deer and rabbit, can be used to make forcemeats with the addition of fat from a different animal or butter, to preserve the meat.

In sausage making, the meat mixture is forced into casings, then either cooked, or further preserved, such as in the case of salumi (see Fermenting Meat, page 210). Terrine and pâté involve cooking the forcemeat (traditionally inside an earthenware terrine) using a hot water bath, called a bain-marie. A gelatin layer may be added on top but is not required. Rillettes are similar to terrines and pâtés, but have a shredded texture to the meat rather than the puréed consistency of pâtés and terrines. Confit is also prepared using a hot water bath, but instead of the meat being mixed with fat, whole pieces of meat (usually legs and wings) are placed into fat in a dish, then poached in a bain-marie. Terrine, pâté, rillettes and confit are generally eaten within a few days or kept in the fridge or freezer because they are not fully preserved.

Getting started

What you need depends on the type of forcemeat you want to make. While sausages necessitate a meat grinder with a sausage-making attachment, terrines, pâtés and rillettes only require a food processor and ovenproof dish such as a ceramic terrine, or glass jars. Confit entails only an ovenproof dish or glass jar.

For pâté cooking instructions, see Rabbit Pâté with Oyster Mushrooms (page 97).

CONFIT DE CANARD (DUCK CONFIT)

Confit may sound super sophisticated, but it's not hard to make. This hot water bath method (bain-marie) simply requires poaching the meat, usually legs or wings, in fat or oil, which is then used to store the meat. I've chosen duck here, but any fatty meat would work, such as goose or wild pig. Leaner meats, such as quail, chicken or rabbit legs, would work with fat from duck or goose added. Confit is a perfect way to use legs and wings, which contain more fat than breasts (birds) or saddles (rabbits). It can be enjoyed warm on toasted baguette, in a bitter-greens salad with arugula, dandelions or chicory, or added to buttery and garlicky pasta.

1 cup (250 mL) pickling salt
¼ cup (60 mL) brown sugar
2 tsp (10 mL) freshly ground pepper
1 Tbsp (15 mL) minced fresh thyme leaves (or 1 tsp/5 mL dried)
Wings and legs from 2 ducks
2–4 cups (475–950 mL) of duck fat
2–4 bay leaves

1. Start by curing the meat. Mix salt, sugar, pepper and thyme leaves in a non-reactive bowl (such as glazed ceramic or glass). Massage the curing mixture into the meat on all surfaces. Place the duck pieces on top of the remaining curing mixture, cover and refrigerate overnight or for up to 24 hours. The longer you leave it, the saltier it will be.

2. Preheat oven to 300F (150C). Heat duck fat in a small saucepan to runny consistency.

3. Remove the duck meat from the fridge and thoroughly brush off the curing mixture. Place the meat into small, clean, oven-safe glass jars just big enough to fit the meat (about 2 cups/475 mL), and add 1 or 2 bay leaves to each jar. Pour duck fat into each jar to completely cover meat.

4. Place jars in a pan filled with boiling water, making sure the water doesn't rise over the tops of the jars (about halfway is fine). Put the pan in the oven—the water should be at a very low simmer while cooking. Cook for 4 to 6 hours until the meat is tender and falling off the bone.

5. Remove the jars from the oven and pan, and allow to cool. Store the jars in the fridge for up to 4 weeks.

MAKES 2 X 2-CUP (475-ML) JARS

Salting and Brining Meat

Salting and brining are important steps in the process of making many dried, smoked or fermented meats, including jerky, bacon, ham, prosciutto/salumi.

Getting started

Commercially, curing salt, also called pink salt, is usually used before meat is smoked or fermented. Curing salt is a mixture of non-iodized table salt (sodium chloride) and preserving salt (sodium nitrate or nitrite). While curing salt is more reliable in killing bacteria than table salt and very popular in large-scale production, it has been linked to negative health effects. It is not required for homestead uses, and instead plain non-iodized table salt works well. Other flavouring agents like herbs, honey and syrup are also often added to salt and brine mixtures.

Sugars help in the curing process by providing food for beneficial microorganisms.

Procedure

Salting meat imbues flavour, removes excess moisture, and inhibits the growth of non-desirable organisms. Salting is used to dry-cure meat when a brine solution (with water) would add too much moisture, such as prior to hanging meat for prosciutto. For instructions on salting meat prior to further preserving, see Confit de Canard (page 204) or Dry-cured Goose Prosciutto (page 211).

A brine is a solution of salt and liquid, so performs the same functions as salting. Brining can be used prior to smoking or drying meat; it also works to tenderize meat, so is useful before cooking tougher meats.

BRINED & COCONUT MISO
MARINATED QUAIL

This method of preparation is especially suitable for older birds, such as laying hens you wish to remove from the flock. Older birds tend to be tough and the brining process tenderizes the meat. The first time Chris came up with the glaze for this recipe, I was a little nervous. It was Thanksgiving and we were serving some older birds we had grown. It was the first time I was hosting dinner for my parents, and as my mom has been putting on extravagant seasonal dinners my whole life, the pressure was on. Going mostly with traditional fixings, I was concerned the miso coconut glaze wouldn't fit in . . . but I needn't have worried (and Chris always pulls it off so I should have known) because the birds were absolutely fabulous! Juicy and tender, they were slightly salty with a subtle coconut flavour.

½ cup (120 mL) salt
8 cups (2 L) water
4 cleaned, plucked quail
1 medium onion, chopped
4 cloves garlic, minced
1 Tbsp (15 mL) grated fresh ginger

2 Tbsp (30 mL) coconut oil
½ cup (120 mL) shiro miso paste
½ cup (120 mL) Rabbit Stock,
    recipe on page 93 (or substitute
    chicken stock)

1. For the brine, use a non-reactive pot, such as stainless steel or enamel, that will fit the water and the quail together. Create the brine by adding the salt and water to the pot and stirring until dissolved. Submerge the quail in the brine, weighing them down with a plate if necessary. Leave the birds in the brine for 2 to 12 hours in the refrigerator, depending on how much you want them to tenderize.

2. Preheat oven to 375F (190C). To make the glaze, sauté onions, garlic and ginger in coconut oil until onions are translucent. Add stock and miso paste and mix until dissolved. Simmer for 5 minutes. Let cool.

3. Remove the birds from the brine and rinse them in cold water in the sink. Place them in a roasting dish and brush the glaze all over: front, back and inside. Put the roasting pan in the oven and cook the birds for about 20 minutes, or until the internal temperature is 135F (57C).

SERVES 4

Smoking Meat

After being salted or brined, meat and fish can be flavoured and preserved with smoke. For example, the distinct flavours of bacon and ham come from brining and smoking. For the urban homesteader, bird meat from quail, chicken, duck and goose can be flavoured with smoke, and fatty fish like salmon, trout, mackerel and herring are also excellent candidates for the smoker.

Procedure

The process can be done on your stovetop (for cooking and flavouring) or in a backyard or balcony smoker. To actually preserve the meat by smoking, it must first be salted long enough to remove moisture, then cooked in the smoking process. If the salting process is only used to provide flavour, it can be shorter. The stovetop smoking method is a good choice for brief smoking. An outdoor smoker will allow you to smoke more pieces of meat at once. It will also allow you to leave the smoke going for longer, which will result in better preserved meat and fish.

For any type of smoking, first brine the meat (see page 205 for instructions), then dry the surface completely so the smoke will adhere better. If you can put it under a fan for an hour or so, that is ideal for a good, quick dry. If not, leave it out in a drafty location for a few hours. Especially for preserving meat and fish, you want a dry layer of skin on top, which will seal out bad bacteria and help the smoky flavour adhere. If you are planning on eating the smoked meat right away, this is not as important.

Getting started

For the stovetop method all you need is a large stockpot, a metal vegetable steamer insert, some aluminum foil, and some wood chips. To smoke outdoors, you will need a backyard or patio smoker, which you can either purchase or build from a metal barrel (there are lots of plans online), and wood chips. Try foraging in your neighbourhood for the wood chips, and experimenting with different types for different flavours in your smoke. There are many types of wood commonly available in urban areas, including alder, maple, cherry and apple. Avoid cedar and cypress. Simply cut into small pieces (1–2 inches/2.5–5 cm long by 1 inch/2.5 cm thick), or find chips from a neighbour doing woodwork with untreated wood.

STOVETOP MAPLE-SMOKED DUCK BREAST

Stovetop smoking is a quick way to get a woodsy and wild campfire taste right in your kitchen. And there's no special equipment required, just a big stockpot and some aluminum foil. Don't worry . . . you seal the pot with foil so you won't fill the kitchen with smoke. This recipe can be used with any type of meat and the smoking time is very flexible—the longer you leave it, the smokier and more preserved the meat will be. My favourite way is to use thicker pieces of meat, such as duck or goose breasts or rabbit loins, and smoke for about 30 minutes, so the smoke will flavour the outside and the inside will be moist. Then slice thinly for a delicious addition to salads or sandwiches, and keep any leftovers in the fridge.

¼ cup (60 mL) + 1 Tbsp (15 mL) pickling salt, divided
4 cups (1 L) water
4 whole duck breasts, skin on
½ cup (120 mL) real maple syrup
½ cup (120 mL) wood shavings (foraged maple, alder, apple and cherry wood work well; avoid cedar and cypress woods)

1. Start by brining the meat. Dissolve ¼ cup (60 mL) of the salt in water. Submerge duck breasts in brine and refrigerate overnight.

2. Remove the breasts from the brine and pat dry. Place the breasts under a fan or in a cool breeze (under 60F/15C) to dry out completely. Drying will ensure a better smoke.

3. Once completely dried, score the skin of each breast, being careful not to pierce the meat. Rub pinches of salt (about 1 tablespoon/15 mL total) all over, then brush with maple syrup.

4. Soak the wood chips in water for about 10 minutes. Place a layer of aluminum foil in the bottom of a large stockpot. Cover the foil with wood chips, then add another layer of aluminum foil. Place a metal steamer in the pot, and then layer the duck breasts on it. Cover the pot with its lid, and then seal all around the top with aluminum foil to prevent any smoke from leaking out.

5. Put the stockpot on the stove over high heat for 5 minutes to start the wood chips burning. Reduce heat to low to smoulder the wood chips for the duration of smoking. Leave breasts to smoke for about 20 to 30 minutes, depending on how well done and smoky you like them (20 to 30 minutes will flavour and cook the meat but not dry and preserve it).

MAKES 4 DUCK BREASTS

SALMON SMOKED OUTDOORS WITH BLACK TEA & HONEY

Smoking salmon has been a very important tradition of Coastal First Nations, and continues to be so to this day. When I was doing fieldwork on the central coast of British Columbia, many of the people in the local communities there smoked salmon over traditional open fires, while others used European-style smokehouses. In the city, we can emulate this by using small outdoor electric smokers, set up on a patio or balcony or wherever a barbeque is permitted. Any wild fatty fish works, but the most popular species for smoking is sockeye salmon. The sweetness of the honey accents the saltiness of the fish, and Earl Grey tea imbues a bergamot aroma.

2 cups (475 mL) honey
1 cup (250 mL) Earl Grey tea leaves
10 lbs (4.5 kg) wild sockeye salmon, filleted
1 cup (250 mL) pickling salt
3 cups (710 mL) brown sugar
10 cups (2.4 L) wood chips (foraged alder, maple, apple and cherry wood work well)

1. Wrap Earl Grey tea leaves in muslin or cheesecloth and tie into a bag (or use tea packaged in fabric tea bags). In a small pot over low to medium heat, heat honey with tea to infuse the flavours into the honey, stirring constantly, about 10 minutes. Scoop wrapped tea out of honey and discard, then divide honey in half and set aside.

2. The first step in preserving fish with smoke is to brine it. Cut the salmon fillets into chunks about 4 to 5 inches (10 to 13 cm) wide to allow the brine to soak in and to ensure even smoking. Stir together 1 cup (250 mL) of the honey infusion, salt, and brown sugar. In a large, flat-bottomed glass dish (or ceramic crock), pour the honey mixture to just cover the bottom. Add a layer of salmon, then cover with more honey mixture. Repeat with more layers of salmon, covering each piece generously with the honey mixture. Cover the container and place in refrigerator for 24 hours, stirring and re-covering with honey mixture periodically (every 6 or 12 hours).

3. The next step is to smoke and cook the fish. Prepare your electric smoker for use according to the manufacturer's directions. Remove salmon from brine, scrape off excess brine and pat dry. Place salmon pieces on grills of electric smoker and leave under a fan or in a cool breeze (under 60F/15C) so the surface develops a shiny skin. This will seal the fish and improve the smoking process.

4. Meanwhile, fill the smoker pans with a small amount of wood chips, and add water to your drip pan, according to product directions. Once the salmon has developed a shiny skin (about 1 hour), insert the grills into the smoker. Start with a small fire for a lower temperature, then gradually build up to about 130 to 140F (55 to 60C) over the course of the first 3 hours, then smoke for an additional 6 hours. This will result in the moistest end product. Every hour, baste the salmon with the other 1 cup (250 mL) of honey infusion, applying with a brush.

5. After 6 hours, remove 1 piece of salmon and cut through at the thickest part. If it has cooked through (is solid and no longer soft), it is done. If not, smoke for longer. In very cold outdoor temperatures, you may need to smoke for 12 or even 24 hours.

6. Once cooked through, remove the salmon and let rest on a cooling rack for 1 hour. Store in an airtight container in the refrigerator for 3 to 4 weeks, or in the freezer for several months.

MAKES 10 LBS (4.5 KG)

Fermenting Meat

Fatty meats and sausages can be covered in spices and hung to cure for weeks or months after salting or brining, to create prosciutto and salumi. During this time, fermentation occurs. This involves beneficial bacteria (*Lactobacillus* and *Leuconostoc*), which break down the sugars to produce lactic acid, which in turn prohibit the growth of detrimental microorganisms.

In urban areas, it can be challenging to source ethically raised pigs, but goose and duck are fatty meats that are good candidates for prosciutto and salumi. Fermenting meats can be one of the more difficult do-it-yourself preservation techniques, so beginning with a duck or goose breast rather than a side of pork might be a better place to start anyway. However, if you have access to it, invasive wild pig meat would also make for great prosciutto and salumi.

Getting started

Other than the basic stuff necessary to salt meat, there is no specialized equipment required. However, the trick with fermenting meat is that you need a place to hang it while it cures that is cooler than room temperature (which is about 70F/21C) and ideally warmer than the refrigerator (which is 40F/4C or less), but it also needs to be more humid than the fridge (which is 20 to 30 percent humidity) and most indoor places (which are 40 to 50 percent). This will inhibit the growth of bad bacteria, and allow the good bacteria to do their jobs. The good bacteria can still live in the cool temperature of the fridge, albeit fermenting more slowly, but the humidity will be low so you may end up with a dried-out breast before the curing process has been achieved.

Ideally, you want to find a place that is between 40 to 60F (4 to 15C) and at about 60 to 85 percent humidity. A root cellar is ideal, or a dry shed outside in cooler weather. If you don't have somewhere cool but humid to cure the meat, you can use the fridge; just keep an eye out that it doesn't get too dry. If it does start getting too dry, simply eat it right away. It will be more like jerky, so slice it thin to eat, or add it to a slow-cook recipe to rehydrate and soften it. Start with shorter ferments (curing times) because this will reduce the chance of something bad growing. Work up to the longer ferments that will give you more complex and subtle flavours.

DRY-CURED GOOSE PROSCIUTTO

In my opinion, fermented charcuterie and cheese making are the pinnacle of urban homesteading. And both take some practice to do well. This recipe for goose prosciutto is a good start for the beginning meat fermenter. If you have backyard space and a pond, raise geese yourself (they are very low maintenance and the fatty meat is ideal for charcuterie), or get one from a local urban farmer, or (where zoning allows) hunt a type of goose or duck whose population is very robust.

¾ cup (180 mL) pickling salt
2 Tbsp (30 mL) sugar
2 Tbsp (30 mL) garlic powder
1 Tbsp (15 mL) paprika
1 Tbsp (15 mL) spicy pepper flakes
1 Tbsp (15 mL) dried oregano, crushed
1 Tbsp (15 mL) freshly ground black pepper
Breasts from 1 goose (or duck), whole with skin
 and fat

1. Mix everything but the breasts in a large, non-reactive bowl (such as glazed ceramic or glass). Massage the rub into the meat on both sides, making sure to cover every part of it. Place the breasts on top of the remaining rub in an airtight container, and leave to cure in the fridge for 3 days (shorter if curing smaller duck breasts), flipping once per day.

2. Remove the breasts from the fridge and rinse off the cure with cold water. Dry the breasts thoroughly (this is very important) by patting with a clean towel and letting the breasts dry on a drying rack or under a fan for 1 to 3 hours.

3. The final step is hanging. Pierce the skin to attach a piece of twine, and hang the meat to dry and cure. Make sure it isn't touching anything (this could introduce bad bugs). Hang it in a cool, moist place. Check on the fermenting meat periodically (start with every few days, then reduce to every few weeks) to make sure it is not too wet, or insects or other pests are getting at it. Don't worry about white or green moulds, these are a normal part of the process. Simply remove them with a cloth soaked in vinegar. However, meat that has developed extensive black mould must be discarded. How long you ferment will depend on what you are making, but generally the larger the cut, the longer you will want to ferment. Longer ferments will also result in more complex flavours. To start with, a duck or goose breast prosciutto can hang to ferment for 6 to 8 weeks.

4. Slice the prosciutto as thinly as possible and serve on a charcuterie plate.

MAKES 2 BREASTS

FERMENTING

People have been preserving food through fermentation for thousands of years, and it has become an important part of food culture all over the world. Not limited to pickles and sauerkraut, fermentation gives us bread, cheese, wine and beer, not to mention so many other delicious and more unusual treats like kombucha and kefir. Here I will introduce you to a few ideas in the amazing world of fermentation and I hope it will inspire you to learn more and experiment yourself.

The basic way fermentation works is to provide food (in the form of sugars) to beneficial microorganisms, such as bacteria and fungi, including yeasts. These bacteria and yeasts then break down the sugars to form compounds that make food tastier, such as lactic and acetic acid and alcohol. They can also enhance food in other ways, such as changing the pH and altering the structure and texture.

Further references

Wild Fermentation: The Flavor, Nutrition, and Craft of Live-Culture Foods by Sandor Katz and Sally Fallon
The Art of Fermentation by Sandor Katz

BREAD

There are a handful of foods where I think the difference between store-bought and homemade or homegrown is particularly dramatic. Tomatoes. Strawberries. Eggs. But the most drastic contrast, at least in our house, is with bread. Chris's sourdough bread is sublime—crusty on the outside with a soft, chewy interior and strong rustic flavour. I absolutely can't go back to mass-produced bread, and even most specialty bakers don't come close to Chris's bread. It's something we are consistently asked to bring to potlucks, and we always try to make it fresh when we have guests.

In bread making, yeasts ferment the dough by eating and breaking down the sugars in the flour and producing carbon dioxide (which creates air in the dough), alcohol, lactic acid and enzymes. These yeasts are naturally present in the air, in your house, even on your hands. With only four ingredients—sourdough yeast starter, flour, salt and water—fermentation is key to flavour in sourdough bread. The longer you let the dough sit while the yeasts eat the sugars in the flour and produce lactic acid and enzymes, the more characteristic sour flavour you will have in your finished loaf. The most important elements for the texture of the bread are stretching and shaping the dough during the slow fermentation, which help give your loaf a light and elastic structure. Finally, baking (and steaming) the bread in a Dutch oven will give a crusty outside and chewy inside to the end product.

Getting started

To make sourdough bread, it's easiest to get a sourdough starter colony from a friend if you can. But it's totally possible to make your own starter too, because the beneficial yeasts you need are already living in most kitchens. Just put out some food for them in a glass jar (one part water to one part flour), cover it with cheesecloth to keep out fruit flies, and see what you get after a day or three. If you get a mixture that starts bubbling and smelling like sourdough, keep it going by feeding it more flour and water. If you get one that smells bad, start over. Your nose is the best instrument to tell you if your ferments are working.

Procedure

Once you have a good colony of yeasts going (or a starter from a friend), you will need to feed them regularly to keep them alive. Keep the starter in a glass jar, topped with cheesecloth to protect it from flies but allow oxygen in. If you're baking bread often (every two to three days), store the starter at room temperature on the countertop. Whenever you make bread, put a few tablespoons aside to keep the colony alive. Feed the colony about every other day by stirring ½ cup (120 mL) of bread flour into ½ cup (120 mL) of water, then mixing this with a few tablespoons of the starter.

Dry the leftover starter to feed your mealworms or chickens (but not your composting red wriggler worms). If you aren't baking bread often, you can keep the starter in the fridge. This will slow down the yeast metabolism so you don't need to feed the colony as often. When you're ready to bake bread, wake up the yeasts by taking the starter out of the fridge, and allowing it to come to room temperature before starting your leaven (see Making Bread Leaven, page 214).

Aside from an active colony of sourdough yeasts, the most important element to making this bread is a Dutch oven, which is a deep cast iron casserole dish with a lid. The bread steams in the Dutch oven with the lid on for the first half of baking, then crisps with the lid off for the second half, which gives you a beautiful soft interior and crusty exterior to your loaf. It also helps to have a food scale, because the proportions of each ingredient are most accurately based on weights and these vary with air moisture, but it is not strictly necessary, and the recipe that follows has been written for use without a food scale.

RUSTIC ROSEMARY SOURDOUGH BREAD

In our kitchen, Chris is the master baker. He has adapted this rustic sourdough approach from a recipe for country bread found in Tartine Bread *by Chad Robertson, a beautiful and informative book about baking bread with excellent tips and recipes. The key is using a Dutch oven, which lets you steam the dough for the first portion of baking to get a warm chewy centre, and then take the lid off for the second half for a crisp crust. The recipe is simple, but definitely slow food: it works well to make the dough in the evening and then let it rise overnight in the fridge, then in the morning fill the house with the smell of baking bread. We like to use homegrown rosemary to add a burst of botanical flavour, but try any other herbs you have handy. And just in case you have any doubts, this bread is definitely worth the time—I recently bet a friend it would be the best she'd ever tasted . . . and won hands down.*

3 cups (710 mL) water, divided
¾ cup (180 mL) leaven (see sidebar for instructions)
¾ cup (180 mL) whole wheat flour
6 cups (1.4 L) bread flour or all-purpose flour
1 rounded Tbsp (20 mL) salt
¼ cup (60 mL) fresh rosemary, finely chopped
¼ cup (60 mL) cornmeal (optional)

1. Make leaven 8 to 12 hours before you plan to bake bread. To start the bread, pour 2¾ cups (650 mL) of warm water into a large mixing bowl, then add the leaven (which should float when you drop it in). Mix the leaven into the water until dissolved. Keep the remaining leaven as your new batch of starter.

2. Add whole wheat and white flours, and mix with clean, bare hands. Let the dough rest for 30 minutes before adding the salt and rosemary. While mixing with your hands, add remaining water tablespoon by tablespoon (up to ¼ cup/60 mL) until the dough has an elastic consistency, and all the flour is no longer dry but the dough is not runny.

3. Cover the bowl with a clean dishtowel, and place the dough somewhere warm, such as near a heater. Let it ferment for about 3 to 4 hours, turning the dough every 30 minutes—to turn it, wet your hands and fold the dough in half 2 or 3 times, making sure not to press too much of the air out. When the dough is ready, it should have taken on a lighter, more airy consistency, pull away from the bowl more easily and hold its shape for several long seconds after being folded. (Note that the longer the dough rises, the stronger the sour flavour will be.)

4. About an hour into the first rise, if desired, the dough can be placed in the fridge to continue to rise slowly overnight (it will need to be brought back to room temperature before shaping).

5. At the end of this first fermentation, turn out the dough onto an unfloured surface such as a smooth counter or table. Dust the top of the dough very lightly with flour. Using a bench knife or dough scraper (another kitchen knife will work in a pinch but a bench knife is very useful for bread making and not expensive), cut the dough into 2 even portions and flip each over onto the floured side, then very lightly dust the other side.

6. With as few movements as possible, use your hands to shape both pieces of dough into rounds. Do this by placing each hand on opposite sides of the dough and tucking the edges underneath with your fingers, then turning the dough about 45 degrees and repeating, continuing until the outer surface is smooth and taut. Lightly cover with a dishtowel and allow to rest for 20 to 30 minutes.

MAKING BREAD LEAVEN

¾ cup (180 mL) whole wheat flour
¾ cup (180 mL) white flour
¾ cup (180 mL) water
Sourdough starter (see page 213 for instructions)

Leaven (also known as active starter) is the robust yeast culture that will ferment the sugars in the flour, releasing enzymes and gases that will cause the bread to rise. Make the leaven the night before you plan to bake bread.

In a clean glass jar, mix the whole wheat flour, white flour and water. Add 1 tablespoon (15 mL) of the sourdough starter, stir thoroughly, then cover with cheesecloth. Dry the remaining starter to feed to your mealworms or chickens.

Leave the flour, water and starter mixture on the counter overnight or for about 8 hours—while the yeasts become more active the leaven should rise in volume by about a quarter. Test to see if your leaven is ready to ferment bread dough by adding a spoonful to a bowl of water. If it floats, it is ready to ferment bread. If it doesn't, leave it in a warm spot for a few more hours. If it still hasn't become active, try repeating the process from the beginning, and if that doesn't work you'll have to use the mixture to try to cultivate new wild yeasts or get a new starter from a friend.

After removing the amount of leaven you need for your bread, place the rest in a clean glass jar and refrigerate. This is your new batch of sourdough starter.

---

7. Next, using a bench knife, being careful not to press air out, flip the dough over on the work surface so it is upside down. Gently grab the edge of the loaf farthest from you, stretch it out (away from your body), then fold it back to the edge closest to you. Repeat clockwise around the loaf until you have folded 4 times, holding the last fold with your hands. Carefully roll the dough over so the final seam is underneath, and shape it lightly by tucking the edges under until it is smooth and taut again. Repeat for the second piece of dough.

8. While the dough is resting for a minute, dust 2 clean (waffle-style are best) kitchen towels with flour or cornmeal, and place them into small mixing bowls (with about a capacity of 4 to 6 cups/1 to 1.4 L). Transfer the balls of dough into the 2 bowls using the bread spatula, and flip the dough so that the seam that was on the bottom is now facing upwards. Leave the bowls of dough somewhere warm for the final fermentation, or final rise, for 2 to 4 hours. Again, you can choose to put the dough somewhere cool (like the fridge) to slow the fermentation and leave it overnight if you have to.

9. When ready to bake, preheat the oven to 500F (260C) with the Dutch oven inside. When it is hot, remove the Dutch oven and take off the lid. Pick up the towel with dough in it from the bowl, and quickly and carefully flip the dough into the hot Dutch oven while peeling off the towel (it should pull away easily if the towel was properly floured). Replace the lid on the Dutch oven and put it back into the oven, immediately turning the temperature down to 450F (230C). Bake for 20 minutes, then remove the lid and continue to bake for another 20 to 25 minutes or until the crust is a dark brown. When the bread is ready it should sound hollow when you tap on the bottom with a knife or spatula. Remove from the Dutch oven and place onto a cooling rack. Listen to the bread crackle and sing as it cools. It's tempting to eat right away but let it sit for 5 to 10 minutes before you enjoy.

10. Being careful to use a pot holder to handle your still-hot Dutch oven, repeat previous step to bake the second loaf.

MAKES 2 LOAVES

BEER, CIDER AND FRUIT WINES

Making beer, cider or wine is one of the best ways to enjoy the benefits of fermentation. Who doesn't love the taste of a fresh pint of a hoppy IPA or dry apple cider? And homemade is always more satisfying.

When Chris and I were working on our Ph.D.s, homebrewing became a major pastime for us and our lab-mates. Chris started many years ago in California, mainly using kits and creating mediocre brews, but the shared interest in yeast cultures and camaraderie amongst friends rekindled the hobby and led to brewing incredible beers with whole grains and homegrown hops. Making beer, cider and wine might sound complicated, but it really just involves inoculating grain or fruit sugars with the right beneficial bugs (yeasts), letting it sit for a while, and then bottling. This results in a quick-ferment, low-alcohol brew, and leaves a ton of room for experimenting with different flavours and foraged ingredients.

In beer, cider and wine making, fermentation happens when yeasts eat the natural sugars that get steeped from grains (in the case of beer) or are present in fruit or berry juice (in the case of cider and fruit wines). One of the main by-products from the beer and cider yeasts is alcohol (which is kind of like yeast pee—gross but cool!). So the more food you give your yeasts (higher sugar content) and the longer you let them eat (longer ferment), the more yeast pee you will get (higher alcohol content). Beer and cider yeasts also produce carbon dioxide (which carbonates the drink if it is prevented from being released by being sealed in a bottle).

Another of Chris's specialties is brewing beer, and he loves to experiment with different flavourings from the garden and woods around our place. Almost every beer he's made has been fantastic, comparable to our favourite craft-brewery beers (and we do sample those a lot too). Chris likes to infuse his beers with whatever happens to be available at the time, adding *Jasmine officinale* blossoms to sweeten up an amber, elderberry flowers to give a distinct nose to our latest French saison, or pumpkin to a fall porter.

Any type of edible fruit, berry or even herb can be used, depending on what is available and what sounds good to you.

While most urbanites don't have the space to grow all the grains needed to make beer, hops are an easy-to-grow ingredient, and take the process all the way from the ground to your belly. A trailing vine that you can grow in a patio container, hops looks very pretty in the summer and produces lovely flowers to add to beer.

Ciders and fruit wines are another great way to preserve the taste of seasonally available fruits and add a little boozy kick. The difference between ciders and fruit wines is a bit of a grey area, but generally ciders are carbonated while fruit wines are not, and fruit wines tend to have a higher alcohol content.

Beer

Chris says that homebrewing beer takes the right gear, a little gumption and a healthy thirst.

Getting started

To get going, it helps to get a starter kit from a beer supply store, which will set you up with a beer-making pot, thermometer, primary and secondary fermenters (one food-grade plastic 6-gallon/23-L bucket with a hole in the lid for the airlock, and one 6-gallon/23-L glass carboy with a small mouth), airlock, plastic tubing with hose clamp and one-way valve, and sanitizer, as well as grains, yeast and hops (if you need them). A small food scale is helpful for measuring out your hops at home. If you want to brew from whole grains rather than using malt extract, you'll also need a mash tun. Wort chillers are totally optional, but can help speed up the process. Finally, get your hands on some used swing-top glass beer bottles, or you can opt for non-screw-top glass bottles with metal bottle caps and a bottle capper. Sanitize the bottles using a bottle brush and solution from the beer or wine-making supply store, or hydrogen peroxide, and rinse thoroughly.

Opposite: Hops, blackberries and elderflowers can be used as aromatic additions to beer, wine or cider, and can be foraged or grown as perennial edible landscaping.

Beer Making 101—know the lingo

Make sure to sanitize all your equipment before using to prevent inoculating your brew with unwanted microorganisms.

When brewing from whole grains, you start with *malted* grains, which means the grains (which are grass seeds) started germinating before being dried, which encourages the seeds to convert their starches into the sugars that are used in the fermentation. The first step in homebrewing from whole grains is called *mashing in.* This is when you steep the grains in a *mash tun* (a food-safe plastic bucket with a spout at the bottom) to extract the sugars from them, creating food for the yeast to eat while producing alcohol. The finished result (like a beer-grain tea) is called the *wort.* Next, you *fly sparge* the wort, which involves adding fresh hot water to the top of the mash tun, while draining the wort from the tap at the bottom into a 6-gallon (23-L) pot, trying to maintain the full volume in the mash tun, then draining the rest into the pot.

In the next step, boil the wort in the pot, at which time you can add flavour elements, such as hops or flowers—how long you let them boil will determine how strong their flavour is, and this is different for each recipe. After the boil, you can use a *wort chiller* to cool down the hot wort, which involves pouring the wort through a coiled tube immersed in cold water. If you don't have a wort chiller, you can also immerse the whole wort pot in a cold water bath in the sink. Using the water-bath method to cool the wort might take several hours (if you make beer regularly, you quickly discover that wort chillers are a good investment!). Chilling the wort faster is better not only because it is more manageable, but also because it reduces the likelihood of any unwanted microorganisms growing in the beer while it cools.

Next, pour the wort (filtering out the solids) into the *primary fermenter*—this is the first container you let the beer ferment in, and is typically a 6-gallon (23-L) food-safe plastic bucket with a tight-sealing lid with a small hole for the airlock. Before putting on the lid, you *pitch*, or add, the yeast. The yeast, of course, is what will turn the sugars in the wort into alcohol. The fermenter is then sealed with an *airlock*, which is a one-way valve that keeps air (and insects) out of the fermenter but allows the carbon dioxide produced by the yeasts to escape.

In the primary fermenter, the yeast will begin to eat the sugars within the first few hours, producing carbon dioxide (and alcohol), and the airlock will bubble vigorously for the next week or so before tailing off, at which point the brew is ready for the *secondary fermenter*—this is the second container you let the beer ferment in, and is typically a 6-gallon (23-L) glass carboy with a small mouth that the airlock fits into. Transferring the brew between containers is called *racking*, and is done using a siphoning technique.

To siphon the brew, place the primary fermenter on a countertop and the secondary on a chair or the floor. Add a tube into the top of the primary about midway down into the liquid (through the airlock hole works). Suck on the end like a straw until the liquid is almost at the end, then stop it with your finger or a hose clamp and place it into the secondary. The key to this is making sure not the suck up the sediments (dead yeast) on the bottom of the primary to prevent a skunky taste in the beer.

After you rack into the secondary, the bubbling may start up again or may not—either is fine. Some recipes call for additional flavour components, such as *dry hops* (which are usually sold as powdered pellets), to be added during the second ferment, which typically lasts another week.

After the secondary ferment, you are ready to bottle, which is the final step of fermentation and captures the carbon dioxide produced by the yeast in order to *carbonate* the beer. The yeasts need more food in order to produce carbon dioxide, so *priming sugar*, or dextrose, is added to the brew at bottling. Dissolve the priming sugar in boiling water, then add it to the clean, empty primary fermenter, and rack the beer from the secondary into the primary. Make sure to leave any sediment on the bottom of the secondary, and to thoroughly mix the sugar in with the beer in the primary with a long-handled spoon or by rotating it gently.

Once it has mixed, rack the beer into bottles using the siphoning technique (a hose clamp and one-way valve on the end going into the bottles makes this easier). And drinking a pint of the fresh, uncarbonated beer during bottling is an unwritten rule, according to Chris.

Cleanliness is the key when bottling, so make sure to thoroughly scrub, sanitize and rinse your bottles before using. Glass swing-top bottles are the best, although used non-screw-top glass bottles also work with fresh metal caps and a bottle capper. Bottling in plastic works, though glass gives a better feel and taste. It is not advisable to bottle into growlers or Mason jars as these aren't designed to withstand the pressures exerted by the carbon dioxide during carbonation, and the glass might break.

Let the beer age in the bottles for a couple of weeks or more. Many beers, especially stronger ones, tend to age well and letting them sit in a cool, dark place longer can really enhance the flavour. Try setting aside a few bottles and aging for few several weeks to taste the difference.

Further reference

The Complete Joy of Homebrewing by Charlie Papazian

Aromatic hops flowers are an essential ingredient for homebrewing—forage these perennial vines in urban parks, admire their beauty as edible landscaping or make good use of vertical space in your stacked urban food forest.

SASSY ELDERFLOWER SAISON HOMEBREW BEER

Chris is the brewer at our house. One day, we were starting up a batch of saison when we noticed the elder shrub outside our door was in full bloom. The flowers had a subtly sweet fragrance that would complement the fruity tones of a saison. The brew ended up with a very flowery nose and complex taste that improved with age. Collect red or blue elderflowers in the spring—just ensure that any elderflowers or berries you consume are well cooked first, as they contain toxins destroyed by cooking.

MASH
6 lbs 10 oz (3 kg) Maris Otter pale malt (grain)
2 lbs 3 oz (1 kg) Munich malt (grain)

BOIL
½ oz (14 gr) Pacific Gem hops, divided
1 oz (28 gr) Mount Hood hops
½ oz (14 gr) Citra hops
16 cups (3.8 L) fresh elderflowers
1 package (5 oz/140 gr) French saison yeast

FERMENTING AND BOTTLING
1 oz (28 gr) Pacific Gem dry hops
1 oz (28 gr) Mount Hood dry hops
1 cup (250 mL) priming sugar (dextrose)

1. Start by sanitizing your equipment. In a mash tun, mash in the malted Marris Otter pale and Munich grains in water. To do this, add 4 gallons (15 L) of 163F (73C) water to the grains. Mash for 75 minutes.

2. Next, fly sparge the wort by slowly adding 2 gallons (7.6 L) of 168F (76C) water to the mash tun while draining into a 6-gallon (23-L) pot at the bottom, and then continue to drain all the liquid into the pot.

3. Place the pot full of wort on the stovetop over high heat. Once it reaches a boil, turn it down to medium heat and maintain a rolling boil for 1 hour. Add the boil hops and elderflowers at the following schedule: when it first comes to the boil, add ¼ oz (7 gr) of the Pacific Gem; with 20 minutes left, add the Mount Hood and remaining Pacific Gem; with 5 minutes left add the Citra and the elderflowers.

4. After 1 hour, remove the wort from the heat and allow to cool. If you have a wort chiller, use it to speed up the process to under an hour; otherwise you can use a cold water bath in the sink.

5. Once the wort has cooled, pour it into a primary fermenter, using a colander to filter out the solids. Pitch (pour in) the yeast on top, then fit the lid on top. Seal with an airlock, adding water or spirits to the airlock.

6. Allow the brew to ferment for 7 to 10 days, then rack it from the primary to a secondary fermenter. Add the airlock onto the top of the secondary fermenter.

7. Allow the brew to ferment for 2 days, then remove the airlock and pour the Pacific Gem and Mount Hood dry hops into the top of the carboy, replacing the airlock afterwards. Allow to ferment for another 5 days, during which you should notice bubbling in the airlock again.

8. Before bottling, boil 1 cup (250 mL) of water and dissolve the priming sugar into it, then add this to the beer. Next, rack the beer into sanitized bottles, leaving about 3 inches (7.5 cm) of headspace. Close the swing-caps or cap the bottles, and put them in a cool, dark place. Let the beer carbonate for a couple of weeks or more—if you can resist. We found a stray bottle of this beer about 6 months after brewing, and it was amazing!

MAKES ABOUT 20 X 4-CUP (1-L) BOTTLES

CALIFORNIA DROOLING CAT SESSIONAL IPA

A delicious light IPA for warm summer months. We affectionately call this brew "Drooling Cat" in honour of Jacob, the kitty who adopted us and now drools in our laps while we sit in the sunshine enjoying this beer.

MASH
5 lbs 8 oz (2.5 kg) 2-row pale malt (grain)
3 lbs 3 oz (1.45 kg) white wheat malt (grain)

BOIL
1 oz (28 gr) Columbus hops, divided
1.9 oz (54 gr) Falconer's Flight hops, divided
1.4 oz (40 gr) Centennial hops, divided
Zest of 3 grapefruits
Zest of 5 oranges
Zest of 5 lemons
Zest of 5 limes
1 oz (28 gr) Nelson Sauvin hops
1 package (5 oz/140 gr) American Ale yeast

FERMENTING AND BOTTLING
1.35 oz (38 gr) Nelson Sauvin dry hops
1 oz (28 gr) Columbus dry hops
1 cup (250 mL) priming sugar (dextrose)

1. See Beer Making 101 on page 218 for basic beer-making instructions.

2. Start by sanitizing your equipment. For the mash, heat 4 gallons (15 L) of water to 168F (76C) and pour onto the 2-row pale and wheat malt grains in a mash tun. Mash for 60 minutes, then fly sparge by slowly adding 2.5 gallons (9.5 L) of 168F (76C) water to the top of the mash tun while draining into a 6-gallon (23-L) pot at the bottom, then continue to drain all the liquid into the pot.

3. Place the wort pot on the stovetop on high heat. Once it reaches a boil, turn it down to medium heat and maintain a rolling boil for 1 hour. Add the boil hops and fruit zest on the following schedule: when it first comes to a boil, add 0.4 oz (11 gr) Columbus; with 15 minutes left add 0.9 oz (26 gr) Falconer's Flight and 0.7 oz (20 gr) Centennial; with 5 minutes left add 0.7 oz (20 gr) Centennial and the fruit zest; remove from heat, then add 1 oz (28 gr) Falconer's Flight, 1 oz (28 gr) Nelson Sauvin and 0.6 oz (17 gr) Columbus.

4. After the boil, remove the wort from heat and cool. If you have a wort chiller, use it to speed up the process, otherwise you can use a cold water bath in the sink. Once the wort has cooled, use a colander to filter out the solids. Pitch (pour in) the yeast on top, then fit the lid on top. Seal with an airlock, adding water or spirits to the airlock.

5. Let ferment in the primary for 7 to 10 days, until the airlock stops bubbling, then rack into the secondary fermenter, and add the airlock.

6. Let ferment in the secondary for another 5 to 6 days, then remove the airlock to add the dry hops (Nelson Sauvin and Columbus). Replace the airlock and allow to ferment for another 4 days, during which time you should notice bubbling in the airlock again.

7. Before bottling, boil 1 cup (250 mL) of water and dissolve the priming sugar into it, then add this to the beer. Next, rack the beer into sanitized bottles, leaving about 3 inches (7.5 cm) of headspace. Close the swing-caps or cap the bottles, and put them in a cool, dark place. Let the beer carbonate for at least 1 week. Enjoy.

MAKES ABOUT 20 X 1-QUART (1-L) BOTTLES

Cider and Fruit Wines

Use your foraged, homegrown or farm-market harvests to make your own refreshing and tasty cider or fruit wines.

Getting started

When starting out, it helps to get a starter kit from a wine or beer-making supply store, which will set you up with the fermenting carboys (the primary fermenter is a 6-gallon/23-L food-grade plastic bucket with a hole in the lid for the airlock, and the secondary is a 6-gallon/23-L glass carboy with a small mouth to fit the airlock); an airlock; plastic tubing with a hose clamp and one-way valve for siphoning; and sanitizer; as well as yeast.

Consult with staff at your local wine or beer-making supply store to choose the right yeast for your fruit of choice, or look up a yeast-strains chart online. The type of yeast to buy will depend on what fruit you are using and what you think you would like—there are several types of wine and champagne yeast. For example, use champagne yeast to create a sparkling cider, red-wine yeast for blackberry wine and white-wine yeast for elderflower wine. Any of these yeasts will achieve the same fermentation . . . it's all about taste when choosing.

You can also make your own cider or fruit-wine yeast culture by leaving a cheesecloth-covered glass jar of sugar water mixed with mashed fruit and seeing what you catch. If you end up with something that smells like cider, wine or beer, try it out; otherwise, just buy the yeast.

You'll also need swing-top bottles for bottling, or a bottle capper, glass bottles and metal caps. Sanitize the bottles using a bottle brush and solution from the beer or wine-making supply store, or hydrogen peroxide, and rinse thoroughly.

Further reference

Jim and George's Home Wine Making: A Beginner's Book by Jim Weathers

WILD BLACKBERRY SPARKLING CIDER

My grandparents had a small apple orchard and a big homemade wooden apple press. In the fall, they would get the family together to press the juice from all the apples that my grandma hadn't made into pies or applesauce. The juice was then fermented to make apple cider (this was my grandpa's specialty). Apparently my teenage parents used to sneak off with a few after bottling day was done, feeling badass, of course, and only found out 30 years later that my grandma knew the whole time, but just didn't worry much about the low-alcohol brew. I've adapted a basic cider recipe for invasive Himalayan blackberries instead.

20 lbs (9 kg) frozen blackberries (or substitute other foraged berries or stone fruit)

4 gallons (15 L) water

16 cups (3.7 L) sugar

3 Tbsp (45 mL) lemon juice

0.176 oz (5 gr) package dry champagne yeast

1 cup (250 mL) brown sugar

1. Start by sanitizing your equipment.

2. In a 6-gallon (23-L) food-safe bucket with a tight-sealing lid with an airlock hole (the primary fermenter), add the frozen berries. Boil the water and dissolve 16 cups (3.8 L) of the sugar in it. Carefully pour the boiling-hot liquid over the frozen berries. Add the lemon juice. Wait for the berries to thaw, then crush with a heavy object, such as a wine bottle. Pitch the yeast (pour over top), stir in thoroughly, and cover tightly with the lid, inserting the airlock in the hole in the top. Fill the airlock with water so that gas (carbon dioxide produced during fermentation) can escape but nothing can get in. Leave it to ferment, stirring daily, until the airlock stops bubbling vigorously (about a week or more, could be up to 4).

3. Use a slotted spoon to remove as much of the berry pulp as possible from the top of the mixture in the primary fermenter, and then rack (or siphon) the brew into a glass carboy with a small mouth to fit the airlock (the secondary fermenter). To do this, put the primary on the countertop, and the secondary on a chair or the ground. Insert a length of plastic tubing into the liquid in the primary, suck on the end like a straw until the liquid is almost at the end, then stop it with your finger and place it into the secondary. Allow gravity to move the liquid from the primary into the secondary. Seal the secondary fermenter with the airlock, fill the airlock with water again and leave to ferment for another 7 to 10 days, or until the airlock stops bubbling. When the airlock hasn't bubbled for a full day, the cider is ready to bottle.

4. For bottling your sparkling cider, you may want to opt for sanitized plastic soda bottles rather than glass bottles, at least for your first few batches. This will allow you to check the pressure in the bottles by squeezing them, and avoid too much gas buildup that could break a glass bottle. At first, squeeze the bottles every few days. If the pressure is high (no give on the sides), gently open the plastic screw-top and allow some gas to escape, then tighten the top back on. After you have successfully brewed a few batches, switch to glass bottles, either re-sealable swing-top bottles or reused glass bottles with new metal caps (and use a bottle capper to cap). If you are worried about bottle breakage, keep the bottles in a plastic storage container with a lid on it.

5. Before bottling, add sugar to reactivate the yeasts to produce carbon dioxide, which will carbonate the cider. To do this, rack the cider into the clean, empty primary fermenter. Boil 1 cup (250 mL) of water and dissolve the brown sugar into it. Allow to cool, then stir into the cider.

6. Next, rack the cider into scrubbed, sanitized and rinsed bottles. Using a hose clamp and a one-way valve on the end of the tube going into the bottles makes it easier to transfer the tube between bottles when racking. Sealing the bottles will prevent the gas from escaping, which will give the cider carbonation. After sealing the bottles, leave them to age. How long you age the cider depends on how dry you want it to be—the longer you let the yeasts eat the sugars, the drier it will become. Of course, it also depends on how long you can stand to wait before enjoying your cider! A good guideline is at least 4 weeks, but more is ideal.

UNCARBONATED BLACKBERRY WINE

If you prefer fruit wine rather than sparkling cider, you can use red-wine yeast rather than champagne yeast, and simply skip the step of adding sugar before bottling, which will result in a fruity and fairly low-alcohol wine. To up the alcohol content, add sugar (up to 1 cup/250 mL per gallon) during the secondary fermentation step. Cider and wine making are creative processes, so play with variations until you come up with something you like.

MAKES ABOUT 20 X 4-CUP (1-L) BOTTLES

SHRUBS

Shrubs are drinking vinegars that were popular in the colonial era and the cocktail culture of the 1920s, and are making a comeback. Infused with fruits and herbs, shrubs make refreshing sodas and cocktails with an unusual and remarkably thirst-quenching combination of sweet and tangy. The basic ingredients are very simple: fruit, sugar and vinegar (and for more on making your own vinegar, see page 230).

Shrubs are non-alcoholic and can simply be added to seltzer water for an afternoon soda. They also pair very well with any number of spirits, depending on the fruit and herbs chosen to make the shrub. When choosing what to use, your imagination and taste buds are the only limit. Look around at what is in season at the time, see what you can forage and think about what fruits and herbs—or even vegetables—might make good combinations in a cocktail. A few ideas are strawberry and basil or peach and rosemary shrubs with gin or vodka. Don't be shy of trying more unusual combinations too: maybe a kale and ginger shrub paired with rum, rhubarb and balsamic shrub with tequila, or blackberry and thyme shrub with bourbon.

Getting started

All you need are the ingredients (fruit, sugar and vinegar), a bowl and clean glass jars with lids.

Procedure

The process involves fermentation of the fruit and sugar from organisms present in the vinegar—this takes a week or two, and creates a cohesive combination of flavours.

HIMALAYAN BLACKBERRY, MINT & PEPPER SHRUB

What better strategy to deal with two very invasive but delicious weeds—blackberry and mint—than by drinking them in this delicious way? Any mint can be used—field mint, spearmint or even lemon balm. When the blackberries are ripe in high summer, it's the perfect time to enjoy a cool, refreshing shrub cocktail in the sunshine. You'll need raw vinegar because the live culture in it is required to further ferment the fruits and sugars to make the shrub. If you don't have homemade vinegar, purchase raw apple cider vinegar. This shrub will continue to ferment slowly in a Mason jar on the countertop for several weeks, or will keep in the fridge for months. To enjoy as a cocktail, mix two ounces (60 mL) shrub with one ounce (30 mL) spirit and top up your glass with sparkling water. Or skip the alcohol for a refreshing summer soda.

1 cup (250 mL) mint (or lemon balm)
2 cups (475 mL) blackberries
2 cups (475 mL) cane sugar
1 tsp (5 mL) peppercorns

2 cups (475 mL) IPA Beer Vinegar, recipe on page 230 (or substitute raw apple cider vinegar)

1. Muddle the mint in a large Mason jar with a muddler or wooden spoon. Add the blackberries, crush and cover with sugar. Leave the jar in the fridge for at least 24 hours or up to 48.

2. Add vinegar and pepper, and mix to dissolve the sugar. Seal the top with a lid, and let sit for a week at room temperature.

3. After 1 week, strain out the solid ingredients. At this point, you can start making beverages with your shrub, or let it sit for another week to let the fermentation add more complexity of flavour.

MAKES 2 CUPS (475 ML)

KOMBUCHA

One of my favourite things to ferment is kombucha—it's so easy! For those who have never tried it, I describe it as a slightly fizzy, cider-like iced tea . . . very refreshing on a hot summer day.

Procedure

The live kombucha culture is a symbiotic colony of bacteria and yeasts, which is used to ferment sweetened black, green or herbal tea. The colony grows as a somewhat mushroom-like culture (remember yeasts are fungi), a rubbery pancake of goodness called a scoby or mother. Some of the bacteria (*Acetobacter* spp.) in the scoby produce acetic acid, much like they do for making vinegar from grain and fruit-juice sugars. This acid gives a wonderful tangy taste to the kombucha, which will intensify as the ferment ages. Once it has reached the tanginess you like, you can remove the scoby and put the drink in a sealed container (such as a swing-top glass bottle) in the fridge for a week or two to let it ferment slowly and build up a bit of carbonation.

After removing the kombucha scoby from a finished batch, separate the older and newer cultures (the scoby pancakes), and use them to create new batches. Give away extra kombucha cultures to your friends (and tell them how easy and delicious it is). If you have more than you can use, feed them to chickens or compost. If you aren't making kombucha regularly, keep your scoby in a jar of sugar water (1 part sugar to 5 parts water) in the fridge, feeding it every 2 to 3 weeks.

If you leave the fermentation for too long, with it becoming too sour to drink, use it to make pickles the same way you would use vinegar (see Vinegar Pickles, page 231). Or if you specifically want to make kombucha vinegar, simply leave the kombucha to ferment for a month or more rather than just a week.

Getting started

When you're first starting out, you'll need to get a kombucha culture (scoby) from a friend or purchase a dehydrated one. You will also require glass jars and cheesecloth. If you can find raw (unpasteurized) kombucha at the store, you can try growing your own scoby by leaving it out at room temperature, covered with cheesecloth, to allow the culture to develop.

FIELD MINT KOMBUCHA

Most people use black or green tea to make kombucha, but I've had a lot of success with herbal teas, especially when made from our own homegrown or foraged mint. The fermenting yeasts and bacteria in the kombucha culture are actually eating the sugar you add, not the tea, so any variation of tea should work fine. If you happen to mess up by leaving the ferment too long—with your kombucha tasting tangier than you like—just leave it even longer to evolve into kombucha vinegar (see Kombucha Pickled Beets, page 231).

½ cup (120 mL) fresh mint
½ cup (120 mL) sugar
2 Tbsp (30 mL) mature kombucha or IPA Beer Vinegar, recipe on page 230 (or apple cider vinegar)
1 kombucha scoby

1. Start by making tea by pouring boiling water over your mint leaves to almost fill the jar you are using—a 1-quart (1-L) jar works well for this. Next, you need to add a sugar because otherwise the bacteria and yeasts have nothing to eat. Regular sugar is the most common, but honey, agave, maple syrup and even fruit juice can also work. The amount to add depends on your own taste and the type of sweetener. With cane sugar I add about ¼ to ½ cup (60 to 120 mL) of sugar for 4 cups (1 L) of tea. Wait for the sweetened tea to cool to room temperature and transfer to a wide-mouthed glass or ceramic vessel, such as a large Mason jar (we use 4-cup/1-L jars).

2. In order to acidify the tea to prevent the growth of unwanted microorganisms, add some mature kombucha, or if you are first starting, add a couple of tablespoons of vinegar. Finally, once the tea has cooled, add the scoby. It's okay if the scoby sinks at first, but it will eventually float on the top, covering the surface of the tea and developing a second culture (like a pancake) attached to the first. Cover the top of the vessel with cheesecloth to prevent flies from getting in, and leave at room temperature.

3. As the ferment ages, it will produce acetic acid, so simply choose the taste and level of acidity you like, and stop the ferment by removing the scoby from the vessel and putting the fermented tea in the fridge. The ferment usually takes about a week, depending on how warm it is (more warmth makes the bugs more active and speeds up the ferment). If you put the kombucha into a sealable vessel, such as a beer bottle with a swing-cap and seal, and leave it in the fridge for another couple weeks, the ferment will continue slowly and carbonate more.

MAKES 4 CUPS (1 L)

VINEGAR

Have you ever wondered why wine starts to taste vinegary a few days after you open the bottle? That's because some of the live microorganism cultures still in the wine are producing acetic acid, which is what gives vinegar its taste.

Procedure

The yeasts that like to eat sugars and produce alcohol don't like air, which is why you need to use airlocks when making beer, cider and wine. But the bacteria that produce acetic acid (*Acetobacter*) do like air, so if you leave alcoholic drinks exposed to air, you'll eventually get vinegar—apple cider vinegar, red-wine vinegar, white-wine vinegar, rice-wine vinegar, fruit-wine vinegar—you get the idea.

Getting started

All you need is some beer, cider or wine that didn't turn out or has started to go off (perfectly good alcohol works too if you're desperate for vinegar), a wide-mouthed Mason jar, some cheesecloth and live vinegar culture. You can start a wild culture by leaving a cheesecloth-covered glass jar of beer, cider or wine exposed to air. Catching a wild vinegar culture is much easier than catching a wild cider or fruit-wine culture. Or use raw, unpasteurized apple cider vinegar (which contains a live culture) or homemade vinegar from previous batches.

Another way to make vinegar is by using kombucha that has fermented for too long, which also produces tangy acetic acid.

BEER VINEGAR

So what is beer vinegar? You've probably had malt vinegar sprinkled over fish and chips. Malt vinegar is produced when malted grains are steeped in water and fermented to produce alcohol (as in beer), then fermented further. But "beer vinegar" sounds way cooler! Super easy to brew with only two ingredients and no equipment, it just takes a bit of waiting while the acetic-acid bacteria do their job of turning the alcohol to vinegar. And it's worth the wait— retaining the maltiness or hoppiness of the beer you started with, this vinegar is perfect for drizzling on roasted veggies or fries. You can adapt this recipe for any lightly alcoholic drink, from cider to white, red, rice or sparkling wine. Use the same proportions and instructions shown here.

1 bottle of California Drooling Cat Sessional IPA, recipe on page 222

¼ volume raw apple cider vinegar, homemade vinegar, or wild vinegar culture (instructions above)

1. Pour out a quarter of the volume of your homebrew (into a glass to drink it!). Fill up the rest of the bottle with raw apple cider vinegar, but don't fill the neck of the bottle (to maximize the surface area that is exposed to air). This will increase the fermentation by the acetic acid-producing bacteria, which need air. Cover securely with cheesecloth to keep out flies.

2. Wait for 3 months, then begin tasting every 2 weeks or so until the vinegar has reached a flavour you like. After this point, strain out the solids. Reserve ½ cup (120 mL) or so for your next batch of vinegar. This will store at room temperature indefinitely, creating more flavour complexity as it ages.

MAKES 1 BOTTLE

Vinegar Pickles

Most pickles you buy from the store, and the majority of the pickles people make at home, simply involve adding hot vinegar to fruits or veggies, which is a quick way to preserve them with acetic acid. All kinds of fruits and vegetables are suitable for vinegar pickles, including the familiar cucumbers, beans, asparagus, beets, onions and garlic, but also root vegetables like carrots and fruit like peaches or plums. Another way to make pickles is by fermenting fruit and veggies using lactic acid (see Lactic-acid Ferments, page 233).

Getting started

For vinegar pickles, you'll need the recipe ingredients and clean glass jars. You'll also need the equipment for the water-bath canning method if you wish to can the pickles for storage (see Water-Bath Canning, page 188). After you enjoy your pickles, save any leftover liquid to make other recipes.

KOMBUCHA-PICKLED BEETS

Anyone making kombucha regularly has on occasion left it for too long on the countertop and ended up with a very zingy brew. It tastes vinegary, and no wonder—some of the bacteria in the kombucha culture are the same as those that make vinegar. So instead of dumping your too-fermented kombucha, use it to make pickles. Pickling with kombucha works the same way as pickling with vinegar (see above)—it's a quick process and the vegetables are not fermented, but the preservation comes from the acetic acid produced in the kombucha fermentation. Simply substitute kombucha vinegar for any other type of vinegar in a vinegar-pickle recipe. Note that you can pickle pretty much any fruit or veggie, even peaches, which I recently tried very successfully. Basically, if it's an edible plant, you can pickle it with delicious results. Instead of beets, try this recipe with bamboo shoots, prickly pear cactus pads and fruits, or kudzu roots and flowers.

10 medium beet roots, (about 1 lb, 455 gr)
⅓ cup (80 mL) pickling salt
2 cups (475 mL) crushed ice
3 cups (710 mL) Field Mint Kombucha (page 229),
   aged over 3 months
1½ cup (350 mL) water
1½ cup (350 mL) sugar
¼ cup (60 mL) pickling spice

1. Boil the beets on the stove until they are tender, about 30 minutes.

2. Rinse beets under cold water and remove the skins (they should come off easily after the beets have been cooked). Slice. Put the beets in a bowl and cover with pickling salt, then ice (this will stop the beets from cooking further and draw out some of the water, which will result in crisper canned beets).

3. After 2 hours, rinse off the salt. In a large non-reactive pot (stainless or enameled), mix kombucha vinegar, water and sugar until sugar is dissolved. Add beets and bring to a boil, then immediately remove from heat.

4. Fill six 1-cup (250-mL) jars with beets and pickling liquid, then top off with 2 teaspoons (10 mL) of pickling spice per jar.

5. To can the pickled beets, follow the Water-Bath Canning procedure on page 188.

MAKES 6 X 1-CUP (250-ML) JARS

KOMBUCHA-PICKLED BEET
& GINGER BELLINI

I've always loved the juice left over from pickled beets—tangy, sweet and a gorgeous deep red. So how better to use it than in a cocktail? This Bellini has a sweet and fruity taste paired with a tangy bite and bit of fizz. Plus, how cool is it that you made your own kombucha vinegar and pickled beets yourself, then transformed it all into something boozy!

1½ oz (45 mL) leftover juice from Kombucha Pickled Beets (page 231)

1½ oz (45 mL) ginger liqueur
½ cup (120 mL) Prosecco

1. Shake beet juice and ginger liqueur with ice until mixture is well chilled. Fill fluted glass with Prosecco and top with beet-juice mixture.

MAKES 1 COCKTAIL

LACTIC-ACID FERMENTS

While creating quick pickles using vinegar (acetic acid) can result in some truly delectable concoctions, it does not actually ferment the produce. However, it's easy to do your own slow fermentation for veggies or even fruit. Instead of acetic acid, this process involves lactic acid, which works as a preservative and results in a slightly less pungent taste than vinegar pickles.

Getting started

You can make slow pickles in glass jars, or for larger batches, use a ceramic crock.

Procedure

When you slow ferment, lactic acid-producing bacteria (namely *Leuconostoc mesenteroides* and *Lactobacillus*) break down the sugars in the produce to create lactic acid and carbon dioxide. This reduces the pH, which inhibits unwanted bacteria and fungi (moulds) from growing. Lactic acid-producing bacteria are present on the food before it ferments, so in this case, you don't have to add a culture. However, if you have left-over whey from cheese making, adding a spoonful or two to your vegetable ferments will help it get off to a roaring start and reduce the potential for unwanted microorganisms to start growing.

KOSHER-STYLE CUCUMBER SLOW PICKLES

Add these delicious pickles to an antipasti plate showcasing your urban-homestead goodies, or pair with a smoked-meat sandwich.

¼ cup (60 mL) pickling salt

4 cups (1 L) water

2 fresh grape leaves (optional)

3 Tbsp (45 mL) dill seeds or fresh dill (and/or 2 or 3 flowers), divided

5 cloves garlic, peeled and whole, divided

6 peppercorns, divided

3¾ cups (890 mL) small cucumbers, whole and cleaned

2 Tbsp (30 mL) whey (optional)

1. First make the brine by dissolving pickling salt in water. Line a clean, wide-mouthed 4-cup (1-L) glass jar with grape leaves, if you have any—these will help keep the pickles crunchy. Place half of the dill, garlic cloves and peppercorns in the bottom of the jar. Fill with cucumbers to halfway, then place the other half of the dill, garlic cloves and peppercorns on top. Fill with remaining cucumbers, no more than 1 inch (2.5 cm) from top of jar.

2. Pour brine into jar, making sure it completely covers the cucumbers. Top with whey, if using. Fill a small narrow-mouthed glass jar with water. Place inside the opening of the pickle jar to keep the cucumbers submerged in the brine. Cover the top with cheesecloth and seal with an elastic.

3. Leave the jar somewhere visible and check the pickles every day or 2. Remove any mould growing on the surface (a bit of white mould growth is normal and not harmful; don't worry). After about a week, start tasting the pickles until they reach a flavour you like. When they are just sour enough, put an airtight lid on the jar and the jar in the refrigerator. The pickles will last for 3 months or more.

MAKES 1 X 4-CUP (1-L) JAR OF PICKLES

PINK KOHLRABI CABBAGE SAUERKRAUT

Sauerkraut is one of the easiest and most common lactic-acid ferments to make. If you've never had homemade sauerkraut, it's nothing like the limp, vinegary stuff you get at the street meat stand. Homemade sauerkraut has a much more complex flavour with a balance between tart, salty and sweet. Using homegrown kohlrabi, which keeps a nice crispness after the ferment, this is our variation on traditional sauerkraut. Chris and I also add red cabbage, which finishes the kraut with a fun pink colour. This sauerkraut makes a perfect condiment for sandwiches or added to the table at dinner, especially for foods like sausages that are nicely complemented by mustard.

2 large kohlrabi, finely chopped
1 head red cabbage, finely chopped
About ¼ cup (60 mL) salt (or more if you prefer
 saltier sauerkraut)
3 Tbsp (45 mL) pickling spice

1. In a large ceramic crock with lid, add a 1.5 to
   2–inch (3.8 to 5-cm) layer of shredded kohlrabi
   and cabbage, then pound the veggies with a large
   muddler or fermenting pounder if you have one
   (we use a wine bottle).

2. Generously sprinkle on salt and a pinch of
   pickling spice, then add another layer of veggies

and repeat. Once you've reached the top of the crock, or run out of veggies, make sure the liquid level is above the solid veggie bits. Use a small plate that fits into the crock and weigh down with a bowl filled with water. How long you let it ferment is up to personal taste.

3. Taste it after a few days, after 1 week, after 2
   weeks and so on until it's just right for you. The
   length of fermentation depends on how sour you
   like your sauerkraut—the longer you leave it to
   ferment, the sourer it will be. We let ours ferment
   for 2 to 6 weeks. You may notice white or green
   mould growth around the top of the liquid. This
   is normal but should be removed, especially
   if it is touching any solids. Also remove soft
   or mouldy parts and make sure all solids are
   covered by liquid.

4. Once it has reached the flavour you prefer,
   transfer the sauerkraut into clean jars and into
   the fridge, where it will store for 3 months or
   more.

MAKES 4 CUPS (1 L)

SEAWEED KIMCHI

This naturally fermented kimchi-style pickled condiment is a delicious addition to sandwiches and suppers, and just as beautiful as it is nutritious. Forage for a brown marine algae, such as ubiquitous bladderwrack or rockweed, which tend to be tougher than green algae and lend themselves better to pickling and fermenting (see Wild and Invasive Edibles at the Seashore, page 48). Seaweed often contains large amounts of gelatinous substances (so much so, they are used commercially to make foaming tooth-paste), so don't worry if the mixture is rather gluey to start with. I find this gelatin lends itself well to kimchi-style ferments, which traditionally use a pastry-flour base anyway. See photo of recipe on page 63.

2 cups (475 mL) rockweed
1 head green cabbage, sliced
1 head red cabbage, sliced
¼ cup (60 mL) pickling salt
2 cups (475 mL) fresh water
¼ cup (60 mL) flour (rice flour is most traditional, but wheat works too)
¼ cup (60 mL) puréed fresh ginger root
8 garlic cloves, puréed
¼ cup (60 mL) puréed onions (about half a medium onion)
1 Tbsp (15 mL) hot pepper flakes (optional)

1. Rinse the freshly collected seaweed by running under tap water to remove any debris or lingering marine water, then slice.

2. Dry salt the sliced cabbage and seaweed by adding the salt and veggies in layers to a large bowl. Leave for a few hours, mixing once or twice. This will soften the seaweed and cabbage. After the dry salting process, rinse thoroughly to remove the excess salt.

3. Create the base for the kimchi by first mixing the flour with water and heating to a simmer on the stovetop, stirring until it thickens. Take off heat, let cool, then mix in ginger, garlic, onions and pepper flakes (if using).

4. Add the base to the rinsed cabbage and seaweed, mixing together. Taste and add salt and hot pepper flakes to desired taste.

5. Pack the mixture into a 4-cup (1-L) crock or glass jar, making sure all the solids are beneath the liquids. I use a smaller jar full of water to weigh down the solids.

6. Cover with crock top, jar lid or cheesecloth, and let the mixture ferment at room temperature for about 3 days, or until it turns a lovely purple and seems to have mixed together. At this point, you can remove any surface moulds (these are normal and not dangerous), put the kimchi in a fresh jar and stick it in the fridge to enjoy right away. Or seal the jar and put it in the back of the fridge to slowly ferment and produce carbon dioxide for a couple of weeks, which will create the coolest fizzy purple seaweed condiment you've ever tasted. Maybe also the only one you've ever tasted.

MAKES 4 CUPS (1 L)

DAIRY

Okay, I'll admit it. My favourite food is cheese. If I could only eat one kind of food for the rest of my life, it would almost certainly be cheese. Cheese goes with everything—cheese and wine, cheese and beer, cheese and cake, cheese on pizza, cheese in soup, cheese and eggs, cheese in salad, cheese in pasta . . . So one of the things I wanted to do most while homesteading was to get raw milk and make my own cheese, as well as other dairy ferments like yogurt and kefir.

Not all cheeses involve fermentation. Unaged cheeses like ricotta, paneer, cottage cheese and quick mozzarella simply require a coagulant (like lemon juice, vinegar or rennet) to curdle the milk so you can separate the curds (the cheese) from the whey (the liquid).

It's in the fermented cheeses like chèvre, cheddar and Swiss that the real flavours happen. Milk contains a sugar called lactose, so adding a bacterial culture (*Lactobacillus* and other bacteria, depending on the cheese) will break down the lactose into lactic acid and enzymes as the cheese ages, giving each type its unique flavour. For mould-ripened cheeses, different forms of fungi (moulds) are also introduced, either within the cheese, such as with blue cheese, or on the outside, as with brie and camembert. These fungi add flavour while softening the texture of the really creamy cheeses.

Through our homesteading adventures, Chris and I have discovered that making good cheese is difficult, and takes more than high-quality ingredients and recipes. It requires some skill, and this has to be learned from a mentor or through a lot of trial and error. So, in this book, I'm only including easier dairy ferments, including yogurt, kefir, ricotta, paneer, mozzarella, feta and a farmer's cheese that's similar to cheddar.

Don't throw out all the whey that's left over from cheese making—it can be used to start lactic-acid ferments for sauerkraut and pickles, or added to homemade bread in the place of water. Whey is full of protein and makes a great nutritional supplement for chickens (and pigs, if you're lucky enough to have them). It will keep in the fridge for up to three days.

TYPES OF MILK FOR DAIRY FERMENTS

The type of milk you use for fermenting is very important. First of all, the flavour of the milk will affect your finished product, so start with milk you think tastes good, whether it is from a cow or a goat. Whole milk makes for the richest-tasting cheeses with the best textures.

It is also very important to know whether or not the milk has been pasteurized. Commercially, milk is pasteurized by being heated to high temperatures in order to kill any potential unwanted microorganisms. This isn't inherently required to make milk safe; it is only a precaution taken by our modern dairy industry because of the health risks large-scale production, processing and transport can pose. Raw milk is perfectly safe, given it has been handled and stored properly.

The problem with pasteurization for the dairy fermenter is that it can kill the good microorganisms in the milk that allow the cultures to ferment to their best taste and consistency. Ultra-high temperature pasteurization is the worst for dairy fermenters because it destroys the chemical structure of the milk, making it unable to coagulate properly. If you can get raw milk (or have your own dairy animals), there is no need to pasteurize your milk before using it for dairy ferments—raw milk will work well for any type of ferment.

The next best thing is organic milk that has been pasteurized at lower temperatures, which you can use to make most dairy ferments if you add calcium chloride, but the cultured cheeses (such as feta, cheddar and aged cheeses) may not turn out as well. Avoid ultra-high temperature pasteurized milks. If this is all you have access to, however, you can try making yogurt and kefir but the other dairy ferments won't work. Each dairy company will process its milk differently, so ask the farmer or your local grocer, or read the label carefully to see if the milk is raw, pasteurized (known as HTST) or ultra-high temperature pasteurized (known as UHT).

Getting started

What you need will depend on what kind of dairy ferment you are making:

For yogurt, you can use storebought plain yogurt as your starter, which contains live cultures, and a non-reactive pot.

For kefir, start with kefir grains that you can buy or get from a friend, and a glass jar.

Cheeses can take more specialized ingredients. Cheese salt, which is used in most recipes, is typically non-iodized, fine-ground table salt. For ricotta, paneer, queso fresco and mozzarella, you need only add a coagulant, which could be lemon juice or vinegar, but citric acid and rennet work the best and are available from cheese-making suppliers. For feta and farmer's cheese, cheese-making ingredients can be ordered online or purchased from a cheese-making store if there is one close to you. These ingredients include lipase, calcium chloride, cheese starter (or culture) and rennet, as well as (optional) cheese moulds and wax. If you are using storebought milk to make cheese, it is a good idea to add calcium chloride to counteract the effects of pasteurization and cold storage during shipping.

In terms of equipment for cheese making, you need a non-reactive pot; a thermometer; a long knife to cut the curds; a slotted spoon to remove the curds; cheesecloth and a colander to drain the curds; and maybe a setup to press the cheese, depending on the type of cheese. If you are making cheese regularly, you may want to invest in a cheese press, which allows you to set the pressure and increase it as the press progresses. However, cheese presses are expensive, and you can achieve the same effect by pressing the cheese between two flat surfaces (such as cutting boards) and weighing down with heavy objects (such as books).

Opposite: Chris and I like to start all of our dairy ferments with fresh raw milk. While miniature dairy goats are allowed in some cities (like Seattle), another option for city dwellers is to source fresh raw milk through a local goat or cow share program (see page 145 for more information).

EASY GREEK-STYLE YOGURT

Yogurt is one of the simplest dairy ferments to make. You don't need a specialized starter to get things going—just use a spoonful of your previous batch or even storebought organic Greek-style yogurt, which contains live cultures. You can purchase a specialized yogurt-making appliance, which keeps the milk and culture warm while it ferments, but I simply use a warm water bath in the sink, or you can use the oven on a very low setting. I've even heard of people wrapping their yogurt pot tenderly in hot water bottles and towels. Whatever works for you is fine.

4 cups (1 L) whole cow or goat milk (see Types of Milk for Dairy Ferments, page 237)

1 Tbsp (15 mL) tapioca, pectin or gelatin for thickening (optional)
2 Tbsp (30 mL) yogurt

1. Add thickener (if using) to milk in a non-reactive stockpot. Heat on medium on the stovetop to 180F (82C), stirring constantly to prevent scalding. Remove from heat and let cool to 110F (43C).

2. Meanwhile, fill the kitchen sink halfway with hot water at a temperature of 110F (43C). If your tap water isn't warm enough, add boiling water to reach the right temperature.

3. Add yogurt to milk and stir well. Place pot in hot water bath in sink, making sure the water doesn't come over the sides of the pot. Cover and let ripen for 6 to 8 hours. Check the temperature every 30 minutes or so to maintain the temperature of 110F (43C). After 6 hours, start to taste. Remove from water bath when desired flavour and consistency is reached. The yogurt will become firmer and increasingly sour the longer it is allowed to ferment.

4. Transfer to a clean glass jar, cover with lid and store in refrigerator for up to 2 weeks. Reserve 2 to 3 tablespoons (30 to 45 mL) of yogurt to make your next batch.

MAKES 4 CUPS (1 L) YOGURT

EFFERVESCENT MILK KEFIR

Another favourite, kefir is even easier to make than yogurt. If you've never had kefir, it's a real treat, kind of like a mild effervescent liquid yogurt—and there is no doubt that homemade is far better than storebought. To make kefir, you need to start with kefir "grains" which are small colonies of a symbiotic yeast and bacterial culture. You can't make this yourself, so ask friends, or order online.

2 cups (475 mL) whole cow or
   goat milk (see Types of Milk for
   Dairy Ferments, page 237)

2 Tbsp (30 mL) kefir grains

1. In a clean glass jar, add the kefir grains to the milk and stir. Cover with an airtight lid. Leave on the counter for at least 12 hours and up to 2 days (warmer rooms will create a faster ferment). Loosen the lid to allow built-up carbon dioxide to be released, and shake twice a day to enhance the ferment. Taste after 12 hours and every few hours after that until it has reached a texture and consistency you like.

2. Strain out the solids—these are the grains you will use for the next batch, so do not discard them. The strained kefir is now ready to enjoy. It will keep in the fridge in an airtight container for a week or two.

3. Add milk to the solids you strained out, which are the kefir grains. Cover with an airtight lid and either leave on the counter to start another batch of kefir, or put the grains and milk into the fridge to slow them down until you are ready to make another batch. Keep your culture happy in the fridge by straining out the grains and feeding them fresh milk at least once a week. If you aren't making kefir that often, you can dehydrate or freeze your grains between uses.

MAKES 2 CUPS (475 ML)

PLUM, HONEY, BOURBON & KEFIR POPS

Remember the Creamsicle? These frozen pops are like the grown-up version.
Careful—they pack a punch! You can also make these without the bourbon (but
what's the fun in that?)—simply sub out the booze with fruit juice.

8 cups (2 L) plums
1 cup (250 mL) honey
2 Tbsp (30 mL) water
¼ tsp (1 mL) cinnamon

3 oz (90 mL) bourbon
2 oz (60 mL) Effervescent Milk
   Kefir, recipe on page 241
3 Tbsp (45 mL) grated orange zest

1. In a small saucepan over medium heat, cook plums, honey, water and cinnamon until plums soften and stew, about 10 minutes. Take off heat and let the mixture cool completely. Strain solids out.

2. In an ice-pop tray, pour ½ ounce (15 mL) of chilled bourbon into each mould, fill almost to top with plum mixture and stir. Drizzle kefir into each pop and sprinkle with orange zest. Top with handles and pop into the freezer.

MAKES 6

RICOTTA, PANEER & QUESO FRESCO

One of the main reasons Chris and I eventually decided to get a little country cottage was because we dreamed of having room for goats so that we could use their raw milk to make cheese. Now that we've got the goats and the kids and the milk, we have discovered that making good cheese is rather difficult. Oops. But ricotta is actually a very easy type of cheese to start with, and one that doesn't require a special cheese culture. Paneer and queso fresco are simply the pressed forms of ricotta, common in Indian and Mexican cuisine.

16 cups (4 L) whole cow or goat milk (see Types of Milk for Dairy Ferments, page 237)
1 cup (250 mL) heavy cream
¼ tsp (1 mL) liquid rennet, diluted in ¼ cup (60 mL) water (or juice from 2 lemons)
½ tsp (2.5 mL) baking soda
3 Tbsp (45 mL) butter, melted
Non-iodized salt to taste

1. Heat the milk and cream over low heat in a non-reactive pot, such as stainless steel or enameled, to just under a boil (195F/90C). Stir often to avoid scalding, and do not boil.

2. Turn off the heat and stir in the rennet (or lemon juice) slowly, stirring up and down rather than in circles. Allow the mixture to stand until it curdles, which it should start to do immediately. As it coagulates, the curds (solids) in the milk separate from the whey (liquid). It will be ready when the liquid is no longer milky, which should be immediate with rennet or may take up to 10 minutes with lemon juice.

3. Using a slotted spoon, transfer the curds into a colander lined with cheesecloth to drain off the whey. Reserve some of the whey to start lactic-acid ferments, or feed it all to the chickens (or pigs) if you have them. Let the cheese drain for 20 to 30 minutes.

4. To make ricotta, place the curds into a bowl, mixing in melted butter, baking soda and salt. Store in an airtight container in the fridge.

5. To make paneer and queso fresco, add the extra step of cinching the cheesecloth into a bag and placing the bag under a weight (bowl filled with water) for 30 to 45 minutes to squeeze out any excess liquid. Store in an airtight container in the fridge. For serving, cut into cubes and lightly sauté in butter for added flavour.

MAKES ABOUT 1½ CUPS (350 ML)

30-MINUTE MOZZARELLA

The quick and dirty way to make mozzarella, resulting in an easy meltable cheese. Mozzarella is a bit more difficult to make than ricotta or paneer because it requires two specialized ingredients for cheese making: citric acid and rennet. However, both of these can be ordered online, and this cheese is fairly foolproof and doesn't require aging. Start with good milk—see Types of Milk for Dairy Ferments (page 237). Chris has become a master at stretching and twisting the mozza so it forms into ropes of delicious string cheese, or we form it into balls like bocconcini for pizza and sandwiches.

16 cups (4 L) whole cow or goat milk (see Types of Milk for Dairy Ferments, page 237)
1½ tsp (7.5 mL) citric acid dissolved in ¼ cup (60 mL) water
¼ tsp (1 mL) liquid rennet diluted in ¼ cup (60 mL) water
Cheese salt, to taste

1. Heat milk over low heat in a large non-reactive pot, such as stainless steel or enameled. Using a good thermometer to monitor temperature, once it reaches 55F (13C), add the citric acid and stir thoroughly. At 90F (32C), add the rennet, stirring up and down rather than in a circle.

2. Continue to heat the milk until it reaches 100F (38C), then turn off the heat and remove the curds with a slotted spoon into a bowl. Once the curds have been removed, turn the heat back on under the pot of whey and heat to about 170F (77C).

3. Meanwhile, gently press the remaining liquid from the curds with your hands. Once the whey is hot, put the ball of curd back in using the slotted spoon and wait for it to get almost too hot to touch (rubber gloves help). Pull it out, then knead and stretch it like taffy until it starts to cool and break apart. Put it back in the hot whey, then remove it and repeat until it's smooth, shiny and looks like taffy when you stretch it (should take 2 or 3 times). Roll into small balls or twist into ropes and store in the refrigerator for up to a week (or eat warm!).

MAKES 2 CUPS (475 ML)

CHIVE & CHEESE-STUFFED
DAYLILY BUDS

Wow guests with these delicious stuffed daylily flower buds (Hemerocallis fulva, see page 32), which are an exciting foraging find in the summer. You can also use squash flowers. Hot, crispy and gooey inside, stuffed flower buds are a creative way to enjoy two easy homestead cheeses (see pages 245 and 246). If you've been wondering what to do with the crusts of the amazing sourdough bread you've been making, worry no more. Chop up the stale bread and pulse it in the food processor until you have breadcrumbs, then simply store in a jar in the freezer until needed for this flowery feast.

½ cup (120 mL) ricotta cheese, recipe on page 245

¼ cup (60 mL) grated 30-minute Mozzarella, recipe on page 246

2 Tbsp (30 mL) chopped chives

1 garlic clove, minced

8 daylily buds

1 cup (250 mL) dry breadcrumbs

2 eggs

¼ cup (60 mL) olive oil

Coarse salt

Freshly ground pepper

1. Mix together ricotta, grated mozzarella, chives and garlic, and transfer to a plastic bag with the bottom corner cut off. Squeeze the cheese mixture into the daylily buds.

2. Place breadcrumbs in a wide, shallow bowl and whisk the eggs in another wide, shallow bowl. In a large skillet, heat oil over medium-high heat.

3. Dip each stuffed blossom into the egg, then roll in the breadcrumbs. Place the bud into the hot skillet and cook until golden brown, about 2 minutes per side.

4. Season with coarse salt and freshly ground pepper and serve hot.

SERVES 4

FARMER'S CHEESE

Okay, I admit it. I wanted to include a recipe for making a perfect creamy and sharp cheddar cheese . . . but didn't because we have yet to make one. Wah wah. But here is a fairly foolproof simple farmer's cheese that we use in place of cheddar.

16 cups (4 L) whole cow or goat milk (see Types of Milk for Dairy Ferments, page 237)
¼ tsp (1 mL) mesophilic starter
½ tsp (2.5 mL) rennet, diluted in ¼ cup (60 mL) water
4 Tbsp (60 mL) cheese salt, divided
Liquid cheese wax (optional)

1. Fill the sink about halfway with 90F (32C) water. Pour the milk into a large, non-reactive pot and place in the water bath, making sure the water doesn't come over the top of the pot. Let the water heat up the pot until the milk reaches 86F (30C) (the water will have cooled down by this time as well).

2. Add the starter and stir to dissolve. Cover and allow to ripen for 30 minutes. Periodically check the temperature and add more hot water to the sink to maintain the temperature at 86F (30C).

3. Add the diluted rennet, stirring up and down rather than in a circle to thoroughly mix. Cover and allow to set for 1 hour, again maintaining the temperature of the water bath at 86F (30C).

4. After 1 hour, check the set of the curds by cutting with a knife. If the curd is solid and moves as 1 piece when cut with the knife, it has set. Cut the curd with a long knife in a ½-inch (1.25-cm) grid all the way to the bottom of the pot. Allow to set for 15 minutes.

5. Drain some of the water from the water bath, then gradually add hot water to heat the curds to 98F (37C), raising the heat no more than 2 degrees every 5 minutes. Gently stir every 10 minutes and maintain the temperature at 98F (37C) for 45 minutes.

6. Next, use a slotted spoon or pour the curds into a colander lined with cheesecloth inside a large bowl. Save some of the whey to start lactic-acid ferments, or feed the rest to the chickens (or pigs) if you have them. Add 2 tablespoons (30 mL) of the cheese salt to the curds and stir gently.

7. Tie up the corners of the cheesecloth to form a bag and transfer into a cheese mould. Press the cheese at 20 lbs (9 kg) of pressure for 15 minutes (you can use heavy books on top of the mould if you don't have a fancy cheese press). After 15 minutes, turn the cheese over in the mould and press with 30 lbs (13.6 kg) of pressure for 1 hour. After an hour, flip the cheese again and press at 50 lbs (22.7 kg) of pressure overnight. Note that you can make this cheese without a mould by pressing the cheesecloth bag of curds between two flat surfaces (such as dinner plates). You just don't get a wheel of cheese as nicely shaped as you would using a mould.

8. In the morning, remove the cheese from the mould and peel away the cheesecloth. Rub remaining salt on all surfaces and let rest on cheese board for 2 days, turning twice a day.

9. At this point, the cheese is ready to eat as a fresh farmer's cheese. If you want to age the cheese to get a taste and texture more like cheddar, paint liquid cheese wax on all surfaces, using 3 or 4 coats. Age at room temperature for 4 to 12 weeks—the longer the cheese ages, the better the texture and taste. After cutting through the wax, keep the cheese in the fridge for up to 2 weeks.

MAKES 4 CUPS (1 L)

RABBIT, HOMEMADE MOZZARELLA & FORAGED GREENS PIZZA

For casual entertaining in the spring, summer and fall, this is an opportunity to share some of your foraging, keeping and preserving know-how. Give everyone homework to hunt for some weedy greens for the pizza. Have them look for chickweed, clover, dandelion, purslane and sorrel—any type of edible leafy green will work, and these are common in organically grown lawns and gardens. Then, get everyone together to make the dough and top the pizzas, carefully confirming each other's plant identification along the way. Experiment with other toppings too, and have your friends bring their own. Our favourite pizza includes rabbit and feta because we grow and make our own, but you could substitute quail or another local, ethical meat you can find, or skip the meat and pile on the veggies.

DOUGH
½ cup (120 mL) leaven (see Making Bread Leaven, page 214)
1½ cup (350 mL) warm water
2 cups (475 mL) flour
2 tsp (10 mL) salt
3 Tbsp (45 mL) Quick Herb-infused Olive Oil, recipe on page 196 (or use avocado oil)
1 small onion, minced
5 cloves garlic, minced
Cornmeal

TOPPINGS
Rustic Roasted Rabbit meat, chopped (recipe on page 95)
1 cup (250 mL) finely chopped foraged greens
1 tomato, thinly sliced
1 cup (250 mL) feta cheese
1 cup (250 mL) grated 30-minute Mozzarella, recipe on page 246
Balsamic vinegar glaze to taste

1. Mix leaven, water and flour with your hands. Allow to rest for 20 minutes. Add salt and mix again by hand. Let rise for 2 to 3 hours.

2. While the dough is rising, sauté onions and garlic in 1 Tbsp (15 mL) oil.

3. Before rolling out dough, preheat oven to 375F (190 C), with pizza stone inside if you have one.

4. Dust counter or tabletop with flour and place dough onto it. Split into halves. Roll each half out separately to fit your pizza stone or baking sheet. Sprinkle cornmeal onto your hot pizza stone or unheated baking sheet, and place dough on top. Brush dough with remaining oil and top with sautéed garlic and onions.

5. Bake for 5 minutes, then pull out to add toppings. Top the toasted pizza dough with half of the rabbit, greens and tomato, and sprinkle on half of the feta and mozzarella cheese, then pop it back in the oven to bake until the cheese melts and the crust turns a golden brown (about 12 to 15 more minutes).

6. Take pizza out of the oven and transfer to a wooden cutting board while you start the other pizza on the stone or baking sheet.

7. Drizzle the finished pizza with balsamic vinegar glaze and serve.

MAKES 2 X 14-INCH (36-CM) PIZZAS

CHEESE, BEER & PROSCIUTTO SOUP IN A SOURDOUGH BOWL

To showcase your awe-inspiring skills as a fermenter, use your own homemade cheese, beer, charcuterie and sourdough bread to make this hearty winter soup.

4 mini loaves of Rustic Rosemary Sourdough Bread, recipe on page 214
1 breast Dry-cured Goose Prosciutto, sliced and chopped (recipe on page 211)
1 Tbsp (15 mL) butter
2 celery stalks, finely chopped
1 large onion, finely chopped
2 large garlic cloves, minced
1 Tbsp (15 mL) fresh thyme, minced, plus leaves for garnish
¼ cup (60 mL) flour
12 oz (355 mL) Sassy Elderflower Saison Homebrew Beer, recipe on page 221, divided (or use a pilsner or even a stout beer, but avoid hoppy brews)
2 cups (475 mL) Rabbit Stock, recipe on page 93 (or use quail or chicken stock)
1 cup (250 mL) heavy cream
2 cups (475 mL) Farmer's Cheese, shredded (recipe on page 249)

1. Prepare the sourdough bread bowls by cutting the top off four small loaves of sourdough and scooping out the soft interior. Reserve for other recipes, or serve with the soup.

2. In a large stockpot or Dutch oven, crisp the prosciutto and thyme leaves for garnish over medium heat. Transfer to a dish, reserving the rendered fat in the pot. Add butter, celery, onion, garlic and thyme. Sauté until slightly softened. Add flour and cook for 5 minutes until onions are translucent.

3. Add half the beer and simmer to reduce by half, about 5 minutes. Add the stock and bring to just under a boil. Slowly add the heavy cream, cheese and remaining beer until just boiling. Reduce heat and simmer until thickened, about 5 minutes. Stir in the prosciutto, reserving some for garnish.

4. Pour the soup into the sourdough bowls, and garnish with crisped thyme leaves and reserved prosciutto.

SERVES 4

ACKNOWLEDGEMENTS

First and foremost, I must acknowledge the immense contribution of my partner, Chris Mull, in all my homesteading and cooking adventures. The completion of this book is as much a testament to his courage, vision and hard work as it is to my writing these words. I couldn't have done it without your ready humour, tireless help and endless support, Poochy, thank you.

I also want to recognize the assistance of my brilliant family, who have all taught me so much and supported my crazy projects: my obliging and talented dad, my industrious and sensible mom, my remarkable and capable uncle Eric, and my brother and fellow DIY food explorer, Ryan.

My heartfelt thanks to the very talented Alison Page for the many hours of brainstorming and styling these photographs with me (we had so much fun!), and for her beautiful, skilled photography. Also, my deepest gratitude to my editor, Carol Pope, for her kind words of support and keen eye. I would also like to thank Nicola Goshulak for her careful editing of the recipes, Patricia Wolfe for her attentive proofreading, Diane Robertson for the cover and text design, Roger Handling for his design and typesetting skills, and Anna Comfort O'Keeffe and the rest of the team at Douglas & McIntyre.

Warm gratitude also to our neighbours, the Sander Family, for their help (especially from Milan) and patience with our many outdoor projects. Thanks to Amanda Kissel and Rylee Murray for their assistance and ideas, and for taking us out bullfrog hunting. And to the many others who have lent a hand along the way, thank you for your indispensable contributions and inspiration: Jacob, Roe, Sharon Hanna, Sherri Elwell, Mike Beakes, Melinda Fowler, Corey Philis, Laurel and Rowan Trebilco, Jenny and Joel Harding, Steph Green, Duncan Frostick, Alejandro Frid, Jon Moore, Brendan Connors, Seb Ibarra, everyone in the barn-raising crew, Sophie St. Hilaire, Deb and Mac at McCarthy Park farm, Mike McDermid at the Fish Counter, Rick Havlak at the Homesteader's Emporium, Sam Philips and Lisa Giroday at Victory Gardens, Clemencia Braraten at Primrose Farms, Brock Dolman and Jim Coleman at Occidental Arts and Ecology Centre, and the incomparable forest-ecology guru, Andy MacKinnon.

INDEX

Page numbers in bold refer to photos
achira, 157, **158**
alfalfa, 149
almond
  Sea Salt, Toasted Almond and Dark
    Chocolate Spread, 160
  trees, 167
amaranth, 46, 47. *See also* greens dishes
appetizers
  Baked Brie, Roasted Garlic & Tree Tip Toffee,
    41
  Chive and Cheese-stuffed Daylily Buds, 247
  Homemade Wasabi Peas, 162
  Mussels Two Ways, 57
  Pickled Quail Eggs, **104**, 105
  Quail Stuffed Three Ways, **110**, 111, **112**,
    113, **114**, 115
  Sesame Panko-crusted Frog Legs, 67, **68**
  Smoked Chili Water Lotus and Taro Root
    Chips with Lemony Herb Dip, 159
  Smoked Wild Salmon Devilled Quail Eggs,
    109
apple tree, 167, 168, 199
apricot tree, 167
aquaponics, 116, 143, 148
  equipment, 117–18
  fish and other organisms, 117, **119**
  plants, grow bed and floating, 116, **119**, 120
  slaughter and processing of seafood, 118,
    120
  See also seafood and freshwater fish dishes
arrowhead. *See* wapato (arrowhead or duck
  potato)
arugula, 166, 173. *See also* greens dishes
asparagus, 31, 46
  Green Bean and Asparagus Gratin, 172
aquatic plants, edible, 155–**58**
autumnberry, 31, 47, 131, 187
azolla, 157, **160**
  Chilled Azolla and Watercress Soup, 161
Baked Brie, Roasted Garlic and Tree Tip
  Toffee, 41
bamboo, 31, 46, 164
basil, 149, 166, 173
bean, 164, 166, 167
beer. *See* brewing: beer
Bee's Knees Cocktail with Homemade Bitters,
  195
bee. *See* honey; honeybee keeping
beet, 149, 166, 231, 232
Bellini, Kombucha-Pickled Beet and Ginger,
  232, **232**
beverages. *See* drinks
Bisque, Crustacean, 121
bitters, 192
  Bee's Knees Cocktail with Homemade
    Bitters, 195
  Burdock Lavender Bitters, 195
black soldier fly, 138
blackberry. *See* Himalayan blackberry

Bloody Nero Cocktail with Pickled Quail Eggs,
  106, 107
blueberry, 31, 46, 47, 131, 167, 168, 187, 199
botulism, 188
bread, 212–13
  Cheese, Beer and Prosciutto Soup in a
    Sourdough Bowl, 251
  Making Bread Leaven, 214
  Rustic Rosemary Sourdough Bread, **213**,
    214–15
  sourdough starter, 212–13
brewing
  beer, 216, 218–19
    Beer Vinegar, 230
    California Drooling Cat Sessional IPA, 222
    Cheese, Beer and Prosciutto Soup in a
      Sourdough Bowl, 251
    Mussels Two Ways, 57
    Sassy Elderflower Saison Homebrew
      Beer, **220**, 221
  cider, 223
    Wild Blackberry Sparkling Cider, 224–25
  fruit wine, 223
    Uncarbonated Blackberry Wine, 225
Brie, Roasted Garlic and Tree Tip Toffee,
  Baked, 41
Brined and Coconut Miso Marinated Quail, 206
brining meat, 205
broccoli, 149, 166
Brown Butter Fiddleheads with Caramelized
  Cattail Shoots, **42**, 43
buckwheat, 149
bullfrog, 23, 65–66, 75
  Sesame Panko-crusted Frog Legs, 67, **68**
bulrush. *See* cattail
burdock, 31, 46, 47
  Burdock Lavender Bitters, 195
button mushroom, 152, **153**
cabbage, 166, 180
  Pink Kohlrabi Cabbage Sauerkraut, **234**,
    235
calendula, 180
California Drooling Cat Sessional IPA, 222
Canned Deer, 191
canning methods
  pressure, 190
  water-bath, 188
carrot, 149, 164, 166
carp
  aquaponics, 117, **119**
  invasive, 71, 75
catfish, 71, 75
cattail, 31, 46, 47, 157
  Brown Butter Fiddleheads with Caramelized
    Cattail Shoots, **42**, 43
cauliflower, 166
chamomile, 31, 46
  Forager's Tea, 37
charcuterie, 203–211
chard, 149, 166, 180

cheese
  Cheese, Beer and Prosciutto Soup in a
    Sourdough Bowl, 251
  Chive and Cheese-stuffed Daylily Buds, 247
  Farmer's Cheese, **248**, 249
  Ricotta, Paneer and Queso Fresco, **244**, 245
  30-minute Mozzarella, 246
  See also dairy fermentation
cherry tree, 167
chicken keeping
  backyard hens, regulations, 85
  eggs, 135
  feed, growing your own, 142
  See also meat dishes: poultry
chickweed, 31, 46. *See also* greens dishes
chicory, 31, 46, 47, 164. *See also* greens dishes
Chilled Azolla and Watercress Soup, 161
Chinese artichoke. *See* crosnes
Chinese mitten crab, 23, 49–50, 75
chives, 166, 173, 180
  Chive and Cheese-stuffed Daylily Buds, 247
chocolate
  Dark and Stormy Chocolate Cupcakes with
    Cricket Flour, **140**, 141
  Sea Salt, Toasted Almond and Dark
    Chocolate Spread, 169
Christmasberry. *See* wolfberry
cider. *See* brewing: cider
cilantro, 164, 166, 173
citrus tree, 167
clam, 23, 48–49
clover, 31, **36**, 46, 149, 164
  Forager's Tea, 37
  See also greens dishes
cocktails. *See* drinks
Coconut Curry Rabbit, 96
Confit de Canard (Duck Confit), 204
container gardening. *See* patio containers;
  vertical planting
corn tortillas, homemade, 72
coypu. *See* nutria
crab. *See* Chinese mitten crab; Dungeness crab;
  European green crab; foraging: seashore
crayfish
  in aquaponics, 117
  signal crayfish, 23, **64**, 71, 75
Creamy Braised Purple Loosestrife and
  Mushroom Risotto, 154
Creamy Roasted Peppers, Corn and Sorrel, 45
cricket
  Dark and Stormy Chocolate Cupcakes with
    Cricket Flour, **140**, 141
  Insect Flour, 139
  keeping, 136–37, 143
crimini mushroom, 152
Crispy Pan-fried Escargot and Arugula Salad,
  70
crosnes, 174
  Gingered Perennial Root Vegetable Soup,
    179
Crustacean Bisque, 121

cucumber, 166, 167
  Kosher-style Cucumber Slow Pickles, 233
Cupcakes with Cricket Flour, Dark and Stormy
  Chocolate, **140**, 141
curing meat. *See* charcuterie
curly dock, 32, 45, 46
  Fire-cooked Wild Salmon with Creamy Dock
    Sauce, 79.
  See also greens dishes
currant, 167, 180
dairy fermentation, 237–38
  Cheese, Beer and Prosciutto Soup in a
    Sourdough Bowl, 251
  Chive and Cheese-stuffed Daylily Buds, 247
  Easy Greek-style Yogurt, 240
  Effervescent Milk Kefir, 241
  Farmer's Cheese, **248**, 249
  Plum, Honey, Bourbon and Kefir Pops, **242**,
    243
  Ricotta, Paneer and Queso Fresco, **244**, 245
  30-minute Mozzarella, 246
dairy share, goat or cow, 145, 238
dandelion, 32, 46, 47, 164. *See also* greens
  dishes
Dark and Stormy Chocolate Cupcakes with
  Cricket Flour, **140**, 141
daylily, 32, 46, 47
  Chive and Cheese-stuffed Daylily Buds, 247
deer. *See* meat dishes: wild game
desserts
  Dark and Stormy Chocolate Cupcakes with
    Cricket Flour, **140**, 141
  Fig and Fennel Clafoutis, **170**, 171
  Patio Container Peach and Cardamom Crisp,
    168
  Plum, Honey, Bourbon and Kefir Pops, **242**,
    243
  Roasted Japanese Knotweed Pannacotta,
    22
  Sea Salt, Toasted Almond and Dark
    Chocolate Spread, 169
Devilled Quail Eggs, Smoked Wild Salmon, 109
dill, dwarf, 164, 166
drinks
  Bee's Knees Cocktail with Homemade
    Bitters, 195
  Bloody Nero Cocktail with Pickled Quail
    Eggs, **106**, 107
  California Drooling Cat Sessional IPA, 222
  Effervescent Milk Kefir, 241
  Field Mint Kombucha, 229
  Forager's Tea, 37
  Himalayan Blackberry, Mint and Pepper
    Shrub, **226**, 227
  Kombucha-Pickled Beet and Ginger Bellini,
    232, **232**
  Rhubarb Gin Fauxtini Cocktail, 194
  Rhubarb-Infused Gin, **193**, 194
  Sassy Elderflower Saison Homebrew Beer,
    220, 221
  Uncarbonated Blackberry Wine, 225

Vancouver Rain Latte, **38**, 39
    Wild Blackberry Sparkling Cider, 224–25
Dry-cured Goose Prosciutto, 211
drying, as food preservation method, 198
    Dry-cured Goose Prosciutto, 211
    Seasonal Fruit Leather, 199, 200, 201
    Sun-dried Tomatoes with Rosemary in
      Olive Oil, 198
    Teriyaki Pineapple Rabbit Jerky, 202
duck
    Confit de Canard (Duck Confit), 204
    preserving, 207, 210
    Stovetop Maple-Smoked Duck Breast, 208
duck potato. *See* wapato (arrowhead or duck
    potato)
duckweed, 157
Dungeness crab, 23, **50**, 50–51
    Steamed Dungeness Crab with Garlic Butter,
      52–53, 54
Easy Greek-style Yogurt, 240
Easy Strawberry Freezer Jam, **186**, 187
edible landscaping, 148, 180
edible flowers, 31–35, 46–47, 120
    Foraged Spring Greens Salad, **28**, 29
    Forager's Tea, 37
Effervescent Milk Kefir, 241
eggplant, 166
egg
    Bloody Nero Cocktail with Pickled Quail
      Eggs, **106**, 107
    Fig and Fennel Clafoutis, **170**, 171
    Hard-Boiled Quail Eggs, 105
    Pickled Quail Eggs, **104**, 105
    Smoked Wild Salmon Devilled Quail Eggs,
      109
    See also chicken keeping; quail keeping
elder (shrub, berry and flower), 32, 47, **217**
    Sassy Elderflower Saison Homebrew Beer,
      220, 221
Enchiladas, Pulled Poultry, 144
escargot. *See* snails
European green crab, 23, 55–56, 75
European grove and garden snail. *See* snails
Farmer's Cheese, **248**, 249
fennel, 32, 46, 47, **170**
    Fig and Fennel Clafoutis, **170**, 171
    Foraged Spring Greens Salad, **28**, 29
fermentation, 212
    beer, cider and fruit wines, 216
    dairy, 237–38
    kombucha, 228
    lactic acid (slow pickles), 233
    meat. *See* prosciutto
    shrubs, 225
    sourdough, 212–214
    vinegar, 230
fiddlehead fern, 32, 46, 180
    Brown Butter Fiddleheads with Caramelized
      Cattail Shoots, **42**, 43
    See also greens dishes
field cress. *See* field mustard
field guide, 20, 21, 47
Field Mint Kombucha, 229
field mustard, 32, 46, 47. *See also* greens dishes
fig
    Fig and Fennel Clafoutis, **170**, 171
    tree, 167

Fire-Cooked Wild Salmon with Creamy Dock
    Sauce, **78**, 79
fireweed, 32, 46. *See also* greens dishes
fir tips. *See* tree tips
fish. *See* aquaponics; carp; catfish; lionfish;
    seafood and freshwater fish dishes
food forests, 148, 163–64, 166–67, 173
Foraged Spring Greens Salad, **28**, 29
Forager's Tea, 37
foraging
    freshwater and inland invasive animals, 20,
      21, **64**, 65–66, 69, 71,
    plants, 15, **18**, 23, 20–21, 26–27, 30, 31–35,
      46–47
    seashore, 20, 21, 48–51, 55–56; 58, **59**, 61
    See also invasive species
forcemeat, 203
Freezer Jam, Easy Strawberry, **186**, 187
freezing, as food preservation method, 184
frog. *See* bullfrog
Fruit Leather, Seasonal, 199, **200**, **201**
fruit trees
    dwarf varieties, 167
    See also food forests; *and individual species*
fruit wine, 223. *See also* brewing: fruit wine
garden sorrel. *See* sorrel
garlic, 149, 164, 166
garlic mustard, 32, 46, 47.
Gingered Perennial Root Vegetable Soup, 179
glasswort. *See* sea asparagus
goji berry. *See* wolfberry
goldenrod, 32, 46, 47. *See also* edible flowers;
    greens dishes
good King Henry, 174, 180
goose
    Dry-cured Goose Prosciutto, 211
    fermenting, 210
    smoking, 207
gooseberry, 180
goosefoot. *See* lamb's quarters
Granola, Honeyed Coconut (with Homemade
    Yogurt), 131
grape, 167, 180
Green Bean and Asparagus Gratin, 172
greens, cooking shortlist, 46
greens dishes
    Brown Butter Fiddleheads with Caramelized
      Cattail Shoots, 43
    Chilled Azolla and Watercress Soup, 161
    Creamy Braised Purple Loosestrife and
      Mushroom Risotto, 154
    Creamy Roasted Peppers, Corn and Sorrel,
      45
    Fire-Cooked Wild Salmon with Creamy Dock
      Sauce, 79
    Foraged Spring Greens Salad, 29
    Miso-Creamed Perennial Greens, 181
    Rabbit, Homemade Mozzarella and Foraged
      Greens Pizza, 250
    Smoked Chili Water Lotus and Taro Root
      Chips with Lemony Herb Dip, 159
    Stinging Nettle Pesto, 19, **19**
    Tree Collard, Mint and Microgreen Salad
      with Peanut Dressing, 151
    Wild Greens Pasta with Periwinkle Sea
      Snails, 60

groundnut, 174
    Gingered Perennial Root Vegetable Soup,
      179
Hard-Boiled Quail Eggs, 105
Himalayan blackberry, 33, 46, 47, 187, **217**
    Foraged Spring Greens Salad, **28**, 29
    Himalayan Blackberry, Mint and Pepper
      Shrub, **226**, 227
    Seasonal Fruit Leather, 199, **200**, **201**
    Uncarbonated Blackberry Wine, 225
    Wild Blackberry Sparkling Cider, 224–25
Homemade Wasabi Peas, 162
honey
    Bee's Knees Cocktail with Homemade
      Bitters, 195
    Honeyed Coconut Granola (with Homemade
      Yogurt), 131
    infusing with herbs, 192
    Plum, Honey, Bourbon and Kefir Pops, 243
    Salmon Smoked Outdoors with Black Tea
      and Honey, 209
    Wild Rosehip and Spice-Infused Honey, 133
    See also honeybee keeping: processing
      honey and beeswax
honeybee keeping, 125–29, 143
    bee gardens, 126
    equipment, 128
    hives and bee handling, 126–28
    processing honey and beeswax, 128–29
hops, **36**, 164, 167, 180, **210**, **216**
    California Drooling Cat Sessional IPA, 222
    Forager's Tea, 37
    Old-fashioned Jelly with Currants and Hops,
      189
    Sassy Elderflower Saison Homebrew Beer,
      220, 221
    See also brewing: beer
huckleberry, 31, 46, 47, 131, 187, 199
infusions, 192
    honey
      Wild Rosehip and Spice-Infused Honey,
        133
    oil
      Quick Herb-infused Olive Oil, 196
      Slow Pine-infused Avocado Oil, 197
    spirits
      Burdock Lavender Bitters, 195
      Rhubarb-Infused Gin, **193**, 194
Insect Flour, 139
insect keeping, 134–37
Invasive Game Carnitas Tacos, 72
invasive species, 18, 20, 21
    animals, 23, 49, 55, 58, 65–66, 69, 71, 75
    plants, 31–35
Japanese knotweed, 21, 27, 30, 33, 46, **123**,
    168, 194
    Japanese Knotweed Chutney on Pan-seared
      Trout, 122
    Roasted Japanese Knotweed Pannacotta,
      22
Japanese silverberry. *See* autumnberry
Japanese sweet flag, 157
Jelly with Currants and Hops, Old-Fashioned,
    189
Jerusalem artichoke. *See* sunchoke
kale, 79, 149, 166, 174, 175, 194
    Rabbit and Kale Stew, **176**, 177

kefir, 241
    Effervescent Milk Kefir, 241
    Plum, Honey, Bourbon and Kefir Pops, 243
Kimchi, Seaweed, 236
kiwi tree, dwarf, 167
kohlrabi, 166, **234**, 235
    Pink Kohlrabi Cabbage Sauerkraut, **234**,
      235
kombucha, 228
    Field Mint Kombucha, 229
    Kombucha-Pickled Beet and Ginger Bellini,
      232, **232**
    Kombucha-Pickled Beets, 231
Kosher-style Cucumber Slow Pickles, 233
kudzu, 33, 46, 47, 131. *See also* greens dishes
lactic-acid fermentation, 233
    Kosher-style Cucumber Slow Pickles, 233
    Pink Kohlrabi Cabbage Sauerkraut, **234**,
      235
    Seaweed Kimchi, 236
lady fern. *See* fiddlehead ferns
lamb's quarters, 33, 46, 47, 180. *See also* greens
    dishes
Latte, Vancouver Rain, **38**, 39
lavender, 164, 166, 180, 195
    Burdock Lavender Bitters, 195
leaven, bread, 214, 250
leek, 166
lemon balm, 33, **36**, 37, 227
lentil, 149
lettuce, 149, 166, 173, 180
licorice flag, 157
lionfish, 75
lion's mane mushrooms, 152, 153
main dishes
    Brined and Coconut Miso Marinated Quail,
      206
    Cheese, Beer and Prosciutto Soup in a
      Sourdough Bowl, 251
    Coconut Curry Rabbit, 96
    Creamy Braised Purple Loosestrife and
      Mushroom Risotto, 154
    Crustacean Bisque, 121
    Fire-Cooked Wild Salmon with Creamy Dock
      Sauce, **78**, 79
    Gingered Perennial Root Vegetable Soup,
      179
    Invasive Game Carnitas Tacos, 72
    Japanese Knotweed Chutney on Pan-seared
      Trout, 122
    Pressure-cooked Red Curry Deer, 73
    Pulled Poultry Enchiladas, 144
    Rabbit, Homemade Mozzarella and Foraged
      Greens Pizza, 250
    Rabbit and Kale Stew, **176**, 177
    Rustic Roasted Rabbit, **94**, 95
    Sesame Panko-crusted Frog Legs, 67, **68**
    Steamed Dungeness Crab with Garlic Butter,
      52–53, 54
    Wild Greens Pasta with Periwinkle Sea
      Snails, 60
maitake mushroom, 153
maple, **24–25**, 33, 46, 47, 131
    Foraged Spring Greens Salad, **28**, 29
mealworm
    Insect Flour, 139
    keeping, 135–37, 143

meat dishes
  poultry
    Brined and Coconut Miso Marinated Quail, 206
    Confit de Canard (Duck Confit), 204
    Dry-cured Goose Prosciutto, 211
    Pulled Poultry Enchiladas, 144
    Quail Stuffed Three Ways, **110**, 111, **112**, **113**, **114**, 115
    Stovetop Maple-smoked Duck Breast, 208
  rabbit
    Coconut Curry Rabbit, 96
    Rabbit, Homemade Mozzarella and Foraged Greens Pizza, 250
    Rabbit and Kale Stew, **176**, 177
    Rabbit Pâté with Oyster Mushrooms, 97
    Rabbit Stock, 93
    Rustic Roasted Rabbit, **94**, 95
    Teriyaki Pineapple Rabbit Jerky, 202
  wild game
    Canned Deer, 191
    Invasive Game Carnitas Tacos, 72
    Pressure-cooked Red Curry Deer, 73
  See also seafood and freshwater fish dishes
melon, dwarf, 166, 167
microgreens, 148–49
  Tree Collard, Mint and Microgreen Salad with Peanut Dressing, **150**, 151
microlivestock, 82–83, 85, 142–43. See also aquaponics; honeybee keeping; insect keeping; quail keeping; rabbit keeping
miner's lettuce, 33, 46. See also greens dishes
mint, 33, 46, 164, 166
  Field Mint Kombucha, 229
  Foraged Spring Greens Salad, **28**, 29
  Forager's Tea, 37
  Himalayan Blackberry, Mint and Pepper Shrub, **226**, 227
  Tree Collard, Mint and Microgreen Salad with Peanut Dressing, **150**, 151
Miso-creamed Perennial Greens, 181
Mozzarella, 30-minute, 246. See also dairy fermentation
mugwort, 33, 46, 47
mung bean, 149
mushroom
  Creamy Braised Purple Loosestrife and Mushroom Risotto, 154
  foraging, 23
  growing, 148, 152–53
  Quail Stuffed Three Ways, **110**, 111, **112**, **113**, **114**, 115
  Rabbit Pâté with Oyster Mushrooms, 97
mussel, 23, 56, **56**
  Mussels Two Ways, 57
mustard, 47, 149
nasturtium, 166, 180
nectarine, 167
nettle. See stinging nettle
nutria, 71, 72, 75
nut tree, dwarf varieties, 167. See also food forests
oil infusions. See infusions: oil
Old-Fashioned Jelly with Currants and Hops, 189
olives, 167
onion, 149, 166

oregano, 164, 166, 173, 180
Oregon grape, 33, 46, 47, 187
ostrich fern. See fiddlehead ferns
oxalis. See sorrel
oxalic acid, 30
oxeye daisy, 34, 46, 47
oyster mushrooms, 152
  Rabbit Pâté with Oyster Mushrooms, 97
  See also mushrooms: growing
oyster, 23, 48, 49, 58, 76
paneer, 245
Pannacotta, Roasted Japanese Knotweed, 22
parsley, 164, 166, 173
parsnip, 164
pasta and pasta sauces
  Confit de Canard (Duck Confit), 204
  Stinging Nettle Pesto, 19, **19**
  Wild Greens Pasta with Periwinkle Sea Snails, 60
pâté, 203
  Quail Stuffed Three Ways, **110**, 111, **112**, **113**, **114**, 115
  Rabbit Pâté with Oyster Mushrooms, 97
patio container, 166–67
Patio Container Peach and Cardamom Crisp, 168
patio pond, 148, 155-156
peach
  Patio Container Peach and Cardamom Crisp, 168
  Seasonal Fruit Leather, 199
  tree, 167
pear
  Seasonal Fruit Leather, 199
  tree, 167
pea, 149, 164, 166, 167
pepper, 166, 180
perennial vegetables, growing, 173–75
periwinkle. See sea snail
Pesto, Stinging Nettle, **19**
pickle
  Kombucha-pickled Beets, 231
  Kosher-style Cucumber Slow Pickles, 233
  Pickled Quail Eggs, **104**, 105
  vinegar, 231
  See also fermentation: lactic acid
pigweed. See amaranth
pineapple weed, 34, 46
  Foraged Spring Greens Salad, **28**, 29
  Forager's Tea, 37
pine tips. See tree tips
Pink Kohlrabi Cabbage Sauerkraut, **234**, 235
Pizza, Rabbit, Homemade Mozzarella and Foraged Greens, 250
plantain, 34, 46. See also greens dishes
plum
  Plum, Honey, Bourbon and Kefir Pops, **242**, 243
  Seasonal Fruit Leather, 199
  tree, 167
pond plants. See aquatic plants, edible
portobello mushroom, 152, **153**
potato, 166

preserving food, 184. See also botulism; canning methods; charcuterie; drying, as food preservation method; infusions; fermentation; prosciutto; salting and brining meat; smoking, as food preservation method
pressure canning, 190
Pressure-cooked Red Curry Deer, 73
prickly pear cactus, 34, 46, 47, 131
prosciutto, 210
  Cheese, Beer and Prosciutto Soup in a Sourdough Bowl, 251
  Dry-cured Goose Prosciutto, 211
  Quail Stuffed Three Ways, **110**, 111, **112**, **113**, **114**, 115
Pulled Poultry Enchiladas, 144
pumpkin, 149
purple loosestrife, 34, 46, **130**
  Creamy Braised Purple Loosestrife and Mushroom Risotto, 154
  See also greens dishes
purslane, 34, 46. See also greens dishes
quail keeping
  equipment for keeping, 102
  raising and breeding, 99–101, 143
  slaughter and processing, 102–3
  See also meat dishes: poultry
queso fresco, 245
Quick Herb-infused Olive Oil, 196
quinoa, 149
Rabbit and Kale Stew, **176**, 177
rabbit keeping, 87, 143
  equipment for keeping, 89
  raising and breeding, 88–89
  slaughter and processing, 89–90, 92
  See also meat dishes: rabbit
radish, 149, 166
raspberry, 167
red tide, 49
red wriggler worm. See worm
reishi mushroom, 153
rhubarb, 168, 173
Rhubarb Gin Fauxtini Cocktail, 194
Rhubarb-Infused Gin, **193**, 194
rice, 157, **158**
Ricotta, Paneer and Queso Fresco, **244**, 245
Roasted Japanese Knotweed Pannacotta, 22
Roasted Sunchokes with Honey Balsamic Glaze, 178
rose and rosehip, 34, 46, 47
  Forager's Tea, 37
  Rosewater Syrup, 39
  Vancouver Rain Latte, **38**, 39
  Wild Rosehip and Spice-Infused Honey, 153
rosemary, 164, 166, 180
  Quick Herb-infused Olive Oil, 196
  Rustic Rosemary Sourdough Bread, **213**, 214–15
Rosewater Syrup, 39
Rustic Roasted Rabbit, **94**, 95 sage, 164, 166, 173, 180, 196
salads
  Crispy Pan-fried Escargot and Arugula Salad, 70
  Foraged Spring Greens Salad, **28**, 29
  Sesame Seaweed Salad, **62**, 63

Tree Collard, Mint and Microgreen Salad with Peanut Dressing, **150**, 151
salal, 34, 46, 47, 187
salmon, 76, 117, 143, 206
  Fire-Cooked Wild Salmon with Creamy Dock Sauce, **78**, 79
  Salmon Smoked Outdoors with Black Tea and Honey, 209
  Smoked Wild Salmon Devilled Quail Eggs, 109
salting and brining meat, 205
Sassy Elderflower Saison Homebrew Beer, **220**, 221
Sauerkraut, Pink Kohlrabi Cabbage, **234**, 235
sea asparagus (glasswort), 23, 61
seafood and freshwater fish dishes
  Crustacean Bisque, 121
  Fire-Cooked Wild Salmon with Creamy Dock Sauce, **78**, 79
  Japanese Knotweed Chutney on Pan-seared Trout, 122
  Mussels Two Ways, 57
  Salmon Smoked Outdoors with Black Tea and Honey, 209
  Smoked Wild Salmon Devilled Quail Eggs, 109
  Steamed Dungeness Crab with Garlic Butter, **52–53**, 54
  Wild Greens Pasta with Periwinkle Sea Snails, 60
sea kale, 174, 180. See also greens dishes
Sea Salt, Toasted Almond and Dark Chocolate Spread, 169
seashore foraging guidelines, 48–49
Seasonal Fruit Leather, 199, **200**, **201**
sea snail (periwinkle), 23, 58, 75
  Wild Greens Pasta with Periwinkle Sea Snails, 60
seaweed, 23, **59**, 61
  Seaweed Kimchi, 236
  Sesame Seaweed Salad, **62**, 63
Sesame Panko-crusted Frog Legs, 67, **68**
Sesame Seaweed Salad, **62**, 63
sheep sorrel. See sorrel
shellfish. See seafood and freshwater fish dishes
shellfish toxicity. See red tide
shiitake mushroom, 152, 153, **153**
shiso, 35, 47
shrubs, drinking vinegars, 225
  Himalayan Blackberry, Mint and Pepper Shrub, **226**, 227
shrubs, fruiting, 164
side dishes
  Brown Butter Fiddleheads with Caramelized Cattail Shoots, **42**, 43
  Creamy Roasted Peppers, Corn and Sorrel, 45
  Green Bean and Asparagus Gratin, 172
  Miso-creamed Perennial Greens, 181
  Roasted Sunchokes with Honey Balsamic Glaze, 178
  See also appetizers; salads; soups
signal crayfish, 23, **64**, 71, 75
Slow Pine-infused Avocado Oil, 197
Smoked Chili Water Lotus and Taro Root Chips with Lemony Herb Dip, 159

Smoked Wild Salmon Devilled Quail Eggs, 109
smoking, as food preservation method, 207
 Salmon Smoked Outdoors with Black Tea
  and Honey, 209
Stovetop Maple-smoked Duck Breast, 209
snail
 Crispy Pan-fried Escargot and Arugula Salad
  70
 European grove and garden snails, 23, 68,
  75
 in aquaponics, 117
snakehead, Northern, 71, 75
society garlic, 157, **158**
sorrel
 Creamy Roasted Peppers, Corn and Sorrel,
  45
 sheep (sour grass) and garden, 34, 44, 46
 wood, 35, 46
 See also greens dishes
soups
 Cheese, Beer and Prosciutto Soup in a
  Sourdough Bowl, 251
 Chilled Azolla and Watercress Soup, 161
 Crustacean Bisque, 121
 Gingered Perennial Root Vegetable Soup,
  179
 Rabbit and Kale Stew, **176**, 177
 Rabbit Stock, 93
sourdough. *See* bread
sour grass. *See* sorrel
soy bean, 149
spinach, 149

sprouts, 148–49
spruce tips. *See* tree tips
squash, 166, 167
staghorn sumac, 35, 47
Steamed Dungeness Crab with Garlic Butter,
 52–53, 54
Stew, Rabbit and Kale, **176**, 177
stinging nettle, **18**, 35, 46
 Forager's Tea, 37
Stinging Nettle Pesto, 19, **19**
 See also greens dishes
Stovetop Maple-smoked Duck Breast, 208
strawberry, 164, 167, 168, 173
Easy Strawberry Freezer Jam, **186**, 187
sunchoke, 174, **175**, 179
 Roasted Sunchokes with Honey Balsamic
  Glaze, 178
Sun-dried Tomatoes with Rosemary in Olive
 Oil, 198
sunflower, 149
sustainable meat and seafood, buying, 75–76,
 145
syrups, 192
 Rosewater Syrup, 39
 Tree Tip Syrup, 41
Tacos, Invasive Game Carnitas, 72
taro, 157, **158**, 179
 Smoked Chili Water Lotus and Taro Root
  Chips with Lemony Herb Dip, 159
teas. *See* drinks
Teriyaki Pineapple Rabbit Jerky, 202
30-minute Mozzarella, 246

thyme, 164, 166, 173, 180, 196
tincture, 192
tomato, 166, 198
tonic, 192
tortillas, homemade corn, 72
tree collard, 175
 Tree Collard, Mint and Microgreen Salad
  with Peanut Dressing, **150**, 151
 See also greens dishes
tree tips, 35, **40**, 47
 Baked Brie, Roasted Garlic and Tree Tip
  Toffee, 41
 Forager's Tea, 37
 Slow Pine-infused Avocado Oil, 197
 Tree Tip Syrup, 41
trout, 117
 Japanese Knotweed Chutney on Pan-seared
  Trout, 122
tsi, 157
Turkish rocket, 175, 180. *See also* greens dishes
Vancouver Rain Latte, **38**, 39
vermiculture. *See* worms
vertical planting, 164, 167, 173
vinegar making, 228, 230
 Beer Vinegar, 230
wapato (arrowhead or duck potato), 35, 46,
 47, 157
wasabi, 117
 Homemade Wasabi Peas, 162
water-bath canning, 188
water caltrop, 157
water celery, 157

water chestnut, 157, 179
watercress, 35, 46, 157
 Chilled Azolla and Watercress Soup, 161
 See also greens dishes
water hyacinth, 35, 46, 47
water lotus, 157, 179
 Smoked Chili Water Lotus and Taro Root
  Chips with Lemony Herb Dip, 159
watermeal, 157
water mimosa, 157
water spinach, 157. *See also* greens dishes
wheat, 149
whey, 233, 237
Wild Blackberry Sparkling Cider, 224–25
Wild Greens Pasta with Periwinkle Sea Snails,
 60
wild pig, 71, 72, 75. *See also* meat dishes: wild
 game
Wild Rosehip and Spice-Infused Honey, 133
wine cap mushroom, 153
wine making. *See* brewing: fruit wines
wolfberry (goji berry), 35, 46, 47, 131, 187
worm
 composting with (vermiculture) 138
 in aquaponics 117
wood sorrel. *See* sorrel
yeast, fermenting, 212–13, 214, 216, 218, 221,
 222, 223, 224, 228
Yogurt, Easy Greek-Style, 240

ABOUT THE AUTHOR & PHOTOGRAPHER

ABOUT THE AUTHOR

Michelle Nelson has completed a Ph.D. in conservation biology and writes about food and conservation for magazines and newspapers. She started homesteading in her one-bedroom East Vancouver apartment five years ago and now keeps chickens, quail, turkeys, geese, rabbits, goats and all kinds of beneficial microorganisms in a tiny cottage on Bowen Island, BC, with her partner in crazy awesomeness, shark biologist Christopher Mull.

ABOUT THE PHOTOGRAPHER

Alison Page is a freelance stylist and photographer who earned a master's degree photo-documenting marine snails before turning her creative attention to food and lifestyle photography. She lives in a high-rise in Vancouver, BC, where she captures the work of local artisans on the leading edge of urban food culture and sustainability.